Astrology Disproved

Lawrence E. Jerome

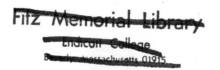
℞ Prometheus Books
Buffalo, N.Y. 14215

Published by Prometheus Books
1203 Kensington Avenue, Buffalo, New York 14215

Copyright © 1977 by Prometheus Books
All Rights Reserved

Library of Congress Catalog Card Number 77-90138
ISBN 0-87975-067-7

Printed in United States of America

Contents

"During the Renaissance, astrology enjoyed once more that universal reign which it had held in the Roman Empire. In the long warfare between theology and the science of the stars, the latter had fairly conquered. *The final disproof of astrology was never written.* So long as the cosmology of Aristotle, and the geocentric astronomy of Ptolemy, held sway in mediaeval schools, a refutation was impossible. With the arrival of the new astronomy of Copernicus, it was no longer necessary."

Theodore Otto Wedel
The Mediaeval Attitude Toward Astrology

Book 1   Historical Perspectives

Is it possible, at this late date, to disprove astrology?

The ancient "art" of divination from the motions of planets and stars is thousands of years old, and the debate over its validity has been raging ever since the Greeks adopted it from the Babylonians in the sixth century B.C. Some of the greatest minds the earth has ever produced have felt compelled to jump into the debate on one side or the other. Yet, as Theodore Wedel's statement in the Preface suggests, the issue has never been settled.

Astrologers today cite this fact—that astrology has never been disproved—as evidence in favor of their "art." Opponents have been losing the battle almost by default. Of the hundreds, even thousands, of books dealing with astrology, only a very few have sought to disprove or debunk the subject; and of the modern works only Robert Eisler's hostile *The Royal Art of Astrology*[1] has been devoted solely to astrology.

Once again, following disastrous declines during the Dark Ages and later during the Enlightenment, astrology's popularity is on the rise. The twentieth century has seen a tremendous upswing in the fortunes of astrologers. Easily one-quarter of the nearly four billion people living on the earth believe in and follow astrology to some extent.

If ever astrology needed to be disproved, it is now.

The modern world is an extremely complex place, precariously balanced between nuclear disaster, ecological destruction, and economic and political chaos. The most careful thinking and action are required today; the simplicity of astrological advice and counseling can provide no real help in today's complex world. The arbitrary and silly "dictates of the stars" can only lead to what must be considered dangerously irrational thoughts and approaches to the problems of contemporary life. The "solution" offered by modern astrologers must be viewed by rational people with extreme distrust and distaste. Astrology arose at a time when humankind was just beginning to become civilized, at a time when the world was a much "smaller" and simpler place. The validity of astrology was not an issue then; the inaccuracy of its predictions was inconsequential.

As I shall show in the first few chapters, astrology arose as a system of magic, a simple pantheistic religion by which Babylonian priests could inspire and control their subjects. The first astrologers cared not a whit whether their "science" was "true" or not; they were interested only in setting up a system by which they could influence and manipulate people. As long as the people thought the planetary "gods" were on their side as a result of the priests' rituals and interpretations, they were encouraged to band together for the common good; of course they dared not disobey their intercessors for fear of angering Marduk (Jupiter) and the other inhabitants of the *bibbu* (wandering "stars").

Thus the earliest forms of astrology served as a societal mechanism for controlling the people and, I will show, that role—however unrecognized—is little changed today. This is the dark side of astrology that astrologers are careful to conceal.

In sum, astrology is a complex subject—not the "art" itself, the casting and interpreting of charts, but the subject: its origins, its history, its arguments pro and con, its relationship to politics, religion, philosophy, and even medicine. It is also a fascinating subject, if approached from the proper perspective. Through a study of astrology, one can gain tremendous insight into a wide variety of fields: astronomy, anthropology, cosmology, philosophy and—perhaps most importantly—the historical development of the human mind.

For, certainly, astrology has played a major role in the history of civilization. During some periods of history, astrology was interwoven with nearly every aspect of life, ranging from the practicalities of daily living (and dying) to inspiring art and abstract thought. As Chapter 2 will demonstrate, astrology as well as astronomy can be traced back to the very roots of civilization, to the European Paleolithic hunters who began spreading across the globe following the end of the last Ice Age.

Thus, understanding astrology requires a strong historical perspective. Some people are surprised to learn that nearly every Renaissance man, woman, and child believed in some form of astrology.[2] Yet, this fact can be misleading unless we ask the question, Why did they believe? What historical factors contributed to that belief? Does their belief have any bearing on the question of astrology's validity for modern man?

As we shall learn, each cultural group had its unique way of looking at the cosmos and its "influence" on life here on earth. To the Babylonians, astrology was a function of the state, to be used in predicting the weather and the fate of kings. To the Egyptians, the stars provided a necessary "cosmic" connection for smooth and proper entry into the next world. It was not until the Greeks and Romans that astrology became the property of the common man and was used to predict individual fortunes and specific events.

During the Dark Ages astrology was banned by the Roman Church as a demonic art, as cavorting with the devil. Eighth- and tenth-century Arabians asked questions about the future and sought answers based on the position of heavenly bodies at the time the question was asked. And following World War I, the German people turned to astrology in large numbers, seeking guidance out of their despair and defeat.

Today astrology has been acquiring even more popularity and influence. More than three-quarters of all newspapers in the United States (1,230 papers) carry a daily horoscope column. Computerized horoscopes are selling at a brisk pace, with prices starting at $9.95 and skyrocketing as "additional services" are provided. Half a dozen universities offer courses in astrology, and private instruction can be found in nearly every city and town.

The reasons for the modern upswing in astrology's fortunes differ considerably from those that were responsible for its rise during the Renaissance, and those were in turn quite different from the reasons for the Greeks taking so passionately to the divinatory "art." Each people, each culture, has had its own rationale, its own collective driving force for its acceptance of astrology. Yet there are common threads: the desire to know what lies ahead, to feel oneself an intimate, important part of the cosmos, and to be absolved of responsibility for social conditions and personal actions.

On the other side—the psychological side—of the coin, astrology has not been without its effects on the various peoples and cultures that have espoused it. In Babylonia astrology was the power wielded by the priests to keep the citizens in line. Among the Greeks astrological thinking inspired powers of abstract reasoning and mathematical logic. During the Renaissance, astrology was so widespread that scarcely one literary work of the period did not contain some allusions or references to the work of the "figure flingers."

It is important to ask, then, what the psychological effects of astrology are. Is astrology as harmless as most people seem to think? Would, for example, Hitler and the Nazis have come to power if astrology and the other occult "sciences" had not helped pave the way for their brand of fuzzy thinking?

These are serious questions, questions that must be answered if we are to gain a full and complete picture of astrology and its influences on the human race.

Because of astrology's long and varied—often confusing—history, its basic assumptions and operating principles have been almost completely obscured. Astrology originated as a system of magic. The planets—or so the priests convinced their people—were omens of the gods and hence represented "signs" to be read, just as the liver and entrails of freshly slaughtered animals were examined for "signs" of the future.

As we shall see in Chapter 6, all such prophesying and "reading of signs" is based on the "principles of correspondences," also known as the "law of analogies." This is the basic assumption behind all magic—white, black, or gray.

Among the early believers, then, astrology was never considered to be anything but magic, many forms of which were quite acceptable in terms of their culture. When astrology came to the Greeks during the sixth and fifth centuries B.C., they began incorporating it into their developing cosmological picture of the world. Thus the stage was set for astrology to be "reinterpreted" by each culture in terms of its own world view.

Since Greek cosmology was man's first faltering step toward modern science, it became traditional for astrologers to interpret their creed in terms of each arising new physical science, thus lending popular credence to their "art" and further obscuring its magical bases.

During the Dark Ages, astrology was still recognized as a demonic art, a system of magic requiring the intervention of devils and planet spirits. Yet at the same time it was generally believed that the planets had some physical effect on earth; however, God alone was considered privy to such knowledge, and any attempt to discern His inner workings was a blasphemous sin and banned by the Church.

With the advent of the Renaissance, continental scholars began to become acquainted with Greek and Roman writings. To the Renaissance mind, the Greek "harmony of the spheres" was a fascinatingly romantic concept, and astrology once again fired man's imagination. Observation of the night sky began in earnest, aided by the technological inventions of the clock, the telescope, and other astronomical instruments.

By this time astrology's magical bases had been almost totally lost and forgotten, its operating principles almost universally ascribed by Renaissance thinkers to the physical "influences" of the planets and stars. Even the most hide-bound skeptics of astrology were willing to grant at least *some* physical "influence" by the stars upon life here on earth; astrology was attacked for the excesses of its practitioners rather than for its faulty assumptions.

As the physical science of astronomy learned more and more about the realities of the universe, particularly the immense distances involved, astrology suffered a decline as great as during the Dark Ages. Scientists of the Enlightenment found no evidence of physical influences by the planets and stars here on earth. By the beginning of the twentieth century, astrology had only scattered adherents in Britain and France; the ancient "art" had been relegated to its proper role of foolish superstition.

During the 1920s, however, scientists in a number of diverse fields began finding evidence of innate rhythms in plants and animals, rhythms triggered by the daily and seasonal changes in sunlight. Also, certain aquatic animals were shown to feed and breed in fairly precise synchronization with the motion and phases of the moon. Statistical studies suggested that sunspots could be correlated with a wide range of phenomena, from economic ups and downs, to the growth of trees, to population fluctuations in the snowshoe rabbit. "Surely, here," announced the astrologers, "is ample evidence that the heavenly bodies influence life here on earth."

Astrology began yet another upsurge, first in Germany after World

War I and then in Britain (where there was already a number of follow-ers), France, and the United States. By World War II, astrology was so prevalent that the German propaganda machine considered it fertile field for psychological warfare.

Today, in the mid 1970s, astrology has become increasingly popu-lar. It claims millions of adherents, thousands of publications, and no doubt tens of millions of customers' dollars, pounds, and francs.

When the ancients ascribed the operation of astrology to physical "influences" of celestial objects, they were unwittingly paving the way for modern astrologers to attach their magical "art" to the physical sciences of biological clocks, astrophysics, and modern cosmology. Chapters 9, 10, and 11 will treat these subjects in full, separating reality from the false claims and statistical fallacies that have marred scientific efforts in those fields and permitted the astrologers to claim the results as their own.

Throughout, however, it must be remembered that astrology is a system of magic, that the alleged stellar "influences" on human charac-ter and future events are strictly analogies based on primitive thought patterns that sought to connect the motion and appearance of planets—seen as abodes and omens of the gods—to people and events here on earth. Thus, the planet Mars, which has a reddish cast in the night sky, has always been associated in astrological lore with war and bloodshed. Mercury, fast moving, dim, and hard to view, has always been ascribed the magical qualities of elusiveness and punctuality.

Astrology, in the way it operates and in the way characteristics of the various celestial objects are assigned to people and events, is a sys-tem of magic. No amount of rhetoric, false claims, or statistical studies can alter that fact. Magic astrology was born, and magic it will remain by definition.

Why, then, do people believe in astrology? Why do thousands of as-trologers and millions of adherents follow the "dictates of the stars" today? If astrology is simple-minded magic, how can modern, educated human beings accept its principles and follow its advice?

Why, indeed? Is the will to believe so strong in man that he will ac-cept almost any theory couched in romantic terminology and promising sufficient rewards? Are the times in which we live so unsettled, so per-sonally stifling, that people long for some "cosmic connection," some proof that they are not so cosmically insignificant as modern science would seem to indicate?

Perhaps. Perhaps the reasons people want to believe in astrology and other occult "sciences" lie deep within the psyche, within the psychological depths of the mind, an indication of the ceaseless struggles between id and ego, complex and archetype. Certainly, there is a psychological side to astrology, both in terms of its acceptance and in its effects upon those who follow it.

Book IV, "The Psychology of Astrology," will discuss these psychological factors. Chapter 14, "Astrological Dowsing," will examine possible psychological reasons for the seeming success of some astrologers, especially when it comes to character analyses of their clients. Chapter 13 will take a look at that branch of astrology that has been misnamed "Humanistic Astrology," combining elements of Jungian psychology with Oriental mysticism.

This book will examine astrology from a number of viewpoints and attitudes, ranging from historical curiosity to scientific skepticism. At all times, I will strive to present an accurate, factual account. Astrology may be a complex subject, but it is not incomprehensible nor, one suspects, unassailable. The widely publicized *Statement by 192 Scientists Objections to Astrology* (reprinted in the Appendix of this book) in *The Humanist* has provided an opening wedge to bring the astrological debate out into the open. For the first time since the Renaissance, astrologers are being called to account for their fallacious assumptions, invalid operating procedures, and false advice to unsuspecting and gullible clients.

The basic premise of this book is that astrology *can* be disproved, that it is possible to clear up the confusion and deception that has long shrouded the ancient "art" in mystery. There is no single "disproof," no single argument that can prove astrology false. Rather, the "disproof" of astrology must rest on the sum total of evidence and arguments; my "disproof" runs like a thread throughout the fabric of this book. One must first understand the historical origins of astrology before the magic in it can be appreciated, and the magical disproof may fail to convince the reader until he or she examines the statistical and scientific evidence. Finally, for those readers who still feel astrology is, at worst, a harmless parlor game, our discussion of the psychology of astrology should make it clear that people can be highly influenced and misled by the advice of untrained astrological "counselors."

Astrologers have a long history of twisting and undermining even the cleverest of arguments. In particular they delight in rejecting embarrassing arguments by shifting ground and dredging up some new approach, some new facet of their "art," of which opponents are hopefully ignorant. Thus, to our proof that astrology is a system of magic, the astrologers counter by claiming that their "science" must be judged on the basis of statistical evidence. And when we point out that all properly conducted statistical studies into astrology have found that its axioms apply to people at no more than chance level, astrologers retort by saying that it must be accepted on "faith," that the subjective "truth" of astrology must be experienced firsthand.

Yet, for all the pitfalls and difficulties, the attempt at disproving astrology must be made. Astrology is the first and foremost of the occult "sciences" and as such greatly encourages public interest in the far more dangerous magical "arts" of alchemy and witchcraft—and worse. As Chapter 12, "Astral Psychological Warfare," amply demonstrates, the irrationality of fuzzy occult thinking can lead to disastrous results for individuals, nations, and the world at large.

Astrologers and occultists in general are playing a dangerous psychological game of which they have little knowledge and less understanding. If this book goes even a small way toward stemming today's occult tide, I shall deem the effort well made and my attempt at "disproving" astrology well taken. I ask only that the reader "suspend belief" and reserve judgment until all the evidence can be weighed and all the arguments can be examined.

And to the astrologers themselves, whether professional or amateur, I would issue a special challenge and appeal to reexamine the facts and reconsider their beliefs, in short, to consider seriously the possibility that they may be mistaken. As the final Book 0, "The Statistical 'Secret' of Astrology," will show, there are good mathematical reasons why astrology *seems* to give accurate character assessments of people.

Astrology is far from the simple predictive "science" it appears to be on the surface; its inner workings are clever, complex, and subtle. Yet, for all that, it remains quite false.

NOTES

1. Robert Eisler, *The Royal Art of Astrology* (London: Herbert Joseph, 1946).
2. Don Cameron Allen, *The Star-Crossed Renaissance* (Durham, N.C.: Duke University Press, 1941), p. viii.

1　Prehistoric Roots of Astrology

Anthropology, the study of prehistoric and primitive man, has unearthed startling new evidence and revelations. No longer does science envision a grunting caveman staring blankly into his fire, moved only by hunger and pure animal instincts. Prehistoric man—even as far back as Peking Man of half a million years ago—had a distinct culture built around developing technology and his evolving cognitive powers.

In fact it is probably no exaggeration to say that anthropology recently has been experiencing a revolution, both in its research techniques and in its general approach to its subject matter. More and more, anthropologists are using broadened comparative techniques, looking at the results of animal behavior studies, and drawing on the growing body of knowledge concerning how the mind operates and develops.

One of the leaders in this anthropological "revolution" is Alexander Marshack. Marshack has pioneered the use of the microscope in examining the artifacts of prehistoric man. Particularly, he has spent long hours in dusty museums examining and analyzing carved pieces of bone and rock containing series of nicks and scratches. Earlier researchers had declared these scratches to be simply "decorative" marks or "hunting tallies," but he discovered that these series of nicks were arranged in groups and that often a different "point" had been used to carve each group.

Figure 1-1 is a photo of a piece of prehistoric carved bone, a phallic, horsehead-shaped "pierced staff" decorated with a stag, hind, and horse, unearthed from a cave at El Pendo and estimated to be ten thousand years old. While the lines and notches on this particular specimen of carved bone could well be simply decorative, there are several series of carved and crossed lines, and such series appear to have been gouged by a different tool (actually a bit of sharpened bone).

Such groupings suggested to Marshack that the nicks had not been carved all at one time, as one might expect if they were meant to be decorative, but rather that the lines had been gouged over a period of time. Further, the fact that a different "point" had been used to carve each group indicated that the person making the notations wanted each group to stand out from the others, perhaps each representing a separate and distinct period of time.

Time? Could it be that early man—and the evidence Marshack presents goes back to Cro-Magnon Man, 32,000 B.C.—had a way of reckoning time, of keeping track of the passage of days and the comings and goings of the seasons? In essence Marshack's evidence suggests just this: prehistoric man kept a crude sort of calendar by carving notations in pieces of bone and rock that he carried with him in his nomadic wanderings.

How and why? How did early man manage to keep track of the days and seasons, and why would he bother going to all that trouble when survival, getting meat in his cave and berries in his belly, was his foremost concern? Why, indeed, unless it *did* enhance man's chances of survival? In other words, would keeping a calendar have had *selective* value to prehistoric man? Can a case be made for such a practice resulting from the natural process of human evolution?

Yes, contends Marshack. Keeping a crude calendar would have been of great selective value in keeping track of the seasonal activities of man's animal prey and plant food. It would serve a nomadic hunting band little good to have the reindeer herd migrate through their valley if they were unprepared for the hunt! Similarly, the band could miss out on a valuable harvest of fruits or berries if they didn't arrive at the proper season before their animal competitors had a chance to eat them out of cave and valley.

So, how did they do it? How did they keep a calendar and know when the bison would be mating and the salmon running? Surprisingly, in much the same way we do: by watching the sky, the orderly procession of celestial objects, sun, moon, and stars.

In particular, suggests Marshack, early man may have watched and kept track of the rapidly changing but periodically recurring phases of the moon. The moon is a prominent object in the sky even in these days of smog and city lights. Earliest man can scarcely have failed to notice the full moon flooding his midnight valley with light, nor could he have failed to notice the full moon diminish in size until five days later it appeared cut in half. A week later, the moon would have virtually disappeared, reduced to a thin sliver rising just before dawn.

Since even the lower animals have been shown to be aware of, and able to use, the changing patterns of the day and night skies (see Chapter 9), it seems reasonable that man, with his "superior" intelligence, should have been able to do at least as well. In a way, we are here discussing the evolutionary transition of instinctual patterns of recognition to the conscious level in man. And, since tool-making evolved during this same period of time (beginning more than half a million years ago), it seems natural that man would use his tools as an aid to remembering and consciously learning the patterns he already instinctively recognized.

But what of the evidence? Do Marshack's groups of notations correspond to the phases of the moon or any other celestial patterns? In other words, can it be shown that the number of lines and nicks in each group roughly correspond to a lunar period?

Marshack thinks so and presents impressive evidence to back up his assertion. First, he constructs a thirty-day lunar model, based on the changing phases of the moon; then he arranges his model alongside the linear series of carved lines and shifts the model until the major phase changes (the new and full moon) line up with the start and finish of the various groups. For example, the freehand drawing in Figure 1-2 suggests a possible lunar model interpretation of the uppermost notations on the El Pendo baton in Figure 1-1.

While the correspondence between model and carving is not precisely one to one, it is close enough to be well within observational error. The moon may not always be visible, and it is very difficult for the naked-eye observer to tell exactly which days are the full and new moons.

So, within the accuracy of a few days, Marshack's lunar model very often fits the groupings of nicks and lines carved into Upper Paleolithic artifacts. The evidence strongly suggests that prehistoric man was keeping a notational and calendric record of the changing phases of the moon. In other words, man was making astronomical observations long before he became "civilized," long before he settled in agricultural villages, and long before there was any form of astrology.

In several of the batons considered by Marshack, there are pictures of plants also carved into the bone, schematic images deliberately placed alongside or in the midst of linear notations. In his detailed analysis of the famous baton from Cueto de la Mina,[1] Marshack identifies two ibex heads and several species of plants in different stages of growth carved beside notational marks. Here we have further evidence that the baton served its maker as a calendar.

If Marshack's calendric thesis—he calls it a "time-factored notation"—is correct, then the baton from Cueto de la Mina represents nearly a year of lunar and seasonal observation beginning in February and ending in late October. The plant and animal images, then, would represent the expected or actual appearances by the plants and animals most important to this late Magdalenian hunter (about 10,000 years ago).

It is also about this same period of time that the walls of caves in France and Spain began to be decorated with exquisite paintings and drawings representing the animals and plants with which prehistoric man was familiar. Previously, anthropologists have attributed ritual and magical significance to these paintings, particularly where an animal was painted over several times and numerous arrows and spears drawn and redrawn over the image of their animal prey.

"Obviously, hunting magic," the anthropologists have always stated. But, in light of recent discoveries such as Marshack's and animal behavior studies of play-learning in primates, one might suggest that such early art and notation may have been much more important as a means of learning and instruction. Certainly it would have been of far greater selective value for the young and inexperienced members of the band to learn the upcoming seasonal and ecological relationships between the plants and animals that served as food than to merely participate in "hunting-magic rituals."

At least at first, then, one would expect the educational and selective values of "time-factored notation" and representational art to take precedence over their ritual and spiritual "values." Perhaps the learning process eventually developed into ritual and attained magical significance, particularly during the Neolithic cultures as man began settling down into agricultural communities. Since magic does not operate on the physical level, but rather only through its psychological effects, it would have had little selective value until civilization had developed to the point where priests had need of some additional "supernatural" power by which to keep the citizens in line. Chapter 2 will follow this line of reasoning more deeply.

PALEOLITHIC STORYTELLING

To recapitulate, then, prehistoric man had a distinct technological and cognitive culture. He had been using fire and making tools for half a million years before any trace of civilization arose. For at least 35,000 years—and probably much longer—man had been making careful astronomical observations of the sky and keeping track of his observations by means of notations on bone and rock. Further, his "art" and representational images of plants and animals indicate that prehistoric man was well aware of the ecology and seasonal changes of the environment around him. He knew that, within a certain period of time following the blooming of a particular plant, he could expect the salmon to begin their yearly spawning run up the river or the reindeer to begin rutting in the valley.

All this suggests that early man was not as "primitive" as he has been pictured in the past, that he had a full, cognitive awareness of the world around him. Prehistoric man may have been "uncivilized," but he wasn't stupid! He may not have been able to speak grammatical sentences, but he certainly knew how to tell a story.

Consider what it took for Peking Man to build and maintain a fire 500,000 years ago. As Marshack points out,[2] it required a fair amount of cooperation between different members of the band in order to maintain the all-important fire during the hardships of the cold, wet winter. Some had to keep the fire alive while others searched for wood—suitable wood, not fresh, green wood that would only sputter out and leave the band to freeze. The fire had to be built in a proper location, protected from rain and snow yet at the same time open enough to permit proper draft to keep suffocating smoke out of the cave and living quarters.

In order to maintain such a fire culture, says Marshack, prehistoric man must have possessed storytelling abilities—not language as we know it but the ability to transmit information concerning necessary or expected action. The information needed only to be in the form of concepts pieced together into a story that transmitted a new, combined idea-of-action, such as "Fire-need-wood, go wood-collecting-place," perhaps just guttural articulations accompanied by sign-language wavings of the hands.

Marshack places great significance on this process of storytelling as man's primary evolutionary step forward, more important to him than the discovery of fire and the development of tool-making. He combines this "storytelling" thesis with his "time-factored notation" to suggest that the notations on bone and rock were more than just a way of keeping track of the passage of days; they were used as mnemonic aids to storytelling. Again, this reminds one of the educational value inherent in such calendric sticks.

Perhaps the hunters kept several sticks or notational rocks from previous years, comparing them, using them to tell the story of the past and what to expect in the future. So, here we have prehistoric man watching the sky—particularly the moon—keeping track by means of notation and at the same time telling tales of events past and future.

Beginning to sound like the first steps toward astrology?

These linear notations combined with pictorial images suggest more than just the beginnings of astrology. It would seem reasonable that this notational storytelling developed with the rise of civilization into the pictographic writings of the Summerians and the Egyptians: cuneiform and hieroglyphics. Certainly the basics were there; the lines and pictures were side by side. It would seem to be a natural extension, to combine the two into a single pictograph character telling the same tale that used to require a number of lines and pictures.

Thus Marshack's "time-factored notation" and storied timetelling goes far toward explaining the development of writing. Of greater interest here is that Marshack's calendric bones and rocks also go far toward setting the stage for the rise of astrology with the advent of civilization. For as man began settling in large civilized groups, it became necessary for the leaders to develop some system of control over the growing number of people. Chapter 2 will suggest that the power of priests was based on magic and that man's magical world view is a relatively recent construct of civilization, a product of man's mind for the purpose of controlling and influencing the minds of others.

Finally, Marshack's lunar notational bones suggest answers to two age-old puzzles involving astrology and its origins.

First, scholars have long speculated on why astrology seemed to be so widespread, with observations of the night sky and its meaning for human events cropping up in Babylonia, Egypt, India, and China. As long as astrology in its various forms was restricted to the Eurasian continent, its widespread presence was attributed to contact between the Babylonians (where astrology was believed to have originated) and the other nations.

China offered the greatest obstacle to this theory since there is indirect evidence of astrology there as early as 2400 B.C., and astrological documents date from the fifth century B.C.[3] Since these dates approximately parallel the development of astrology in Babylonia (though there are astrological records from Babylon as early as 1800 B.C.),[4] the theory that astrology originated in Babylonia and spread from there becomes hard to accept.

Then, when scholars discovered that a form of astrology had also arisen in the New World among the Mayas and the Aztecs, the thesis for the Babylonian origin of astrology became totally untenable, for certainly nobody was about to seriously suggest that there was any cultural contact between the Babylonians of 2000 B.C. to 200 A.D., and the Mayans of 800 to 1400 A.D. Yet it seemed unlikely that such an abstract concept as astrology would arise virtually simultaneously and independently all over the globe.

However, Marshack's Paleolithic time-factored notation provides a key to the solution of the problem. First, it must be recognized that the Paleolithic nomads had a high degree of mobility, with technological and cultural diffusion taking place between the various European and Asian cultures and splinter groups.[5] In other words, this knowledge of lunar notation and seasonal storied time-telling was widespread over both Europe and Asia. Here we are dealing with tens of thousands, perhaps even hundreds of thousands of years, for the diffusion and spread of a tradition, whereas in the case of astrology proper, there are only a few thousands of years available for the idea to spread across the globe.

Hence it seems much more reasonable to expect the practice of lunar notation to be widespread by the beginning of the last Ice Age and that astrology in all its diverse forms arose more or less simultaneously and independently in Babylonia and China. Later, it arose in yet another form in Central America, where the late Paleolithic hunters had settled following their migration across the Bering Strait during the last Ice Age.

The other puzzle for which Marshack's excellent book suggests an answer is the age-old question of why abstractly shaped constellations were given the names of animals. Almost all writers have suggested that ancient man somehow "saw" these shapes among the randomly scattered stars. However, since early man was used to associating celestial objects with the seasonal comings and goings of plants and animals, it seems natural that when man began his more formal observations of the sky as civilization took root, he continued the practice and assigned animal names to the stars he was studying, thus maintaining a continuity between prehistoric seasonal notation and the developing "civilized" system of astrology.

NOTES

1. Alexander Marshack, *The Roots of Civilization* (New York: McGraw-Hill, 1972), pp. 214-17.
2. Ibid., pp. 112-14.
3. Rupert Gleadow, *The Origin of the Zodiac* (New York: Atheneum, 1969), pp. 92-93.
4. Ibid., p. 152.
5. Marshack, *The Roots of Civilization.* p. 95.

2   Astrology, Civilization, and Man's Magical World View

As the last Ice Age drew to a close and the glaciers began receding, the late Paleolithic hunters began changing their lifestyle. Glacial runoffs created broad, rich deposits in the flood plains of the river valleys, and agriculture began to be a viable way of life. The increasing warmth, the moisture, and the rich soil combined to entice man to abandon his nomadic huntings and settle down to a comfortable life of farming.

Neolithic man had arrived on the scene.

When man began raising his food rather than gathering it, much of his previous ecological and seasonal knowledge became obsolete. There was much to be learned anew. Yet we can be sure that the old, traditional ways of learning and remembering—Marshack's storied time-factored notation—were not abandoned to the hoe and plow. The old traditions would have been put to use in new ways to provide new answers to new problems.

First, and perhaps most important, was the weather. To the earlier nomads the weather was just a part of the environment, something to be accepted or endured; regardless of the weather, the salmon would still run and the berries would ripen. But, to agricultural man, the weather took on new significance, becoming almost a matter of life and death. If the rains failed to come in time, the grains might not ripen; untimely storms could wipe out an entire crop, perhaps forcing the neophyte farmers to revert for a time to their former nomadic existence.

So it behooved Neolithic man to search for ways of understanding and anticipating the weather. No doubt, many tribes, many agricultural communities, relied on their existing knowledge and instincts of the weather. Others, whose leaders were perhaps more ambitious, began examining the old traditions for new clues, new hints for ways of predicting the weather. Since watching the sky and relating it to seasonal events was one of those traditions, it became natural for the burgeoning agriculturalists to look to the sky for clues for predicting the weather.

The evolving agricultural states had more problems than just the weather, however. For the first time, people were living in groups that were larger than the simple family unit. More elaborate forms of organization were needed. No longer could each individual work for the good of the family alone; now he was also required to work for the good of the community, a much more abstract concept.

In practical terms, then, the leaders needed some way of controlling people, of convincing them they should work for the good of a larger entity, the state. In order to produce more and more crops, citizens had to work together to clear fields, plant seeds, weed, tend, and harvest.

Life had become more complex; civilization was on its way.

MAGIC, THE WORD, AND RITUAL

In the fertile river valleys of the Tigris and Euphrates, and southward in the broad flood plain of the Nile, the Neolithic farmers settled in growing numbers. It was in these places that civilization first arose. Unfortunately, we know little of the nature of this transition.

Was it a peaceful settlement? Probably not, particularly at first. Each tribal group had its own leaders, its own hierarchy, and considerable friction undoubtedly arose as groups settled near one another and began combining forces into larger and larger communities. There was a need not only to coordinate the activities of large numbers of people, but there was also a need for authority, some mechanism by which strong leaders could maintain control and ensure the loyalty of their followers, particularly those leaders who had recently been subordinated.

So it was natural that a hierarchy arose within the communities, a hierarchy that provided roles for the displaced leaders and yet gave them enough authority so that both they and their followers would work for the good of the state. Anthropologists have demonstrated a number of mechanisms for establishing and maintaining such a hierarchy. Potlatch, or competitive feasting, is one of the more interesting examples of later primitive societies.

In competitive feasting, the chief/big man throws a huge feast during which he gives away nearly everything he owns just to impress his neighbors, thus ensuring their cooperation in community affairs and farming. Marvin Harris offers the following evolutionary sequence of cultural development: reciprocity (humble sharing) becomes competitive feasting, which then evolves into monarchy.[1]

Another such cultural mechanism is magic. In all its various forms and systems, the operation of magic required specialists, a priestly class that alone could understand the mysteries and read the "signs." Magic, then, became the cultural mechanism by which the leaders of the Nile and Tigris and Euphrates valleys exercised their authority and established the hierarchy that gave their states cohesiveness.

Magic is poorly understood today, perhaps because modern man is so used to thinking in terms of scientific cause and effect. As we shall see in Chapter 6, "The Magic in Astrology," magic does not operate through any physical cause and effect. It relies on analogies, on any sort of connection envisioned by an active imagination. It must be remembered that language was still a relatively recent invention and that primitive minds attached great significance to the power of words.

As Gleadow suggests,[2] to the primitive mind, the spoken word itself was a form of magic. A man merely needed to speak the words, "bring food," and others in his band would bring him food, *as if by magic*. So, throughout man's evolutionary development of language, there was a tradition, or at least the germ of a tradition, that there was some sort of magic in the spoken word itself. Later, as writing developed, that same magical significance was attached to the written word.

Let us reexamine the evidence. We have the need for a cultural mechanism for maintaining the hierarchy of society. We have the Paleolithic traditions of storied time-keeping and the magic of words. Just one more piece of the puzzle is needed to establish magic as one of the major cultural forces that welded the Neolithic peoples into coherent societies: ritual.

Magic is nothing without ritual.

But we already have the earliest elements of ritual inherent in Marshack's storied time-keeping, for the telling of a story is itself a form of ritual. And if the same stories are repeated year after year, the telling takes on even more ritualistic significance. The final evidence for ritualistic story telling during the close of the last Ice Age can be found in the Magdalenian caves of France and Spain. Deep within the inner recesses of caves, often in almost inaccessible caves, located virtually all over the globe, late Paleolithic man left drawings and paintings of animals, plants, spears, and men. These paintings reached their finest level of development in the caves of France and Spain.

But what is important here is not the artistic merit of these cave paintings but rather their evidence of ritual. Many of the images, particularly of animals and spears, have been redrawn over and over in the same spot on the cave walls, as if the *act* of painting, not the painting itself, was important—as if the painter had gone through a ritualistic reenactment of the scene each time he repainted it.

Figure 2-1 gives a picture of one such cave wall with its dubbed-over animals and spears.

Anthropologists have long described these drawn-over paintings as evidence of ritual "hunting magic," and perhaps it did form part of the ritual. But one is led to suggest, with Marshack, that these paintings represent more than simple hunting magic. All we see on the cave walls is the physical evidence; we can only speculate on the nature of the rituals themselves, but since there was a long tradition of storied time-telling—of telling tales with the aid of time-factored notation—it seems reasonable that this tradition was continued and expanded in the dark recesses of the caves.

In other words, late Paleolithic man gathered in difficult-to-reach caves for ritualistic story-telling, perhaps initiation rites centering on the retelling of the traditional stories about his ecological and seasonal world. Perhaps it was within these ritual caves that the priestly class, the natural leaders who could tell the best tales and most entertain the group, was born. When these men emerged from their caves and began settling in the river valleys, the story-telling rituals, the magic-in-words, and the budding priests went with them.

The stage was set for the magical civilizations of Babylonia and Egypt.

BABYLONIA AND EGYPT: MAGIC FOR THE STATE

By the time we have recorded evidence from the Babylonian civilization (about 4000 B.C.), its culture already possessed a structure and hierarchy not so different from our own. At the top were the king and his family with an administrative hierarchy for seeing that his commands were carried out. The priests formed their own hierarchy and performed their own functions and rituals designed to entertain and impress the citizens, all, of course, on behalf of the state and the king.

The Babylonians were a practical people, concerned with their crops, the weather, and the general state of the kingdom. So the priests developed ritualistic techniques of foretelling such information that also entertained the populace and put them in awe of their king's all-important value and "influence" in and by the outside world. To the Babylonians the state of the world was dependent upon the king, and vice versa. Needless to say, the priests, as primary architects and keepers of the cultural edifice, derived great power and influence from the authority of these rituals.

The Babylonian priests became very "skilled" in the reading of omens, forecasting the fate of kings and the state of the weather by interpreting "signs" and natural phenomena, such as eclipses and comets and the condition of animal entrails. In essence, then, the Babylonian priests had two major techniques for predicting the future: inspecting the liver of sacrificial animals (performed by the *haruspex*) and hemerology (the reading of sky omens).

Scholars usually assign greater early importance to the *haruspex*, who concentrated mainly on the liver because its weight and bulk so impressed the Babylonians.[3] However, there is also considerable evidence that the reading of sky omens, particularly in the case of eclipses and comets, played an important early role in the Babylonian magical hierarchy. Perhaps we are more familiar with the *haruspices* because their clay and bronze models of livers preserved so well (see Figure 2.2).

How did the priest "read" the future in the fresh, bloody entrails extracted in sacrificial ceremony? This is precisely where magic enters the picture. The priest interpreted the omens according to strict rules relating to the size, shape, color, and unusual features of the liver. For instance, a liver with a right twist would indicate favorable aspects, while length foretold success and long life.

This is magic, pure and simple: the priests made mental analogies or connections between the condition of the entrails and the external world. Again, this is the magical "principle of correspondences" (see Chapter 6) applied to the reading of omens in entrails; the same principle could be applied to the reading of omens in anything, provided the priest could see some sort of connection between the state of the object and the external world. Livers and celestial bodies were only the more popular and impressive omens; the behavior of domestic animals, the flight of birds, in fact any everyday occurrence might be interpreted as an omen in the same way.

Then, as now, the only limitation rested in the imagination of the interpreter!

The Babylonian *haruspices* usually limited their liver forecasts to political affairs and left—perhaps naturally to their minds—the forecasting of the weather to the reading of sky omens (hemerology).

As in the case of the *haruspices,* the priests who watched the Babylonian skies interpreted their findings via the "principle of correspondences." Thus eclipses were considered to be dangerous because the omen/god was being "eaten up," disappearing before their eyes. If the moon—and certainly the sun—were actually to disappear physically from the sky, it *would* be a most disastrous moment, so in that sense the primitives were right. They had no idea that eclipses were caused by shadows from the very objects they were watching (or standing on), so to them eclipses were a real danger to the sun and moon and the gods they represented and thus to the earth and nations under their dominion.

Of course, this primitive reading of sky-omens was still a far cry from horoscope astrology, which did not begin its full development in Babylonia until the sixth century B.C. But it was a major step in that direction. During the several thousand years the Babylonians developed this system of hemerology, the rules of interpretation were laid down and codified. In the last millennia of the Babylonian empire, a more advanced and structured form of these magical rules of interpretation was used in horoscope astrology, a more sophisticated form of omen-reading very similar to the astrology practiced today.

At the same time that they were developing these magical rules, the Babylonians were also making careful physical observations of the sky, noting the comings and goings of the stars, the planets (which they called *bibbu,* or wanderers), eclipses, comets, and novae. In short, astronomy, begun by Paleolithic hunters watching the changing phases of the moon, continued to develop alongside magic. And it is important to remember that the Babylonians placed the moon above the sun in importance, adding further support to Marshack's theory of moon-phase observation and lunar notation among Stone Age hunters.

As the cult of the sky grew more important, the Babylonians built huge observational temples, broad, flat pyramids called *ziggurats,* for their priests. From atop these temples, the astronomer-priests of Babylonia could view virtually the entire hemisphere of their crystal-clear desert sky. They were able to plot the courses—the Way of Anu—of the planet *bibbu* against the stars of the ecliptic. They replaced their simple, inaccurate lunar calendar with a reasonably accurate lunar-solar calendar, much like the one we use today. Finally, they developed numerical tables that enabled them to chart the cyclic movements of celestial objects so that they were able to make accurate forecasts of major occurrences in the sky, mainly eclipses and conjunctions. This feat so impressed the Egyptians and the Greeks that Babylonian astrology fired their imaginations and was eagerly assimilated into their cosmology.

But such assimilation did not begin until the sixth century B.C., preceding by a few centuries the invasion of Babylonia by Alexander the Great. Needless to say, the Egyptians and Greeks already possessed some measure of sky lore themselves, as did nearly every tribe and nation from the Eskimos to the Gauls to the Australian Bushmen. But Babylonian astrology was the most highly developed sky lore of its age. Astrology and its ancestral sky cults did not develop accidentally; they were the result of strong cultural factors and powerful evolutionary selective forces.

In Egypt, the counterpart hierarchical mechanism to Babylonian liver-reading was dream interpretation (they also engaged in ordeals, cup-reading and necromancy).[4] Again, as with the Babylonians, a strong class of priests who alone could interpret the dreams and give their significance for the state rose to power. The priest would lead the person requesting a "reading" to a special room deep within the temple. Following certain rites, the person was instructed to relax and fall asleep (perhaps with the aid of drugs) and to remember the dreams of that night. In the morning, the priest would come, waken the subject, listen to his dreams, and interpret them. The interpretation touched on the petitioner's problems or questions.

Needless to say, these early Egyptian dream interpretations differed considerably from modern psychological methods of interpreting dreams. Like all omen-reading techniques the interpretations were steeped in magic and based on the principle of correspondences.

The Egyptians also had their star lore, but there is a curious lack of evidence that they used their astronomical observations in magical omen-readings and forecasts. The Egyptians were more interested in the sky in order to establish their calendar; in fact the Egyptians had developed a very accurate calendar at least a millennia before the Babylonian predictive methods surpassed their own capabilities.

Egyptian economy and agriculture were totally dependent on the flooding of the Nile; for them, life began with that yearly phenomenon. At the beginning of each year, the Egyptian priests would watch for the rising of the star Sirius because they knew that the all-important flooding of the Nile would soon follow. So it was natural that the Egyptian year began with the day that they first sighted that brightest star shimmering through the early morning light just before sunrise.

However, the Egyptians also put their celestial observations to an entirely different, nonmundane use: to aid "souls" of the dead rise through the celestial spheres and find the appropriate planet to which they were pledged.[5] Much like the Babylonians, the Egyptians associated their gods with celestial objects; for instance, Venus was considered the offspring of dead kings, Ra was their sun god, and the constellation Orion was associated with Osiris. Anyone familiar with ancient mythology can name many more.

The Egyptian kingdom was a very settled, orderly place compared to the unrest and political intrigue of Babylonia, so perhaps it's to be expected that the Egyptians were less interested in predicting events here on earth than in providing a smooth and orderly transition to the "next world," their main preoccupation in life. It was especially important for the pharaoh to make a successful journey through the heavens to be united with the sun and certain stars. The soul, or *ba,* of the departing king was supposed to make a pact with the gods to ensure a smooth transition of power to the next pharaoh and to convince the gods to smile with favor upon the new reign.

This is why the Egyptians spent so much effort building their huge pyramids as tombs for their kings. Their purpose was to provide the proper vehicle for the ascension of their souls. There also seems to be considerable evidence that the pyramids were built with certain astronomical features in mind. For instance, the bases appear to have been lined up within a few degrees of their Polar Star, Thuban, and the windows slanting into the interior may have been used for astronomical sightings of certain stars at particular times of the year (see also p. 33 for a similar use of Mayan temples).

Perhaps the Egyptian priests used the astronomical sighting windows to determine propitious times for ceremonial events or even to ascertain when the planets and stars were at the proper angles for the soul to be assisted in its journey to its assigned resting place. Of course much of this is speculative. All we really know is that the angles the planets make with each other was an important concept to the Egyptians. Centuries later, when astrology began to be assimilated by the Greeks, this concept of planetary *places* was incorporated into the Babylonian Way of Anu, becoming what we know today as "planetary aspects."

Modern astrologers are also indebted to the Egyptians for yet a further refinement of their horoscope techniques. In their search for ever greater accuracy in their calendar, the Egyptians divided the ecliptic into thirty-six equal divisions of 10° each. Each division was called a *dekan* (originally, *dekans* were constellations rising ten days apart). Much later, when astrologers divided the zodiac into equal 30° "houses," it became natural for them to further divide each house into three subdivisions of 10° each.

So we see that the early Egyptians, while possessing some sky lore and omen-reading abilities, did not use a system of astrology as did the Babylonians. In fact, it was not until the Hellenistic period that Babylonian astrology infiltrated Egyptian cosmology, at about the same time it was being discovered by the Greeks.

To be more precise, it was just before the Hellenistic period that astrology developed in Babylonia into a form recognizable as a prototype of horoscope astrology. And it was this late (about sixth century B.C.) Babylonian flowering of astrology proper that captured the imaginations of Greek and Egyptian scholars. The accuracy of their *astronomical* predictions combined with their impressive mathematics and symbology gave astrology then the same appeal that it has today.

During this late flowering of Egyptian astrology under Babylonian and Hellenistic influences, the Egyptian priests began to relate their long-standing plant lore and herbal medicine to planetary "influences." This astrological system of Iotromathematics formed the basis of medicine for the next two thousand years, especially after the "father" of modern medicine, Hippocrates, declared that no doctor could afford to be ignorant of astrology. It was with the Egyptians and Greeks that the Babylonian "art" of celestial divination began its long history of association with man's first attempts at physical science.

Centuries, even millennia, of Babylonian development had built astrology into a complex, refined system that almost totally obscured its magical bases. Then, when the Greeks took astrology over and wove it into their mathematical, logical, and romantic cosmology, the stage was set for the Babylonian ancient cultural mechanism to become part of the occult religions of Rome.

GRECO-ROMAN COSMOLOGICAL ASTROLOGY

The Greeks, of course, had their own stories, myths, and traditions, all stemming from the basic Paleolithic pattern of ritualistic story-telling. They also had their omen-reading techniques, but they were inordinately fond of oracles, prophetic readings by specially gifted (and often drugged) priests or priestesses. What part the oracles actually played in the priestly hierarchy is a bit unclear; the Greek political structure was considerably looser and more locally oriented than either the Babylonians or the Egyptians, so in that sense the early Greeks were less "civilized," lower in the evolutionary cultural scale.

But this also left the Greeks freer and more open to new ideas. They had more leisure time (so it would seem) to pursue intellectual concepts and try to build a coherent picture of the world they observed. Where the Babylonians were practical, the Greeks were abstract; where the Egyptians sought ways to ensure a successful journey of the "soul" to the stars, the Greeks sought ways of relating life here on earth to the entire cosmos.

In short, the Greeks felt compelled to find "the meaning of life," and in their searchings they became the precursors of modern scientists. But Greek cosmology was *not* a science, however much it did to develop the mathematics and logic so necessary to the later development of modern science during the Renaissance.

What can we say about Greek cosmology? Their passion for abstract thinking, their readiness to incorporate foreign concepts, their pantheon of deities, and their fondness for mysticism? They were a unique, creative people. Their philosophers and mathematicians set the "scientific" standards for the entire Western world for two millennia. Democritus created the concept of the atom—and the necessity for it—strictly on the basis of abstract thought. Likewise, Zeno—through his paradoxes—established the thought patterns that eventually led to the invention of calculus.

Yet, at the same time these same Greeks were quite willing to not only cling to their own myths but readily to accept and assimilate the magical myths of their Assyrian neighbors. No doubt their own magical lore had primed them, establishing fertile soil in which the new and exciting Babylonian astrology could take easy root as early as the sixth century B.C.

It seems, too, that the Greeks possessed one important, nearly all-encompassing myth: the idea that the world is one organic entity, one interrelated being or "cosmos."

So, when Babylonian astrology, with its assumption that there is a correspondence between celestial objects and events here on earth, began infiltrating across the Mediterranean into Greece, they readily seized upon it as support for their own concept of the unity of the cosmos. With the aid of Hellenized Chaldeans, such as Kidenas and Berosus, the Greeks modified and adjusted their own cosmology to include astrology, adding star lore to their own myths and transporting most of their own gods into the heavens.

Thus they added many characteristics of their own gods and myths to the already established Babylonian influences and in the process used the same underlying principle of correspondences. In hermetic literature—supposedly handed down by the Greek god, Hermes—this principle is described by the well-known phrase, "As above, so below."

In other words, the characteristics of the planet gods were ascribed to events here on earth through the mathematical formula of the horoscope.

It was during the early Greek period of assimilation that horoscopes began to be drawn up for the common man. This was a luxury previously reserved only for royalty. The practice of predicting celestial fortunes for commoners began first in Babylonia following the Persian conquests, which left astrology in a much weaker political position (and it must be remembered that astrology arose basically as a political mechanism). So perhaps, finally, it was this forecasts-for-everyone approach that won the Greeks over; certainly it would appeal to their famous sense of democracy to make this previously royal "art" available to the masses.

Suffice it to say that a number of cultural factors were operating to speed the assimilation. In a few short centuries astrology had become fully integrated into Greek thought and cosmology. In fact, nearly every Greek school of thought believed in the astrological "influences" of the stars in one way or another and incorporated it into its particular system of cosmology. Socrates, Plato, and especially Aristotle sung praises of the "harmony of the spheres."

Even before the invasion of Persia by Alexander the Great (ca. 330 B.C.), Eudoxus of Cnidus, the greatest mathematician of his time, had written his famous work *Phaenomena,* which made astrology logically and mathematically acceptable to the Greeks.[6] A century later, the great poet Aratus of Soli popularized Eudoxus's astrological concepts in a poem based on the *Phaenomena.* For centuries this poem was admired, translated, and eulogized in other poetry by both Greeks and Romans. So it was that astrology gained entry into Greek thought and literature, soon to be transported to the Roman Empire and spread throughout the Western world.

What exactly was this Greek cosmology, this romantic, appealing concept of astrological unity? Did the Greeks do more than merely borrow Babylonian magic and dress it up for popular consumption? Is there any hint of modern scientific reality in Greek cosmology?

Basically, the Greeks saw the universe as a cosmological whole, a single living organism growing, as it were, out of the Primal Egg (also a Babylonian idea).[7] Every part of the cosmos was supposedly linked to every other part through correspondences between high and low, between heaven and earth. Up to this point, we find little difference between Greek cosmology and the Babylonian system, which was also based on a strong system of correspondences. But the Greeks imposed a mathematical geometry on the system, attributing the correspondences to physical interactions and interconnections between the various celestial spheres and the earth.

Thus the distances to the planets were established according to a mathematical progression, or harmonics. Earth, as the center of the universe, corresponded to the first harmonic; Saturn, the farthest of the planets (a fact recognized by the ancients due to its slow motion), was assigned the thirty-sixth harmonic, and the other planets were placed at varying harmonic distances in between (see Figure 2-3).

Even the ancient Greeks recognized that you can't have harmonic vibrations without a medium through which to transmit them. So, naturally, they envisioned the entire cosmos as permeated by a "subtle essence," the aether. It was this aether that thus held the universe together and gave it its structural unity.

Needless to say, it was this same concept of aether that led scientists astray two thousand years later as they searched for the medium by which light is transmitted (eventually arriving at Einstein's theory of relativity and Heisenberg's uncertainty principle, the very bases of modern quantum mechanics). But this does *not* mean that Greek cosmology was in any way "scientific." The Greeks combined existing myths and basic assumptions about the universe—accepting them virtually unchallenged—with their own experiental observations to come up with what might be described as a magical-scientific cosmology.

In other words, there were elements of both magic and science, both fantasy and reality. What was really important about Greek cosmology, however, was the logic and mathematics involved and the sense of rational reasoning that characterizes modern man.

The Greeks added one further refinement to astrology: the philosophical concept of free will. As long as the Babylonian astrological predictions were limited to kings and realms, the question of individual free will never entered the picture. But, when the Babylonians began predicting individual fates and transmitting their astrological "art" to the Hellenes, the democratic Greeks soon discovered a paradoxical flaw in the new astrology. If one's fate, one's entire life, is determined by the stars, they argued, how can one possibly make decisions? Those decisions would already have been decided by Fate, by the stellar positions and influences! Therefore, if astrology is true, man possesses no free will, no ability to make decisions, a conclusion that seems contrary to common sense and experience.

The Greeks, although great abstract thinkers, also placed great stock in common sense, man's innate intuitive ability to make the correct decisions for his survival.

They got out of this "free-will dilemma" by refining or modifying Babylonian "fatalistic" astrology into what they called, "catarchic astrology" (from the Greek word for beginning, *katarché*). Since the Greeks were unwilling to give up their freedom, their free will, they limited the scope of astrology to certain areas of their lives; in particular, they decided that astrology could only provide an indication of favorable periods and auspicious times for beginning projects, making decisions, etc.

The Stoics represented the school of thought most adhering to the concept of fatalistic astrology, while most of the other schools leaned toward the catarchic interpretation. This controversy between free will and fate formed a major part of astrological arguments pro and con for the next two thousand years, with the cultural winds blowing first one way, then the other.

It was the Romans who most developed and believed in fatalistic astrology, so that by the middle of the second century A.D., emperors of the Roman Empire literally lived and died according to the "dictates of the stars."

Astrology came to the Romans via Greek slaves (who often tutored young nobelmen) and Stoic diplomats. While astrology had been drifting into Rome in fits and starts for over a hundred years, the Babylonian "art" became popularly introduced to the masses of Rome in 156 B.C. as the result of a diplomatic mission on behalf of Athens, which had been fined 500 talents by the Roman Senate for pillaging Oropus.[8]

Athens sent as its ambassadors three famous Greek philosophers: Critolaus, head of Peripatetic school; Carneades, head of the Academy and founder of the New Academy; and the great orator, Diogenes the Babylonian, head of the Stoic school. While biding their time before talking to the Senate, the three ambassadors held public speeches and debates, expounding upon Greek philosophy and cosmology and fascinating the staid Roman public with their concepts of astrology and celestial fate.

So rapidly did astrology fire the Roman imagination that by 139 B.C. the Senate issued a *senatum consultum* expelling astrologers and other disruptive foreigners in a political move to quell revolutionary ideas.

Thus the die was cast for astrology to play an increasingly important role in Roman politics.

The Romans of course had their own native systems of divination, primitive systems based on omens (they were particularly superstitious about comets) and entrails, much like the early Babylonians. And, also like the Babylonians, the Romans were a practical people, so astrology rapidly worked its way into the political arena. This role is finely detailed in Frederick H. Cramer's *Astrology in Roman Law and Politics*. For those who feel that astrology is a harmless pastime, Cramer's Chapter 3, "Astrologers—the Power behind the Throne, from Augustus to Domitian," is recommended reading.

For over 150 years the family of the astrologer Thrasyllus used astrological "predictions" to manipulate the political decisions and unending intrigues during the reigns of nearly every emperor from Tiberius to Domitian. If Thrasyllus or his son Balbillus said that the stars (or more often comets) indicated blood needed to be spilled, the emperors were all too eager to comply. The astrologers were present in court nearly all the time, and their advice was sought on many if not all issues.

In Rome, astrology became such a political and psychological weapon that astrologers decided the fate of several emperors simply by convincing their opponents that the "stars were with them" and that their conspiracies were "fated" to succeed. Even the assassination of Julius Caesar had been foretold in advance by astrological means; this does not imply that astrology predicted his death on the Ides of March, but rather that the conspiracy was generally known and that friends, including Spurinna the *haruspex,* tried to warn Caesar through the medium of prediction

After Julius Caesar's death, a comet happened to appear, and the famous "casterization of Caesar" (from *astre,* star) occurred. One of the beliefs of primitive people was that their "souls" departed earth upon death and took up residence in the sky as stars. When the comet appeared, it was rumored to be Caesar's "soul," a positive sign of his divinity. Octavius took the opportunity to declare publicly the "casterization of Caesar," a popular political move that ensured his own rising "star."[9]

At the same time, astrology became completely and confidently accepted by Roman nobility. Perhaps even more than the Babylonians, the Romans recognized the political and psychological values of astrology for controlling the masses and manipulating the rich and powerful. Most writers credit the many Oriental cults that sprung up in Rome as responsible for the popularity of astrology, since most of the cults incorporated astrological theory. However, they may be putting the cart before the horse; without political sanction, the cults could not have existed, nor could astrology have been used as a political tool.

It wasn't long after the "casterization of Caesar" that astrologers were making predictions of the death of the emperor. This upset Augustus to such an extent that he published his "real" horoscope in 11 A.D., proving his time was not up yet and at the same time prohibiting such astrological predictions of death in an imperial edict. However, throughout Roman history this and similar edicts only affected the lower classes, the street soothsayer; nobels continued to rely on their astrologers and to employ astrology in their political stratagems.

For instance, Thrasyllus had predicted the building of a pontoon bridge between Baine and Puteoli, with the result that Emperor Caligula exhausted his funds in fulfilling the prophecy. Soon, violent death was popularly predicted for mad Caligula, and his assassination in 41 A.D. proved the "prophecies" right. When a comet appeared in 64 A.D., Balbillus revealed the "Piso conspiracy" to Nero. The consequences of this prophecy was the death of Seneca, who apparently was innocent, because comets required the shedding of noble blood as a substitute for the emperor's own.

Emperor Titus so believed in the astrological predictions of his death that he died cursing the stars even though he apparently enjoyed good health at the time.[10] This is astrological magic, pure and simple, with the same psychological forces at work that produce similar deaths in cases of witchcraft and voodoo.

Finally, it was Emperor Domitian's belief in his predicted death during the fifth hour of September 18, 96 A.D. that inspired the conspirators to choose that "fated" moment to assassinate him as he prepared for his bath without having taken any precautions to protect himself. In his rise to power, Domitian had murdered his own mother, just as his birth horoscope had predicted!

Does astrology still appear to be harmless? If so, perhaps Book IV, particularly Chapter 12, "Astral Psychological Warfare," will further demonstrate the political and psychological dangers of blindly following the "dictates of the stars."

ORIENTAL AND MAYAN ASTROLOGY

If, as I have suggested, late Paleolithic man throughout Asia and Europe possessed lunar notation and associated story-telling lore, we should expect something like astrology to arise wherever civilized communities appeared. We would expect Neolithic man to use and develop the techniques for keeping track of the seasons that had proved so successful for his Paleolithic ancestors. The evidence, although sparse, indicates that both astronomical and astrological methods arose independently in China and Central America and possibly in India as well.

The first documented evidence of astrology in China occurs in the *Book of History* compiled by Confucius during the fifth century B.C.[11] However, indirect evidence places Chinese astrology—or at least its star lore, which was analogous to Babylonian hemerology—before 2000 B.C..

The Chinese used a number of astrological systems. The similarity of one of these systems to the Babylonian zodiacal system makes it very difficult to unravel their various origins and possible influence by the West. At first the Chinese apparently used the stars surrounding the North Pole, perhaps, as Rupert Gleadow suggests, because the circumpolar constellations are visible throughout the year if the skies are clear.

At some point, the Chinese divided the equator into twenty-eight equal divisions (probably corresponding to the twenty-eight days in a lunar month). These twenty-eight asterisms, or mansions, were used primarily for telling time, while most astrological predictions relied on the polar stars. To confuse the issue, the Chinese also used a circle of twelve divisions, called the Twelve Kung, which may be an older system than the mansions.[12] According to Gleadow, the Twelve Kung were definitely used for making astrological predictions of the fate of the state by noting the color, brilliance, and motion of the planet Jupiter through the twelve divisions.

By the time Western astrology was introduced into China around the third century B.C., the Chinese were quite ready to incorporate appealing concepts and ideas into their own system. Since their cosmology was based on the opposing forces of the Yin and Yang, they associated the Yin with the moon and the Yang with the sun; then, each planet was given two names, depending on whether it was closer to the sun or the moon.

The zodiacal signs—the Chinese didn't give a name to the ecliptic until the second century A.D.—were assigned animal names and alternated in "quality" from Yin to Yang. Further support to the idea that astrology arose from seasonal time-keeping comes from Gustave Schlegel, who observed that "the choice of animals was made from the seasons at which their activity was most conspicuous."[13]

In the case of India, we are much less able to separate native astrological ideas from possible Babylonian imports. However, they too seem to have developed their system of lunar mansions independently. When Hellenistic ideas began pouring into India around 300 A.D., there was at first opposition between the two systems; then, as astrology began to flourish, both methods were used.

When we turn to Central America, however, we find abundant evidence of a totally independent astronomy and astrological cosmology. As in the case of the Babylonians, the Mayans associated their gods with celestial objects; especially, they identified Kukulcan-Quetzalcoatl with the sun and the planet Venus.[14]

And just as the Egyptians built their pyramids with astronomical observation windows, the Mayans built temples for making important observations of certain stellar phenomena at special times of the year. Aveni, Gibbs, and Hartung show that particular lines of sight formed by pillars and windows in the temples correspond within less than 2° (and often within 1°) to astronomical events such as sunrise at summer solstice, Venus at maximum northern declination, and the rising and setting of important stars.

Thus the Mayans would seem to have been as interested in accurate astronomical observation as the Gaulic builders of Stonehenge, no doubt for similar practical and religious reasons.

The Mayans seem to have developed a cosmology much like the Greeks, linking man to celestial objects. According to Aztec and Mayan legend, the gods were playing a "game" in the sky, using the stars and planets as balls. In sympathy with their cosmology, these ancient Central Americans played a "cosmological handball game" (thought to have originated as early as 800 B.C.),[15] which no doubt served to link man with the gods and stars and helped to keep the cosmos running smoothly. The long I-shaped court represented the world, and the ball stood for the sun or moon; the object of the game was for two teams to try and pass the ball (sun) through a stone ring at the side of the court (perhaps representing the precision with which celestial objects return to their same position each year).

So we have seen that astrology essentially arose simultaneously and independently all over the globe, supporting our contention that the concept of astrology derived from Paleolithic man's lunar and seasonal notation and storied time-keeping. The next chapter will trace the decline of astrology during the last days of the Roman empire (thus leaving medieval Europe free of the predictive "art") and give some indication of its survival in Arabian mathematics and science.

NOTES

1. Marvin Harris, *Cows, Pigs, Wars and Witches: The Riddles of Culture* (New York: Random House, 1974).
2. Rupert Gleadow, *Magic and Divination* (London: Faber & Faber, 1941), p. 41.
3. Jack Lindsay, *Origins of Astrology* (London: Frederick Muller, 1971), pp. 9, 15.
4. Ibid., p. 145.
5. Rupert Gleadow, *The Origin of the Zodiac* (New York: Atheneum, 1969), p. 195.
6. Frederick H. Cramer, *Astrology in Roman Law and Politics* (Philadelphia: American Philosophical Society, 1954), p. 26.
7. Lindsay, *Origins of Astrology,* p. 116-23.
8. Cramer, *Astrology in Roman Law and Politics,* pp. 53-56.
9. Ibid., pp. 78-80.
10. Ibid., pp. 141-142.
11. Gleadow, *Origin of the Zodiac,* p. 93.
12. Ibid., p. 99.
13. Ibid., p. 90.

14. Anthony Aveni, Sharon Gibbs, and Horst Hartung, "The Caracol Tower at Chichen Itza: An Ancient Astronomical Observatory?" *Science* June 6, 1975, p. 980.
15. Christopher McIntosh, *The Astrologers and their Creed: An Historical Outline* (London: Hutchinson, 1969), pp. 13-14.

3 Dark Age Decline and Arabian Survival

Astrology reached its peak in the Roman Empire during the first and second centuries A.D. With the death of Domitian, fatalistic astrology began giving way to the more moderate catarchic interpretation. Until the end of the Empire, some emperors, particularly Marcus Aurelius and Hadrian, still relied heavily on astrology; others, like Trajan, were either skeptical or at least disinterested.

At the height of its Roman popularity, astrology was codified and set forth as a sister "science" to astronomy by the Provincial astrologer and writer Claudius Ptolemy. In his *Tetrabiblos,* Ptolemy drew together all existing astrological knowledge into four books that systematically ordered the operating theories and alleged planetary influences. Astrologers today essentially use Ptolemy's methods of setting up a chart and interpretation, so it might be of interest to look a bit closer at his famous work.

In Book I he sets up the theoretical bases: "That certain power, derived from the aetheral nature, is diffused over and pervades the whole atmosphere of the earth, is clearly evident to all men."[1] He then sets up the primacy of the sun: "The power of the Sun, however, predominates, because it is more generally distributed; the others either cooperate with his power or diminish its effect . . . ."[2]

In Book II Ptolemy establishes the rules for the general application of astrology to nations and races by assigning various geographical regions of the earth to the "influence" of particular signs and planets. In the last two books, he sets down the rules for astrological interpretations related to health, wealth, and death of individuals. Needless to say, his rules of interpretation are nothing more than the application of the magical "principle of correspondences"—what the Babylonians and Greeks had used for centuries.

No doubt, Ptolemy's other great work, the *Almagest,* a similar compendium of ancient knowledge of astronomy, added to the prestige of the *Tetrabiblos.* But Ptolemy's great efforts notwithstanding, astrology began its long decline during the same century in which the *Tetrabiblos* was written.

There were two major forces in the Roman Empire that opposed astrology: religious mysticism and rational skepticism, both forces opposed to each other as well. By 218 A.D., when the fourteen-year-old emperor Elagabalus tried to introduce the revolutionary religion solar monotheism, the more moderate catarchic astrology was the only form permitted at court. Fatalistic astrology did not leave sufficient freedom for a diety that could be influenced by rituals, prayers, and sacrifices; thus the decline of fatalistic astrology and the growing interest in monotheism were necessary preludes to the later adoption of Christianity by the Romans.

The debate between fate and free will was leaning heavily in favor of the latter.

It was in Roman North Africa, in the city of Alexandria, that Ptolemy wrote his famous work extolling astrology. It was also in Roman North Africa that astrology was dealt a near-fatal blow by the opposition and writings of St. Augustine, Bishop of Hippo, head of the Eastern portion of the Holy Roman Church.

As a young man, Augustine was a believer in astrology, as was nearly everybody in North Africa at the time. However, a friend's wife got pregnant at the same time as their slave woman, and the ensuing simultaneous births of a noble and a slave convinced Augustine that the astrological "influences" of the stars were nonexistent. Today, however, astrologers would argue that—regardless of their social stations—the two astrological twins would lead remarkably parallel lives. (See Chapters 8 and 10 for a complete treatment of such coincidental phenomena.)

Augustine is considered the greatest religious thinker of his time, and no doubt religious questions concerning fate, free will, and devotion to God influenced his attitude toward astrology. Already, by the time he had written the *Confessions*, Augustine had turned against astrology so that when he became head of the Church at Hippo shortly before 400 A.D., his opposition influenced the entire Holy Roman Church to turn officially against astrology.

Since the Church was much more the law of the land than the weak feudal states that struggled into existence following the collapse of the Roman Empire, astrology virtually disappeared from Western medieval Europe for the next eight centuries. Astrology was classified officially as magic by both Isidore of Seville's *Etymologicae* and the Bishop of Fulda's *De Universo*, and as such its practice was forbidden by the Church.

Not so, however, in the Byzantine Empire. Astrology survived until the sixth century A.D., and in the eighth and ninth centuries it made a comeback in Byzantium as a result of Arabian influxes. As astrology declined and disappeared from the West, the Arabs became fascinated with Greek cosmology, mathematics, astronomy, and of course astrology, which was so closely tied up with the others. While astrology was frowned upon in the West as magical cavorting with devils, the Arabians improved Greek astronomical methods and extended the applications of astrological interpretations.

The most famous Arabian astrologer was Abu Ma'shar, who reinterpreted astrological influences in terms of Aristotelian science (Ptolemy's work, as well as that of earlier Greeks, helped set the stage). In so doing, Abu Ma'shar paved the way for astrology to be accepted by medieval Europe four centuries later; he made astrology palatable by ascribing celestial influences to physical causes, thus greatly contributing to the obscuring of astrology's magical bases.

One of his surviving works, *The Thousands of Abu Ma'shar*, must rank as one of the most esoteric and obscurant in all of astrological literature, the writings of twentieth century Aleister Crowley notwithstanding! Another of his works, *Introductiorum in Astronomian*, "solved" the question of free will by distinguishing between necessary and contingent action (i.e. the Arabs used catarchic astrology).

A half-century later, Al-Battan simplified the complex Greek astrological computations by introducing the concept of equal houses, or signs, which divided the ecliptic into twelve equal divisions of 30° each.

Unfortunately, there has long existed much confusion in astrological writings concerning the term *house*. Ptolemy used the term to indicate the sign to which particular planets are assigned according to their astrological "affinities." (See Chapter 7 for a discussion of the various uses of the term.)

Ptolemy followed traditional astrological lore in using the principle of correspondences to assign the planets to their "houses"; for instance, "Mars is dry in nature, and beneath the sphere of Jupiter: he takes the next two signs, of a nature similar to his own, viz. Aries and Scorpio, whose relative distances from the houses of the luminaries are injurious and discordant."[3]

Perhaps it was Ptolemy's association of the planets with pairs of signs that induced the Arabians to place more emphasis on planetary positions and angles rather than on the fixed stars or the precessional signs. Perhaps, also, it was this Arabian interest in planetary angles that persuaded Al-Battan to simplify the zodiac to make such angular calculations easier.

The Arabs insisted on great accuracy in their horoscopes because they were mainly concerned with short-range forecasts. In order to achieve such accuracy, the Arabs set up astronomical observatories and invented a number of astronomical instruments (including primitive sextants and astrolabes for charting planetary positions). The Arabs took their astrology very seriously indeed and went far beyond the Greeks in applying the ancient "art" to everyday affairs.

In particular, the Arabs developed the branches of astrology called *interrogationes* and *electiones*. In the former system, questions are asked (say, about lost items or the future of a business venture) and the answer obtained from a horoscope cast for the moment of questioning; in *electiones*, the most propitious moment for engaging in projects is sought. Arabian interest in the exact moment of questioning and starting ventures accounts for their great passion for the accuracy of horoscopes.

These novel applications of astrology to *interrogationes* and *electiones* would, in a few centuries, contribute to medieval and Renaissance revival of interest in the ancient "art." The Arabian attachment of astrology to Aristotelian science would serve the same purpose. In fact, it was through Latin translations of Arabian works that Greek science and thought were introduced to medieval Europe during the twelfth century A.D. It was inevitable that astrology, so much a part of Greek cosmology, would come along with the science and mathematics.

NOTES

1. Ptolemy, *Tetrabiblos* or *Quadripartite: Being Four Books of the Influence of the Stars,* trans. by J.M. Ashmand (London: Davis & Dickson, 1822, 1896), p. 2.
2. Ptolemy, *Tetrabiblos,* p. 4.
3. Ptolemy, *Tetrabiblos,* p. 43.

4 Renaissance Revival

Astrology had begun creeping into medieval Europe perhaps as early as the tenth century; by the middle of the twelfth century, there was already an underground cult of astrology closely aligned with alchemy and the other magical occult "sciences." Strangely enough, astrology gained its first mass popularity in Europe as the result of a widely publicized prediction of disaster that failed to materialize!

John of Toledo predicted that the seven known planets would appear in conjunction together in the sign of Libra in the year 1186. When the planets *did* appear together as predicted, people were so impressed by his astronomical prowess that they ignored the fact that his further astro*logical* prediction that this would signify storms and earthquakes was totally false.

Thus did astrology gain entry into the popular medieval mind. The pattern was set for periodic predictions of disasters that would send people scurrying for the mountaintops or hording their grain against predicted pestilence and famine. If it could be calculated, no doubt the adverse economic effects of such astrological predictions during late medieval and Renaissance Europe would stand as mute testimony to the dangers of believing in and following such false "dictates of the stars."

Nearly everybody who lived during the Renaissance believed in astrology in one way or another. Even the staunchest opponents of astrology were willing to admit some general influence of the stars, though they denied any particular or predictive "influence." However, before such widespread belief in astrology could catch hold in medieval Europe, the opposition of the Church had to be allayed.

It was not enough that Greek and Arabian cosmologies contained astrology as part of their modus operandi, for the Church was officially opposed to all forms of divination, however scientific they might claim to be. Astrology had to be aligned with Church doctrine and its fatalistic contradictions of the Christian concept of divine will removed.

Church scientists set to work. By the thirteenth century, the Church already distinguished between a "true" and "false" astrology; enthusiasm waxed strong for Ptolemy's moderate catarchic "science," while vulgar forms of astrological magic (talismans, using the planets to help evoke devils, etc.) were held in contempt.[1]

So astrology became part of the intellectual climate of late medieval and Renaissance Europe. Universities established chairs in astrology and offered courses in the technical aspects of the ancient "art." As in the Hellenistic period, astrology became virtually indistinguishable from astronomy. And, once again, court astrologer became an official position (beginning in Italy and soon spreading to France).

Belief in celestial "influences" was so ingrained that it was difficult for even the founders of modern science to look at the motions of the planets and stars without some measure of astrological thought and theory intruding into their calculations and hypotheses. Chapter 5 will illustrate how astrological theory led Kepler astray in his search for planetary laws in the "harmony of the spheres" (in spite of the fact that he didn't believe in astrology itself).

Not all Renaissance thinkers and writers were believers in astrology, and a lively controversy arose between opponents and defenders, a debate that would extend over two hundred years only to be ended by the decline of astrology during the scientific revolution of the seventeenth and eighteenth centuries.

THE RENAISSANCE DEBATE

The debate may be pinpointed as beginning in the late fifteenth century with an unpublished manuscript written by the great physician Marsilio Ficino. His work, "Disputationes contra Astrologorum judicia," was circulated among the intelligentsia of Italy and established many of the classical arguments against astrology, particularly those dealing with the question of providence and free will.[2]

A portion of Ficino's arguments against astrology appeared in a twenty-page section of his treatise on Plotinus, so at least some of his "Disputationes" was preserved for posterity. And it seems that its title was taken over by Pico della Mirandola, whose *Disputationes adversus astrologiam* is considered to be the first great book against astrology in modern times.

Pico's treatise is a massive, rambling work in twelve books, the first ten attacking astrology as a "science," the last two as an "art." While the question of free will forms an important part of Pico's work, it is not his central theme, and he only presents traditional attitudes of philosophers and astrologers. Apparently Pico intended his *Disputationes* as an encyclopedia of arguments against astrology rather than as a single coherent work. This accounts to some extent for its disorderliness.

One of Pico's more original approaches is his claim to have checked the weather predictions of astrologers during the winter and found them correct only 7 times out of a total of 130 days[3] (an almost unbelievable rate of failure). Thus Pico may be considered one of the first to perform a statistical study of astrological claims. He also tackles the question of what are now called "astrological twins" (people born at the same time and place) and says that "if the skies were true causes, these people would be identical."[4] Pico so rejects celestial influences on earth that he even denies that the moon has anything to do with the tides!

For the next two centuries, Pico's encyclopedic tome against astrology stood as *the* standard, establishing the majority of the classical arguments that would be cited time and time again. Most classical scholars consider the opponents of astrology to be less original than the defenders in that they merely repeated the same polemics ad nauseum. This is a somewhat unfair charge, since occultism permits imaginative flights of fancy—in fact, thrives on it! In contrast, defenders of the rational point of view often seem dull and unimaginative, especially from the popular point of view. (Sometimes, however, these tables were turned, as we shall soon see in the famous Chambers/Heydon controversy.)

The defenders of astrology used three basic methods in presenting their case, methods which are still popular today. The first technique used by astrologers (adopted by Heydon as well as Bellanti and others) was to refute a single opponent's arguments point by point. A second method was to write a general essay in favor of astrology followed by a manual of its basic methods and applications. A third and more imaginative approach was to present case histories of famous people and show how their horoscopes predicted and set the courses of their various careers.

In Britain, William Fulke published in the sixteenth century his *Antiprognosticon,* the most scholarly of the books against astrology. In his book Fulke refutes the arguments of the astrologer Doctor Cuningham, who had tried to claim Hippocrates as a disciple of astrology (which, in a sense, he was). Fulke finds that Cuningham had told of only two accurate predictions and humorously states that such a small number over the two-thousand-year history of astrology does little to verify its validity.

In 1601, John Chamber continued the British attack on astrology with his publication of *A Treatise against Iudicial Astrologie,* a light-hearted, witty, and pious work inveighing against the foolishness and evils of astrology. Like most opponents, Chamber's arguments are not particularly original, but he presents them in a novel, popular manner that served to keep his book in the public eye for decades.

Chamber's first technical argument invokes the lack of precision in the total number of stars known. In one of his most humorous arguments Chamber points out that the skies are not always clear in Britain, nor does every peasant own a watch: "It may be also that even in the night they may misse, if the night be misty and foggy . . . Because therefore the figure-flinger hath not marked himselfe the birth-houre, but taketh it by the relation of an unskilfull messenger, it remaineth, that no certaine prediction, but errour, and deceit rather must ensure of this fantasticall and false arte."[5]

Chamber also considers the usual debate concerning the question of birth hour versus the hour of conception, as well as the question of "astral twins." The more original sections of Chamber's book are Chapter X, "Of the small use of predictions, though they were true," and Chapter XIX, "Foure causes why Astrologers seeme often to say true, and that for their true saying, they are never a whit the more to be trusted."

In 1603, two years after Chamber's book came out, Sir Christopher Heydon published a point-by-point refutation, numbering and titling each chapter in the same order as Chamber. While Heydon is by far the better scholar, his heavy style and pedantic manner makes his book rough as well as lengthy reading. (It is four times as long as Chamber's more popular volume.)

In response to Chamber's term for astrologers, "figure-flingers," Heydon refers to his opponents as "astrologie-whippers." In replying to Chamber's argument concerning "misty" nights, he points out that astrologers have tables for determining the positions of the stars, and even if errors in birth time occur, "For as the case (unskillfull messenger) is admitted, it concerneth such nativities only, in which error happeneth through false information, and yet thereupon contrary to all Logicke, he concludeth universally against the whole arte."[6]

POPULARITY AND SATIRIZATION

Heydon was right: astrology *is* an "art," an "art" in the way it convinces people they are exactly what they are: diverse beings with a number of characteristics and attributes; an "art" in its language and descriptions of people and the universe; an "art" in the way astrologers convince people that their vague readings and false predictions are worth coin of the realm.

The language, imagery, and terminology of astrology became part and parcel of the Renaissance world. Everyday events were commonly described in astrological terms, and large numbers of commoners and nobles alike regularly consulted astrologers and almanacs. Renaissance Europe was a rough-and-tumble world, rife with wars and pestilence, thievery, and oppression. Astrology offered a port in the storm, a simplistic if random guide to living. Further, astrology offered Renaissance man a common bond, a common language, thus occupying much the same social role as sports and television today.

In sharp contrast to its unsavory occult role in Roman politics, astrology during the Renaissance was a lively, open property of the people. Everybody believed in it to some extent; many practiced and followed it; writers such as Shakespeare and Chaucer wrote about it (or in terms of it); even the Church accepted it to such an extent that many an altar was adorned with astrological art and symbolism.

Astrology became inseparable from the life and times of the Renaissance.

We have already seen how the Romans and their emperors were concerned with political fate, much like the earlier Babylonians. But what about Renaissance man? What sort of advice did he seek? What sort of questions did he ask? What answers did he get?

Since astrology was introduced to Renaissance Europe via the Arabs, who were fond of *interrogationes* and *electiones,* it's not surprising to find Renaissance clients of astrologers asking much the same sort of questions: Where can I find my lost brooch? When should our ship set sail to avoid the tempests?

The astrologer would cast a horoscope based on the time of questioning and give a reply supposedly based on the planetary positions and attributes. "Venus is in Gemini; your brooch will be found behind the dresser." "Sail on the fifth of the month when Jupiter will be in Pisces."

Close examination of such Renaissance astrological questions and answers reveals that it was during this time that the modern language and techniques for "interpreting" horoscopes were developed into the fine "art" we know today as astrology. The Renaissance astrologer was called upon to answer precise questions, to make specific predictions for large numbers of people. He had to become adept in wording his answers in such a way that he seemed "to say true," no matter what actually happened. He had to learn to play the odds, to make predictions that had a fair chance of coming true. Small wonder astrologers often became the leading mathematicians and statisticians of their time!

It was also during the Renaissance that astrology split into the dichotomy we still have today. On the one hand were the serious, scholarly "scientific astrologers," such as Sir Christopher Heydon and Roger Bacon. On the other hand were the popularizers, the charlatans, and the almanac makers.

The prototype of the astrological almanac was first introduced in Rome by Tubero's *parapegma* and Julius Caesar's *de astris.* Renaissance almanacs first began on the continent as a sort of astrological weather guide for the year, much like their Roman prototypes. The printing press made it possible for large numbers of these almanacs to be distributed, and they soon gained popularity as they spread from Italy to France to Germany and finally across the channel to Britain. The almanac makers, quick to seize an opportunity, expanded the material in their almanacs to include general predictions, good and bad days, homilies, advice, and medical suggestions. The almanacs became the encyclopedias of the Renaissance, as indispensable to Renaissance life as TV is to ours.

By the 1600s, almanac circulation totaled well over 100,000 and approached 500,000 at its peak before astrology's popularity began to decline as modern science arose and turned man's magical concepts of the cosmos topsy-turvy. Yet, before it was over, Don Cameron Allen claims, almanacs "probably had in the long run almost as much influence on the life of the times as the Scriptures."[7]

The growing discontent with astrology toward the end of the Renaissance can be clearly seen in the great popularity of almanac parodies and satires. Rabelais's *Pantagueline Prognostication,* published in 1533, became the classic satire on the almanac. In Britain, almanac parodies were often published under such pseudonyms as Ffrauncis Fayre Weather and Adam Fouleweather.

This tradition of almanac satirization took a humorous historical turn in 1707, when Jonathan Swift published his *Predictions for the year 1708* under the pseudonym Issac Bickerstaff. Swift's pseudo almanac predicted the death of the popular almanac writer, Partridge, on March 29, 1708.

When Partridge failed to die on the appointed day, he became angry and indignant and was considering how to get back at his mysterious protagonist who dared make such false predictions, when he received a worse shock: a pamphlet entitled, *An Account of the death of Mr. Partridge, the Almanack Maker, upon the 29th instant, in a letter from a Revenue Officer to a Person of Honour.* The author, of course, was none other than Jonathan Swift, revealing the joke on Partridge and poking fun at astrology.

Both the almanac maker and his "art" suffered great embarrassment as the result of Swift's joke.

Twenty-six years later, Benjamin Franklin played the same trick on the successful Philadelphia almanac publisher, Titan Leeds. In launching his *Poor Richard's Almanac,* Franklin predicted the death of his "good friend and student," Leeds, who, needless to say, replied angrily that he was quite alive and planned to stay that way. Instead of revealing the joke as Swift did, Franklin continued the farce by calling Leeds an imposter, since his "friend" would never utter such blasphemies against him.[8] Franklin had established his genius for publicity; as we well know, sales of *Poor Richard's Almanac* soared, and Franklin was launched on his illustrious public career.

Astrology, of course, had already begun its decline in the face of science. It was only in America that it hung on for a few more unglamorous decades. By the middle of the eighteenth century, the Western world had become infatuated with science and technology. The Darwins, Newtons, and Herschels of the world wrested public attention away from the ancient "art."

But not without a battle. Astrologers continued to chart their clients' fortunes and to publish polemics against the "blindness" of a science that could not see the "truth" of astrology. They also attempted to mold their own "science" to the new science of forces, energies, and immense astronomical distances. Each new ray, each new type of energy discovered by science, was cited by the astrologers as evidence of some possible "influence."

But they fought a losing battle. The realities of science were far more marvelous to seventeenth- and eighteenth-century man than the fantasies of astrology. The darling of the Renaissance became the goat of the Age of Enlightenment, but not before it had left an immense impact on Western society. Our concepts of fate and fortune were mainly set and patterned by the astrological beliefs of Renaissance man. Our language for the future, success, and failure is steeped in astrological magic. Thus, we have movie "stars" hitching their wagons to a "star." Favorable "aspects" for the future often appear all too "mercurial," etc.

Astrology, for better or for worse, played a very large role during the Renaissance, a much larger role than generally recognized. How, then, shall we judge it? Was it beneficial, or does the balance swing the other way? Since astrology is a system of magic and has no basis in physical reality, did Renaissance astrological predictions do more harm or more good? Did the money paid the astrologers balance the solace received or advice given to one who perhaps sorely needed it?

Certainly, a number of predictions *did* cause harm, particularly the widely publicized predictions of disasters that terrorized the people and caused large sums and time to be spent in preparation. Certainly, too, the poverty-strickened peasant could ill afford even the few pennies he or she gave for vulgar advice from charlatans.

On the credit side of the astrological ledger, we have the part astrology played in stimulating Renaissance art, literature, and thinking, much as during the Hellenistic period. Or did it? An equally good case could be made for astrology standing as a stumbling block in the development of Renaissance science and thought. Along with astrology came a host of superstitions, new and old, products of prehistoric man's analogical way of thinking.

If Greek science, logic, and mathematics had come to the Renaissance unencumbered by the magic of astrology, how much more rapidly would have Renaissance thought developed? As we shall see in Chapter 5, Kepler wasted years trying to adapt a geometric version of the Greek "harmony of the spheres" to his model of the planets and their orbits. Roger Bacon wasted much of his scientific genius trying to create a new "rational astrology" (which turned out to be disappointingly similar to the traditional variety).

Yet, in spite of astrology, progress *was* made. The Renaissance saw the rise of rationality, the development of the scientific method, the close observation of physical fact. The most we can say for Renaissance astrology is that it did not impede civilization too much; it never created the stultifying occult atmosphere that characterized the Roman Empire and post–World War I Germany.

Astrology may appear to have enriched the language and art of the Renaissance, but we can be sure that the genius of Shakespeare would have found other metaphors, other—perhaps more imagina-tive—figures of speech. And, certainly, modern science arose indepen-dently of astrology; even Kepler, part of whose salary came from astro-logical duties, sought his planetary laws out of scientific curiosity rather than in an attempt to prove the tenets of astrology.

While it was Copernicus who conceptually moved the center of the universe from the earth to the sun and thus set the stage for the downfall of geocentric astrology, it was Kepler—a competent astrologer in his own right—who sounded the death knell for the ancient "art" with his Three Laws of Planetary Motion.

NOTES

1. Theodore Otto Wedel, *The Mediaeval Attitude Toward Astrology* (New Haven, Conn.: Yale Univ. Press, 1920), p. 112.
2. Don Cameron Allen, *The Star-Crossed Renaissance* (Durham, N.C.: Duke University Press, 1941), pp. 14-17.
3. Ibid., p. 25.
4. Ibid., p. 27.
5. John Chamber, *A Treatise Against Iudicial Astrologie,* 1601, pp. 24-25 (Bender Room, Stanford University).
6. Sir Christopher Heydon, *A Defence of Judicial Astrologie, in answer to John Chamber,* 1603, p. 144 (Bender Room, Stanford University).
7. Allen, *The Star-Crossed Renaissance,* p. 210.
8. *The Autobiography and Other Writings of Benjamin Franklin,* (New York: Dodd, Mead & Co., 1963), p. 183.

5　Kepler and the Decline of Astrology

Of all the founders of modern science from Copernicus to Newton, the least understood is Kepler, Johannes Kepler, Imperial Mathematician for Rudolph II of Germany. Kepler has been called a fanatical astrologer and "sleepwalker." He has been accused of being a mystic and occultist; during his own time his own mother was accused of being a witch and nearly tortured, all because of one of his most obscure books, *Somnium, Sive Astronomia Lunaris.*

None of these accusations is warranted.

Kepler lived during a very tumultuous time, the end of the Renaissance and the dawning of the Age of Enlightenment. Superstition and magic, feudalism and imperialism, still abounded; yet, there was a dawning rationality, a growing interest in reality. The Western world was experiencing the birth pangs of modern science.

Into this world came Kepler, one of many children of unhappy peasant parents; he was unhealthy, choleric, and brilliant. His mathematical and cosmological meanderings would set the stage for modern physics and astronomy. At age fourteen he was sent to a Lutheran university where his talents for mathematics and quarrels soon earned him a reputation as a maverick, sincere but difficult to get along with. By age nineteen, young, impetuous Kepler was ready to throw himself into the

Copernican controversy on the side of the Polish astronomer who dared to claim that the sun was the center of the universe.

Kepler's public discussions of Copernicus's heliocentric theory of the solar system no doubt played a role in the offer, in 1594, of a chair in astronomy and mathematics at the University at Gratz. It was felt he would be far safer as a teacher than a priest.

How wrong they were!

One of Kepler's chores at Gratz was the publication of the annual almanac, a task he loathed, on the one hand, yet in which he took a certain pride when his predictions turned out surprisingly accurate, particularly his weather forecasts. (In later chapters, we shall discuss reasons for such apparent astrological successes.) In his numerous letters to various colleagues, Kepler often complained of having to perform the onerous duties of preparing almanacs and casting occasional charts.

Yet, at the same time, he would speak of astrology as containing a grain of truth. Astrologers and writers are fond of quoting from one of Kepler's papers on astrology, ". . . while justly rejecting the stargazers' superstitions, they should not throw out the child with the bath water."[1] It must be remembered that Kepler lived during the Renaissance; nearly everybody believed in astrology. And even astrology's staunchest opponents believed in some general "influences" by the planets and stars, so it's not surprising that the founders of modern science had many superstitions and fallacious ideas to discard before they could get down to the hard scientific core of reality.

Kepler's path to the truth of the universe was a tortuous one, full of blind alleys and missed opportunities. It is a testament to his genius that, in spite of hardships, ill health, personal disasters, and fallacious assumptions, he was able to arrive at the correct answers at all!

Why then, does Arthur Koestler call Kepler a "sleepwalker"? Is it true, as Koestler claims, that Kepler's basic assumptions were steeped in mysticism and held no relationship to reality?

No. Koestler himself points out that Kepler's comprehension of gravity was startlingly close to the truth. In the preface to *A New Astronomy,* Kepler speaks of the attraction between two bodies as being proportional to each other's masses.[2] Elsewhere, Kepler speaks of a force, "emanating from the sun," which varies "as does the force of light."[3]

Since the density of light from a point source varies inversely with the square of the distance, exactly in the same mathematical manner as gravity, it would clearly seem that Kepler verbally anticipated by seventy five years Newton's law of gravitational force between two bodies, $F = gm_1m_2/r^2$ (where g is a constant, m_1 and m_2 are the masses, and r the distance between the two bodies).

Strangely, Kepler never used his concepts of gravity in his attempts to discover a universal law for the motion of planets. Koestler finds this fact very paradoxical and faults Kepler for confusing the two opposing forces, gravity and inertia. Yet how many students of physics today still find it difficult to digest these two concepts at first sight? Or even the hundredth? Can the father of such ideas be rightfully condemned for experiencing some difficulty when biting them off for the initial chew?

BAROQUE GENIUS

A major part of the trouble in understanding and interpreting Kepler is his writing style, breathless, baroque, demanding, rambling, taking the reader down every tortuous channel of his thoughts. Kepler examines every wrong turn, every mistaken assumption.

In addition, the times in which Kepler wrote were fraught with political intrigue and superstitious dogma; the Inquisition eagerly sought heretics and witches. It was common practice for the scholars and savants of the day to couch their discoveries and discussions in obscurant language. Often they employed astrological and religious imagery while clarifying the text for their colleagues in obscure footnotes.

Kepler's book concerning the moon—the same *Somnium, Sive Astronomia Lunaris* that nearly sent his aging crone mother to the stake for witchcraft—is a classic in this late Renaissance scholarly writing style.[4] The book is an allegory, a dream allegory of the new science of astronomy discovered by Kepler, Copernicus, and Galileo. The language of *Somnium* is mystical, couched in the magical superstitions of the day, so much so that Kepler's creative genius nearly got his poor mother condemned as a witch. He spent the greater portion of the remainder of his life adding footnote upon footnote, trying in vain to explain his mystical-scientific work.

Small wonder, then, that Koestler feels Kepler stood at the "watershed," one foot in the mysticism of the past, the other feeling about tentatively for the solid ground of the new science. However, Kepler's head was *not* buried in the clouds. He had a clear view of the stars and wanted desperately to chart the orbits of the planets accurately, even if he couldn't afford the expensive measuring instruments of Tycho or even a simple telescope like Galileo's.

Why, then, did Kepler look for his planetary laws in the Greek "harmony of the spheres"? Why did he devote his years at Gratz and his first book, *Mysterium Cosmographicum,* trying to fit the five regular solids between the orbits of the planets?

Between the orbits of Saturn and Jupiter he assigned a cube, between Jupiter and Mars he fitted a tetrahedron, between Mars and the earth a dodecadron, and so on. Kepler's first "model of the universe" is shown in Figure 5-1.

Why? Why did Kepler come up with such an abstract theory? Did he really think that there are regular solids placed between the planets, much as the Babylonians and Greeks pictured the stars and planets attached to transparent spheres in the heavens?

We can't really tell what Kepler's motive, his driving force, was here. Koestler calles it an *idée fixe,* a mystical delusion proving that Kepler was operating in a fog. However, another interpretation is possible. Kepler wanted to find some fixed mathematical relation between the orbits and motions of the planets. So he tried as his first hypothesis a Chinese box of regular solids with the Greek concept of harmonic relationships between planets as his guide. No doubt he felt that the volumetric relations between the solids might give some hint of the functional relationship between planetary orbits.

Thus Kepler tried to keep the last of the astrological "bath water," but he was finally forced to throw it out when he found that it served only to muddy the picture. The father of modern cosmological science would accept only the hard facts of reality. Much later he would similarly throw out his off-center-circle model for the orbit of Mars because of a discrepancy between prediction and observation of only 8′ of arc.

Eight minutes of arc. Little more than an eighth of a degree. Not bad vision for a "sleepwalker"!

This is not to say that "luck," or circumstance, did not play a role in Kepler's career. He knew that before he could draw up his mathematical model of the solar system, he had to have accurate data of the planetary positions—much more accurate data than Ptolemy or Copernicus, who could not be trusted within 10′ of arc and were often off in their predictions of planetary conjunctions by several days. The Imperial Mathematician realized the key lay with Tycho de Brahe, the secretive, rich Danish astronomer who had been making precisely such accurate observations of the sky for over thirty years. Tycho, however, held court on his lavish island observatory, Uraniborg, and refused to divulge his data.

Professional jealousy is no stranger to science.

Finally, a year and a half before Tycho's death, the two astronomers found themselves in semi-exile in Germany. Tycho was setting up a new observatory on another island, this one near Prague, and realized he needed the brilliant young mathematician, Kepler, to put together the model of the universe they both were searching for.

So Kepler came to work as Tycho's assistant and was assigned the troublesome planet, Mars, as his special charge.

Kepler set to work on Tycho's planetary tables, trying to fit the data to various models, beginning first with the off-center circle, then graduating to the oval (Koestler jokes about Kepler's new fixation with the "primal egg"), finally settling on the ellipse.

How perfect! In *A New Astronomy* Kepler breaks into estatic raptures of prose when he finally hits upon the ellipse. And how absurd, he notes (echoed by Koestler), that he had previously discarded the ellipse as too geometric, too simple, merely an analogy he had been using to describe the data. A classic study in the evolution of an idea, of the devious, intuitive paths tread by genius.

The ellipse as the mathematical model for the shape of planetary orbits became Kepler's Second Law. The first had already been derived: each planet, in its motion about the sun, traces out equal area in equal times, a result Kepler had derived from considering the hypothesis that the closer a planet is to the sun, the faster it moves, while the farther away it is, the slower it moves. Figure 5-2 illustrates Kepler's first two Laws of Planetary Motion.

MODERN DOWNS AND UPS

With the advent of Kepler's laws, astrology began its long, slow decline into the oblivion it existed in during the nineteenth century. Man at last had a rational picture of the universe, a picture that at least had some chance of corresponding to reality. Gone was the simple-minded magic that had lain at the base of man's cosmological thinking for millennia. Mars would no longer be seen as the abode of the god of war, magically "influencing" those born under its "sway" to be aggressive, masculine, warlike.

With the discoveries of Copernicus, Galileo, and Kepler, the planets assumed their rightful positions in the order of things—huge celestial objects like the earth, circling the sun according to known physical laws that could be checked and verified by anyone who would take the trouble to do so.

And how much more marvelous was the new cosmology! No longer was man imprisoned in a tiny world made especially for him. No longer were the stars mere symbolic signposts attached to concentric spheres, but immense suns extending virtually without number into the farthest reaches of space that the mind could conceive.

The real world, a world composed of atoms and infinity, containing unthinkable power and black holes, caught man's fancy. With Kepler and his associates was born the scientific revolution. The next three centuries would see momentous discoveries: Newton's law of gravitation, Descartes's calculus, Darwin's theory of evolution, and Mendel's genetic laws.

Each discovery seemed to pound yet another nail into the coffin of astrology. The planets were no longer seen as the cause of biological diversity. Heredity, the inheritance of genetic material from one's parents, replaced the planets' mystical role in determining character. Germs and other environmental factors were recognized as the causes of disease, robbing the stars of another of their age-old magical "influences."

Astrology's role in determining fate and fortune, too, was soon forgotten. Man became far too interested in using his new science, his new, rational view of the universe, to his own ends to improve his lot and learn to make the forces of nature do his work for him.

The world of modern science had come to stay.

Yet astrology's decline during the Age of Enlightenment would not be its final fall from grace. Much encouraged by the popularity of spiritualism and parlor séances, occultists, with astrologers in the lead, would once again find adherents in late nineteenth-century England. Soon, astrology was experiencing a revival in Germany and France, again in concert with occultism, particularly in the cases of the Theosophists and Rosicrusians.

Then, in post–World War I Germany, astrology would reach its modern peak of popularity and influence. Once again, astrology would play a role in the political affairs of a nation and the world (see Chapter 12 for a full discussion).

Today—amid the complexities and uncertainties of the last quarter of the twentieth century—astrology is more popular than ever, though the extent of its present influence is poorly documented. A recent Gallup poll indicated that 32 million Americans believe in astrology. Nearly every newspaper carries a daily horoscope column. Hundreds of astrological books, magazines, and pamphlets are being rushed into print.

Astrology has shown amazing staying power. It had a powerful hold on the minds of the Babylonians, the Greeks, and the Romans. It withstood the opposition of the Church by surviving in Arabia. During the Renaissance, astrology once again became part of man's cosmology and was believed in and followed by nearly everyone. And now, seemingly, astrology has survived the onslaught of modern science. It seems amazing to the modern rational mind that the simple-minded magic of astrology could hold any real interest for twentieth-century man. Astrology must hold some mystical appeal, some fascination for the irrational, perhaps archetypical, side of man. Or perhaps astrology's popularity is a sign of a growing discontent with science and technology, a revolt against mass production and the impersonality of modern monolithic institutions.

This growth of interest in occultism has it ominous sides. Witness the similar rise of astrology and occultism that occurred in Germany just prior to the rise of Nazism. Could people today be experiencing the same despair, the same loss of confidence that characterized the Germans following their defeat in World War I? Could it be the nuclear age, pollution, political manipulation, or any combination of such similar woes?

Whatever the cause, astrology is once again a part of man's society, though its role is still far from what it was in Roman or Renaissance times. Its present popularity is a testament to astrology's appeal to the human mind, to its hold upon the public fancy, helping us gain some appreciation for its tremendous impact upon ancient societies. If astrology can still gain large numbers of believers today, can we doubt that it captured the minds of entire empires, that it helped shape, for better or worse, the course of history?

In the next section, "Inside the Inner Temple," I shall begin the search for the secret of astrology's appeal, for the key that unlocks its inner workings. There are psychological and mathematical "secrets" to astrology, to its success in describing people and influencing their psyches. However, the answers lie not in the stars, which are only incidentally involved. The stars are conveniently always present, always marking the paths of the planets and the motion of our own earth.

In a way, the stars are the scapegoats, the convenient coathooks upon which can be placed the psychological ills of the human race. For these and many other reasons, it may well be a long time before man sees the final decline of astrology.

NOTES

1. Arthur Koestler, *The Watershed* (Garden City, N.Y.: Anchor Books, Doubleday & Co., 1960), p. 39.
2. Ibid., p. 152.
3. Arthur Koestler, *The Sleepwalkers* (New York: Macmillan 1959), p. 258.
4. John Lear, *Kepler's Dream* (Berkeley: University of California Press, 1965).

Book II   Inside the Inner Temple

Welcome to astrology's Inner Temple. It's dark and mysterious, isn't it? It's designed that way; the darkness helps shroud the inner workings of the "art"; it helps obscure what is actually going on. Note, too, the engraved decorations, esoteric symbology, and cabalistic scribblings—all designed to impress and obfuscate. An astrological talisman lies carelessly on a crude altar, awaiting the magical ritual and rich client that will give it its "power."

In the deepest recesses of the temple, one is likely to find faint, circular chalk marks, angular lines and scribbles still visible through the dust on the floor. Here, some power-hungry magician attempted to summon evil spirits with the help of astrological "powers."

The Inner Temple of astrology contains many secrets, many hidden recesses and little-known rooms. But, above all, the Inner Temple must remain dark, not so much to permit the stars to shine as to focus the vision of astrology's visitors on the heavens and their "influences."

For it wouldn't pay for the high priests of astrology to permit too much light. The disciples must not be allowed to see too much too quickly. The secret knowledge must be administered in small, regularly applied doses. First, give them a hint, then promise them the world. Let them see only on a need-to-know basis. Get them thoroughly hooked, then lead them gently through the outer halls of the temple.

Admit to the Inner Temple only those who are able to discover the key and unlock the inner doors on their own initiative. These shall become the innovators, the leaders of the astrological priestly class who, knowing the innermost secrets, are able to mold and fit the "art" to the times, to introduce those changes that will make astrology compatible with current thought and politics.

Thus, by means of its Inner Temple, astrology has managed to maintain its first rank among the occult "sciences."

The Inner Temple is both a place and a concept. Within its mysterious walls lie many secrets considered by many to be the most important secrets of the occult world. The millennia of darkness, the thousands of subtle changes in the liturgy and ritual, each new symbology and ceremony, have all helped shape the temple, adding new defensive walls here, deepening the shadows there, creating new rooms and labyrinths to lead the disciple astray and distract his attention from the innermost secrets.

Historically, the Inner Temple might be a tiny room hidden within the labyrinthine recesses of one of the Egyptian pyramids or Mayan temples. At various stops along the route, there might be tiny observation rooms where, on certain days of the year, the light of an important star or planet might intrude, its presence dutifully recorded on the Great Tables so essential to the astrologer's "art."

In Babylonia, the Inner Temple was located at the tops of the *ziggurats,* where the astrologer-priests would be closer to the heavens and thus have a clearer view. In Greece, the Inner Temple became entrusted to the minds of philosophers, the most respected men of their time, usually the heads of schools. In Rome, there was no Inner Temple for centuries; the secrets were kept safely hidden in the Provinces, in Jerusalem, in Alexandria. It was only during the brief realm of the fanatic sun-emperor Elagabalus that Rome possessed its own Inner Temple, a weak flimsy thing grounded in the moderate catarchic side of the "art."

During the Renaissance, however, the doors of the Inner Temple remained closed for the most part, except possibly to the most visionary of the adepts like Bacon and Kepler. No doubt, some Renaissance astrologers gained some inkling, some intuitive feel, for what it was they were doing. But the majority of Renaissance astrologers followed the traditional liturgy, performing the latest ceremonies without question.

Astrology was so accepted during the Renaissance that there was no need for an active Inner Temple, no need to erect new walls or create new secret chambers. The old traditions—newly introduced to the Renaissance—were romantic enough to capture the popular fancy. Friend and foe alike repeated the same old rituals and reiterated the same old arguments that have kept astrology alive for centuries.

With the end of the Renaissance, the doors of the Inner Temple seemed closed for good; astrology appeared to be a dead "art." However, the end of the nineteenth and the beginning of the twentieth centuries saw many attempts to reopen the doors of the Inner Temple. Theosophists and the Rosicrusians claimed to have taken over maintenance of the Inner Temple, further obscuring its features by adding more rooms and furniture, attempting to learn the secret of the "cosmic mystery" by combining with astrology nearly every form of occult "science" they could imagine.

Turn-of-the-century mystics, such as Aleister Crowley and Gurdjieff, added their own rooms to the temple, dark, rambling chambers that were obscure not only to their closest disciples, but probably even to themselves.

The ancient core of the Inner Temple became nearly totally lost in the maze of modern thought. Occultism, except in Nazi Germany, seemed about to smother of its own weight. The flame of the Inner Temple was about to be snuffed out.

Then modern science discovered the biological clock.

All forms of life, scientists found, from the tiniest plants to the largest animals, display daily rhythms, life processes that wax and wane with the daily movement of the sun across the earth's sky. "Aha," cried the astrologers. "Isn't that just what we've been saying all along? That the motions of the planets and stars affect life here on earth?"

The doors of the Inner Temple seemed to fly open.

In America as well as in Russia, researchers found evidence of relationships between sunspots and all sorts of phenomena, ranging from biology to economics. In Germany, led by the famous Nazi astrologer/mathematician Karl Ernst Krafft, astrologers began using statistics to correlate planetary motions and events here on earth. After the war, the Austrian naturalist Karl von Frisch showed that bees possess a sort of sun compass that tells them the position of the sun even on cloudy days.

With each new discovery, each new promising study, the astrologers gained renewed confidence and attracted new followers. They began to talk of finally being able to throw open the doors of the Inner

Temple to everyone and at last being able to base their ancient "art" on scientific principles. They dreamed of the old secrets giving way to the new. As we shall see in "Book III: Biological versus Cosmic Clocks," they dreamed in vain.

For the old secrets of astrology are of an entirely different order, from an essentially different universe: the magical world of our pre-historic ancestors. Astrology is steeped in magic and as such can never be a science. The theoretical basis of astrology is the magical "principle of correspondences," or the "law of analogies" (see Chapter 6). Even the psychological operating principles of astrology are startlingly similar to the psychology of voodoo and witchcraft. Book IV will attempt to un-cover the psychology of astrology, traditionally not part of the Inner Temple since the unconscious and the way in which it operates was not discovered until late in the nineteenth century.

Yet, of course, the psychological aspects were always there. The most successful astrologers—Thrasylus, Merlin, John Dee, for in-stance—used the psychological powers of astrology to their own great advantage. Had more astrologers been conscious of how they arrived at their "predictions" and how they manipulated their clients, astrology might have become a far more potent political force.

Today, despite the popularity of astrology, its Inner Temple lies in disarray, its secret chambers plundered, its rich symbology looted. The wealth of the temple is now serving other causes, other occult mysteries and wisdoms of the East.

Astrologers today must be content with the bare bones, the slim pickings left by the ungrateful jackals of less scrupulous cults. No longer can the astrologer claim to hold the secret of your soul; no longer can he chart the destiny of kings or the fate of nations. No longer can the astrol-oger claim to cure your every ill, to know even the moment of your death. He can only chart trends, indicate possibilities, suggest alterna-tives.

The great cosmic mysteries are no longer available to the astrol-oger. The Inner Temple lies in ruins, in part from the efforts of astrol-ogers themselves to cleanse their temple, to make their "art" scientific. Astrology may be popular today, but it lies on weakened footings, teetering like a bombed, burned-out ruin. Only the ramshackle props of statistics, popularity, and the new discoveries in biological clocks are holding the structure up.

Let us, then, make our way through the rubble and gently pick the lock to the Inner Temple. First, in Chapter 6, we will show how the magic in astrology, the ancient "principle of correspondences," operates and how it is used in astrological interpretations. Then Chapter 7, "Horoscopy," will show as simply as possible how to set up a chart based on local time positions of the planets, with emphasis on astronomical realities. Finally, Chapter 8 will take a quick look at the astrological debate that has been raging off and on for more than two thousand years.

The arguments, teachings, and information we shall find within the Inner Temple are the traditional material presented by astrologers to their disciples, yet we shall be examining it from a different point of view, pushing aside rusty doors, and flooding dusty chambers with the new light of modern science and rationality. We must tread lightly, though: one strong push, one crucial block dislodged, and the entire structure of astrology's Inner Temple may come tumbling down!

6   The Magic in Astrology

Of all the occult "sciences" none appears as scientific as astrology. Its horoscopes are based on the positions of the stars and planets; elaborate calculations are required to translate zodiacal and planetary positions from the ephemerides tables to the astrologer's horoscope. Local time must be translated into Greenwich mean time, which in turn must be transformed into sidereal time by more tables.

It all *seems* so scientific.

Like the stage magician who distracts the audience's attention from what he is really doing by elaborate flourishes and rituals, the astrologer disguises *his* magic behind the façade of the horoscope. The magic does not even begin to enter astrology until long after the horoscope is cast—when the astrologer goes to *interpret* the chart.

The magic in astrology rests in its interpretations, in the assignment of planetary "influences," in the magical correlations between zodiac sign and events here on earth. "As above, so below," goes the astrological litany. Whatever is "writ" in the stars is "mirrored" here on earth. Man is a "microcosm," a tiny replica of the "macrocosm" of the universe.

These are just a few of the literary creations that—over the ages—have polished and obscured the magical correlations that lie hidden at the base of astrology. The planets and stars are always conveniently present; the horoscope can always be drawn up. However, it requires the application of the magical "principle of correspondences" for the astrologer to be able to "read" the chart, to be able to relate planetary and stellar positions to human events.

THE PRINCIPLE OF CORRESPONDENCES

The "principle of correspondences," usually referred to by astrologers as the "law of analogies," is the basic assumption behind all magic: white, black, voodoo, alchemical or astrological. The "principle of correspondences" arose with man's use of language. There is "magic" in the spoken word, the "magic" of imagery and conception, the "magic" of thought before action (see Chapter 2). There was "magic," too, in prehistoric art and notation—magic and ritual, learning and experience.

What exactly is this "principle of correspondences"? What role does it play in magic and astrology?

The "principle of correspondences" is based on the simple, basic idea of analogy. Any sort of connection, any sort of analogy, that can be seen in the omen object (or in the magician's mind) is then transferred to the magical subject via the "principle of correspondences."

Figure 6-1 illustrates the principle. The omen, O (e.g. zodiac sign), is reputed to have qualities, Q; hence, the corresponding analog object, $\mathcal{O}$ (the magical subject) has similar corresponding qualities, $\mathcal{Q}$.

A simple example will illustrate this principle. The planet Mars has a reddish cast in the sky. To the primitive mind, this meant that Mars was associated with blood, war, and aggressive behavior. Once Mars had been associated with the god of war, additional analogies became possible. The metal iron, for instance, became associated with the planet Mars because iron proved such a superior metal to bronze in warfare.

In fact, once the planets became associated with gods, the entire mythology connected with each god could then be used in making magical correspondences between the planet and analogous events here on earth. Thus, once the goddess of love became associated with the planet Venus (as the brightest, most lovely of the planets), all of her characteristics of beauty, sensitivity, and motherhood could then be associated by the astrologer to people under her "influence."

Table 6-1 provides a list of the planets, their observational characteristics, and their corresponding magical association with gods and astrological "influences."[1] Note that the observational characteristics of the planets determine the characters of their godly namesakes. Thus the Greeks associated Mercury—which moves rapidly in the vicinity of the sun and is very difficult to view with the naked eye—with their shrewd, unpredictable messenger of the gods. Jupiter, moving slowly and majestically across the sky, became the ruler of the gods for both the Babylonians and the Greeks; thus astrologers consider Jupiter's "influence" to be beneficial, providing leadership qualities for those lucky people born under its sway.

Table 6-1   The Planets and their Magical Influences

Planet symbol	Observational characteristics	Godly namesake	Astrological influences
Mercury ☿	Close to Sun, moves rapidly, difficult to view.	Messenger of the gods, who was shrewd, swift, unpredictable.	unpredictable skillful deceitful
Venus ♀	Inside Earth's orbit, appears as a bright morning and evening 'star'.	Goddess of love and beauty, who was soft, weak, treacherous.	harmonious emotional sensitive love for beauty
Mars ♂	Distinctly red, moves slowly, then rapidly.	God of war, who was hateful, murderous, cowardly.	aggressive impatient fighting instinct
Jupiter ♃	Very bright, moves slowly and majestically across the sky.	Ruler of the gods, awesome and majestic, adulterous.	lucky sincere strong handsome
Saturn ♄	Moderately bright, slower than Jupiter.	Ruler of the Titans, father of Jupiter, brought about Golden Age.	gloomy scholarly punctual
Uranus ♅	Discovered in 1781, barely visible	Father of Saturn.	Only a few 'radicals' include the outer planets

Source: L. E. Jerome, "Astrology and Modern Science," *Leonardo* 6 (1973): 126.

These same magical "qualities" of the planets are still used by astrologers today. There were no statistical observations made to determine the reality of such planetary "influences," as has often been
claimed by astrologers past and present. Magic alone, in the form of the
"principle of correspondences," determines the astrological role played
by the planets in horoscope interpretations. Thus Mars imparts aggressiveness, Venus rules affairs of the heart, and Saturn makes one punc-
tual.

Magic, pure and simple.

Similarly the signs of the zodiac play their magical roles as well. A
person born under Aries the Ram is considered to be "headstrong, im-
pulsive." Those born under the sign of Scorpio are naturally "secretive,
troublesome, and aggressive," just like their earthly counterpart. And
when Pisces the Fish comes into play in one's horoscope, beware the sea
and alcohol!

Table 6-2   Signs of the Zodiac and their Magical Characteristics

Constellation and symbol	Animal namesake	Selected characteristics
Aries ♈	ram	headstrong, inpulsive, quick-tempered
Taurus ♉	bull	plodding, patient, stubborn
Gemini ♊	twins	vacillating, split personality
Cancer ♋	crab	clinging, protective exterior shell
Leo ♌	lion	proud, forceful, born leader
Virgo ♍	virgin	reticent, modest
Libra ♎	scales	just, harmonious, balanced
Scorpius ♏	scorpion	secretive, troublesome, aggressive
Sagittarius ♐	archer/horse	active, aims for target
Capricornus ♑	goat/fish	tenacious
Aquarius ♒	water carrier	humanitarian, serving mankind
Pisces ♓	fish	attracted to sea and alcohol

Source: L. E. Jerome, *Leonardo* 6 (1973): 126.

Table 6-2 gives a list of the signs of the zodiac, their animal namesakes, and selected characteristics used by astrologers today.[2]

Magic, then, lies at the basis of astrology. When Peking Man spoke
of fire, he associated the magic of abstract thought with the spoken

word. When Paleolithic man carved images on bone and associated those images with lunar notation, he began associating the "magic" of art and notation with celestial objects and the seasonal comings and goings of the animals he depended upon for his livelihood. By the time late Paleolithic man began painting and repainting ritual images on the walls of caves, magic had long been a part of his culture, his way of life.

With the rise of civilization and Neolithic man, magic began to be used by the priestly class to institute power and hierarchy into the growing political structure of their small city-states. As we saw in Book I, Babylonian priests magically interpreted the omens provided by animal entrails and celestial events. Thus the intestine of a sacrificial animal that coiled to the left was considered a weak and sinister "sign" (since most people are right handed). Similarly darkness and the setting of planets were considered ominous due to the magical association of blackness with death.

In China, as well as in Babylonia, comets were considered especially ominous since they appeared at unpredictable times and their "hairy" tails always stretched out away from the sun. To the ancient Mayans the sun and planets were analogous to a gigantic cosmological handball game played by the gods.

The key to magic is analogy: "as above, so below"—"one nature delights another."

As the Babylonians began codifying their magical system of correspondences between heaven and earth, the priests realized that here was the perfect medium for playing their games of political intrigue and control. The planets and stars are always available, even when they're not visible. Unlike the *haruspex,* who had to perform his magical interpretations based on a limited number of possible entrail configurations, the astrologer dealt with an infinite number of possible planetary and stellar permutations.

In addition, astrology deals with symbols, numbers, and geometrical constructions, concepts that had magical significance to primitive man. It did not take long for the many advantages of astrology to manifest themselves; it was clean, impressively complicated, and intuitively "logical" in terms of man's magical world view.

With its magical bases in the "principle of correspondences" safely hidden amid the complexities of mathematical computation and philosophical obfuscation, astrology was a natural to capture the Greek mind, itself already steeped in the magic of mythology and the divination of oracles. Once the Greeks began ascribing these same magical correspondences to physical "influences" by the stars and planets, the magic in astrology became thoroughly disguised and essentially forgotten.

By the second century A.D., Ptolemy describes astrology as a physical "science," complete with an ethereal medium for propagating the planetary "influences." Yet even Ptolemy carefully separated the science of astronomy from the practice of astrology.

The magic was hidden but not totally unrecognized.

The Roman Empire saw magic unabashedly creep back into astrology. Chaldean *haruspices* plied their trade side by side with the street astrologers. Astrological talismans, herbs, and elixirs competed for clients' money. Provincial alchemists sought to harness the planetary powers to produce gold from lead and immortality from foul-tasting drinks.

Perhaps more than anything else, the astrological talisman illustrates the magic in astrology, as well as the converse role that astrology played in the development of the other magical occult "sciences."

Talismans are magic amulets to be carried or worn. Their special magical significance was alleged to contain the power to ward off specific diseases and evil spirits or to protect one from the magic of one's enemies. Talismans have to be made of certain materials at specified times in order to magically contain the desired magical power; usually, the magician inscribes symbols on and recites incantations over the talisman before it is considered sufficiently "charged" and ready for sale.

Magic always requires ritual.

Undoubtedly the magician's own belief, combined with the psychological effect of having performed the ancient forbidden rituals, creates a "magic state of mind" easily transferred to the gullible client. As William Seabrook first pointed out, magic relies heavily on the power of suggestion.[3] It is this aspect of the occult, this creation and fostering of highly suggestible states of mind, that makes occult "sciences" potentially dangerous.

Suggestion, then, played a major role in the "efficacy" of talismans. In the case of astrological talismans, it is the "power" of the planets that is being captured and focused. Since nearly everybody believed in at least some general "influence" by the planets, and the planets are always available to exert their "power," the astrological talisman was more generally believed in than talismans constructed according to more vulgar magical rituals.

In fact nearly all talismans were at least partly astrological, the magician taking advantage of all available "powers." For instance, a "love" talisman might be made of tin for good luck (Jupiter rules the metal, tin) and cast when Venus is found in her own houses, Virgo or Taurus, or exalted in Pisces.[4] Even when the talisman was based on other occult practices such as necromancy or the summoning of spirits, astrological principles were adhered to. The magician who failed to enlist the "powers" of the planets in his behalf might find his struggles to subdue the darker forces of nature thwarted.

THE "POWER" OF MAGIC

For those who dabble in the black arts, there is always a danger; usually, their will-to-believe and their suggestibility are very high. Should their magic turn against them, this suggestible magic state of mind makes them psychologically vulnerable to the very "powers" they are trying to control.

Modern astrologers of course would rather forget that astrological talismans ever existed. So, just to remind them and the reader, Figure 6-2 pictures such a talisman for capturing the "powers" of the planets, and the ritualistic chant that was supposed to "charge it up" magically. With talismans, as in all magic, any observed "effects" occur strictly in the mind of the believer. If the talisman succeeds in warding off illness or the magic of one's enemies, it does so because the wearer himself has been "charged" with the power of suggestion.

As I shall show in Chapter 14, "Astrological Dowsing," the effect of astrology upon its believers is entirely due to the power of suggestion. In a deeper sense, that's precisely what *all* belief is: a highly suggestible psychological state of mind. Belief in any system, whether magic, astrology, or politics, carries with it the psychological dangers inherent in the power of suggestion. We need only picture grim thousands cheering Hitler as he spouted occult nonsense to support his racial theories.

There may appear to be a vast gulf between astrology and Hitler's racial pogroms, but consider what might have happened if Hitler had been able to fit astrology into his "cosmic scheme." Belief in astrology was very widespread in Germany before World War II; if Hitler had realized that Ptolemy's *Tetrabiblos* provided astrological "reasons" for the differences among people and races, he might have found astrology a far more potent psychological warfare tool than Horbigger's Cosmic Ice theory or Nostradamus's *Prophecies!*

Astrology, then, has played a major role in all the magical "sciences," alchemy, black magic, the conjuring of spirits, necromancy, and even in the simpler magical practices such as the use of talismans. Astrology, too, in its full magical form played a major role in early medicine. Virtually no Renaissance doctor would think of operating when the moon was waxing, or touch a particular part of the body when its planet or sign were badly "aspected."

Herbs and plants, too, became part of the astrological magical lore. Just as certain parts of the body were associated with their corresponding planet and signs, so herbs were "ruled" by particular planets. Again, the "principle of correspondences" was evoked to magically determine which plants would be assigned which planets and stars. Figure 6-3 gives the astrological assignments of the various parts of the human body along with the corresponding herbs recommended by Culpepper for treating ailments and disorders "ruled" by each planet or sign.

Early medicine, then, like the alchemy that led to the modern science of chemistry, used the astrological theory of sympathy ("principle of correspondences") for its working hypothesis. For instance, since Scorpio was associated with the sexual organs, and the plant hops was "ruled" by Scorpio, Culpepper naturally suggests in all seriousness that hops be used as a cure for venereal disease![5]

To modern man, it's a wonder that anybody got cured before the Enlightenment. Since, of course, the doctors were simply applying astrological magic, the power of suggestion no doubt played an important part in most of their "successful" cures. Not all the cures were simple magic, however; as modern pharmacology is learning, some herbs *do* contain drugs and medicines of value. The beautiful flower foxglove, for instance, is a source of the drug digitalis which is useful in preventing heart attacks; likewise, the poppy provides morphine, a very important drug. Therefore, on a chance level alone, some of the astrological herbs and medicines could be expected to have some curative powers.

Knowledge of a plant's effect upon a particular disease may have led to its assignment under the "rulership" of the planet or sign associated astrologically with the disease or part of the body ailing. Perhaps, once pharmacology has taken a complete look at astrology's herbal associations, we will learn which plants may have been assigned on the basis of their effects rather than appearance or other nonessential attribute.

As Kepler once said of astrology itself, "one must be careful not to throw out the baby with the bath water"! However, just because modern chemistry arose from alchemy, and modern medicine from astrological medicine, this does not imply any validity to astrology. The modern counterparts are *not* based on magic, and the only resemblance to their ancient "protosciences" lay in their operating materials: chemicals, drugs, and the human body.

Kepler was probably referring to the magic in astrology when he commented about "tossing out the bath water." For, once the magic is removed from astrology, what remains but Kepler's "baby," the modern science of astronomy?

Likewise, once doctors threw out the astrological magic and began applying the new scientific method of data collecting, theorizing, and testing, modern medicine was born kicking and eager to attack the problems and misery of mankind. Astrologers who hope to use the horoscope to achieve even a small measure of the same success as modern medicine are seriously deluding themselves and their clients. The magic of astrology can operate only through the power of suggestion; therefore any apparent astrological "cures" can only be due to the client's belief and suggestibility.

Faith healing—whether astrological, mystical, or modern technological—will always remain popular as long as psychosomatic illnesses exist that are amenable to the power of suggestion. This, perhaps, suggests one reason why astrology is becoming so popular today: our modern civilization may have taken the magic out of science and medicine, but the mind-body link remains so strong that the magic of our ancestors in the form of suggestion can still operate today.

Modern man may not be as modern as he thinks!

Magic, then, plays a double role in astrology. Magic in the form of the "principle of correspondences" lies at the very basis of astrology—its operating assumption, if you will. Magic via the power of suggestion is also the means by which astrology operates on the "physical plane."

The "effects" of the stars are really only the effects of the power of suggestion. As Henry Howard, Earl of Northampton, wrote, "If the planet has an influence, it is probably more in the mind of the observer than in the planet."[6]

The medieval Church fathers were right, then, in classifying astrology as magic, as a demonic art that could usurp the power of the Church. The magic of astrology is a haughty, self-centered thing, quite contrary to the humility required by religion. Astrology magically links man to the entire cosmos, raising him to the level of the stars.

As in all occultism, the magic of astrology offers direct competition to institutional religion. When astrology was first gaining acceptance during the Middle Ages, the Church first frowned upon and then began persecuting astrologers; more than a few were burned at the stake. It was only when the magic of astrology was made compatible with religious assumptions that the Church could accept astrology into its fold. It's interesting that today, when nearly all organized religions are witnessing a strong decline in membership, the occult "sciences," and especially astrology, are experiencing a "spiritual revival."

So, the ancient magic is making a comeback here in the latter half of the twentieth century. Astrology, more than the other occult "sciences," seems to appeal to the new spirit of searching, of looking for old, easy answers to new, difficult problems. One might even be tempted to call it a "sign" of the times!

NOTES

1. Lawrence Jerome, "Astrology and Modern Science: A Critical Analysis," *Leonardo* 6, no. 2 (1973):126.
2. Ibid.
3. William Seabrook, *Witchcraft: Its Powers in the World Today* (New York: Harcourt, Brace, 1940).
4. Richard Cavendish, *The Black Arts* (New York: G. P. Putnam's Sons, 1967), p. 221.
5. Derek Parker and Julia Parker, *The Compleat Astrologer* (New York: McGraw-Hill, 1971), p. 29.
6. Don Cameron Allen, *The Star-Crossed Renaissance* (Durham, N.C.: Duke University Press, 1941), p. 115.

7   Horoscopy

It is the casting of charts, the locating of planets in the ephemerides, the calculations of sidereal time, and the like that give astrology its "scientific" character. Horoscopy is the key to the astrological door behind which lie vast chambers of magic.

Horoscopy pulls a "scientific" veil over the magic, disguising the anthropomorphic dark roots of the ancient "art." For the uninitiated it is the horoscope that fascinates and attracts. At first, drawing up the horoscope is a complex mathematical puzzle, the sort of puzzle sure to interest those who like to solve problems, to come up with a final answer to questions.

The horoscope looks so "scientific"—so mathematically precise—and it is! That's the beauty and charm of astrology: one first has to calculate and plot an accurate map of the heavens, a map showing the actual positions of the sun, moon, and planets. The fact that they are plotted against an arbitrary reference frame of signs rather than real stars matters not at all. The planets are still there, accurately plotted, ready as always to exert their astrological "influences."

By the time most people learn to cast a chart, to read ephemerides and all the rest, the magic in the subsequent *interpretation* process has been lost in the welter of calculations and plots. Part of the problem lies in the complexity of the various horoscope systems (at least a half-dozen major ones exist). The astrologer has at his disposal a number of different methods, all of which will lead to different results and hence differing interpretations. If one system doesn't happen to fit the case at hand, there's a good chance that another will!

Most astrologers today use the same basic system of horoscopy as contained in Ptolemy's *Tetrabiblos,* with, of course, endless variations. Due to the slow astronomical wobble in the earth's axis of rotation (see Figure 7-1), the stars do not always return to the same spot in the sky each year. If one made accurate measurements of a particular star over a long period of time, one would notice the star slipping "backward"; after twenty years, the star would have slipped back a measurable amount—about a tenth of a degree. This astronomical peculiarity, called *precession,* is the reason Ptolemy talked of signs rather than constellations.

If one were able to keep track of the marker star over thousands of years, one would notice the star slipping back almost a twelfth of the whole celestial circle every two thousand years. The astrologers would say that the tropical zodiac has slipped back yet another sign with respect to the sidereal zodiac. Note in Figure 7-1 that the sidereal zodiac is attached to the stars, while the astrologer's tropical zodiac is merely a fictional construct of signs placed where the stars *used* to be in Hipparchus's time (second century B.C.).

Hipparchus, a Greek astronomer from Nicaea, noticed that the positions of the "fixed" stars no longer matched the positions indicated by the earlier Greeks and Babylonians. Thus he was the first to detect the phenomenon of precession, one of the most important astronomical discoveries of ancient times.

Since the theory of astrology was based on the relative positions of the planets and stars, one might have expected that the discovery of precession would spell trouble for the astrologers. Since the relative positions of the stars and planets constantly changed over a very long period of time, how could these same relative positions impart any fixed "character" or "quality" to people and events here on earth?

The astrologers, ever ready to attach new scientific discoveries to their magic "art," responded by shifting their zodiac from the stars to an arbitrary fixed position in space, fixed at least to the earth's precessional axis. This new tropical zodiac rotates with respect to the stars or sidereal zodiac once every 25,868 years. Their reasoning, though faulty, no doubt ran in this track: since astrology had shown the efficacy of planetary "influences" over the previous four hundred years, it must be *that part* of the sky which is important, not the stars themselves.

In other words, since it was the relative positions which were "significant," and Hipparchus had demonstrated that stars change their relative positions, the system of astrology had to be disconnected from the stars. The Greeks realized you couldn't have fixed "influences" based on changing patterns.

Three hundred years after Hipparchus discovered precession, Ptolemy codified the astrological result of his discovery, the tropical zodiac, in his *Tetrabiblos*. The signs had become a permanent fixture of astrology; in the course of the next two millennia, the concept of signs would become an integral part of man's civilization and language.

Note, too, how the term astrological *sign* is intimately connected with the magical concepts of omens and signs. The astrologers have never been able to totally rid their "science" of its magic. When the astrologer draws up his chart, he is not actually drawing up a real plot of the sky as it exists. He is concocting a magical diagram of the sky as viewed from the tropical zodiac reference frame of omens and signs. Yet, in order to be able to plot the positions of the planets with respect to their tropical zodiac, the astrologers must still use astronomical data; they merely shift the planetary right ascensions to their own reference frame. By such stratagems, astrologers have managed to make their magical "art" look "scientific."

Astronomers base all their planetary positions on Greenwich standard time, which they convert to the more useful sidereal time (based on the time taken by the earth to revolve on its axis with respect to the stars rather than the sun). Herein lies the major complexity in drawing up accurate charts. In order to be able to look up planetary positions in their ephemerides (tables of planetary angles within the zodiac), astrologers must first convert birth times to Greenwich mean time, which in turn must be converted to Greenwich sidereal time, which finally must be converted to local sidereal time. All of these conversions and calculations could be eliminated if the astrologers dealt only with *local time*. The loss in accuracy (as we shall see) is nearly negligible. In short, the conversion to Greenwich sidereal time would be unnecessary if the astrologers knew their planetary positions in terms of local time.

Surprisingly, there is just such a source of current planetary positions given in terms of local time—or *almost* in local time. A little subtracting is still necessary, but once the position of the horizon at the local time of birth is located with respect to the astronomers' right ascension, we need only look on a star chart and find the planets directly. No tables, no sidereal or Greenwich times are required.

For several years now, *Astronomy* magazine (as well as *Sky and Telescope*) has been providing its readers with a monthly planet-finder star chart showing the changing positions of the planets along the ecliptic (see Figure 7-2). This is the same reference frame as the astrologers' sidereal zodiac.

First, note the rectangular "crosshatched" region toward the center of the chart in Figure 7-2. This gives the astronomical position of the sun during the month of February 1975 beginning at the right on the first of the month and moving progressively to the left, where the cross-hatched region ends with the sun's location on February 28.

LOCAL TIME ASTROLOGY

Local time is very similar to the astronomer's *right ascension,* which is the horizontal scale in Figure 7-2. We all know approximately what time the sun rises in local time: some hour between 6:00 and 8:00 A.M., depending upon local variations and daylight savings, etc. By checking the local newspaper, we can obtain the exact local time of sunrise and sunset. This establishes our local time reference frame.

We merely place the local time scale next to the horizontal right ascension scale in Figure 7-2, with the sun's rising time corresponding to the sun's position on the chart. On February 1, 1975, the sun rose in New York City at precisely 7:06 A.M., local time, and set at 5:12 P.M. (according to the *New York Times*), so our local time scale in Figure 7-2 is placed with 7:06 A.M. directly below the sun's position on February 1. Since local hours are exactly the same length as the astronomer's right ascension hours, it is an easy matter to lay out the local time scale as we have done in the lower scale of Figure 7-2.

This local time scale gives us the local sidereal time at which each portion of the sky appears on the eastern horizon. The sidereal zodiac can be erected directly upon our local time scale. If we use an "unequal house" system (similar to the popular system of Placidus), the sidereal zodiac superimposes on *Astronomy* magazine's Planet-Finder Chart as in Figure 7-2. Note that we have used the time difference between the sun's rising and setting to estimate the length of the celestial arc that will be in view above the horizon. The placement of the cusp separating the large from the small houses is tricky, but it can be estimated from the formula: sun's position $\pm$ Mod_{30} (Date $-$ Dec. 21)/30 $\cdot$ (sunset time $-$ sunrise time)/12 $\cdot$ 30, where $+$ applies to the fall and $-$ to the spring. We then divide each unequal half of the zodiac into six equal houses, measured from the cusp that has been calculated.

The sidereal horoscope elements, the signs and planetary positions, can be read directly from Figure 7-2. For instance, a person born on February 1, 1975, at 8:00 P.M., would have the constellation Leo just rising on the eastern horizon. In astrological terms, this person would have the sidereal sign, Leo, in the ascendancy of his chart. Also, from Figure 7-2 we can see that his sidereal sun sign would be Capricorn, since the sun is located in that constellation during the first part of the month of February.

We are now in a position to erect the sidereal horoscope for anyone born during the month of February 1975. All that is required is to adjust our local time scale according to the local time at which the sun rises and sets on the day the client is born. If he were born on February 21, we would simply move the local time scale about three-quarters of an hour to the right. We would then erect the sidereal zodiac with the ascendancy placed at the birth time on the local time scale.

In the case of our hypothetical person born on February 1, 1975, at 8:00 P.M., we can now read off the sidereal positions of each of the planets directly from Figure 7-2. Venus is located at 22 hours, 23 minutes, right ascension, or 8:45 A.M. local time, nearly 30° behind the sun (i.e. Venus appears as an "evening star"). Mars, on the other hand, is located at 18 hours, 35 minutes, right ascension, or 4:50 A.M. rising local time, which places it in the constellation of Sagittarius, which of course means to the astrologer that Mars is found in the sidereal sign of Sagittarius.

Once we have located the ascendant sidereal sign and placed the eleven planets within their appropriate signs, we have all the data necessary to erect our sidereal horoscope for February 1, 1975, 8:00 P.M. Figure 7-3 gives the result.

The most important thing to notice about Figure 7-3 is *not* its appearance—the mysterious symbols, numbers, angles and aspects—but the fact that this sidereal horoscope is reasonably accurate for anyone born anywhere in the northern hemisphere at 8:00 P.M. local time, February 1, 1975. Differences in latitude merely raise or lower the horoscope horizon (taken care of if the local rising and setting times of the sun are obtained). While the earth rotated one complete twenty-four hour turn on February 1, 1975, none of the planets in our horoscope of Figure 7-3 would have moved much more than a single degree!

The sun, of course, moves about a degree every twenty-four hours (since there are an average of thirty days per month, and a month is one-twelfth of 360°, or 30°). The fastest moving planet during the month of February 1975 was Venus which, we see from Figure 7-1, traversed 1 hour, 5 minutes, right ascension during the first half of the month, or just over 1° per day (2 hours right ascension equal approximately 30°). During the same period of time, Mercury only traversed 56 minutes right ascension (0.93° per day) while Mars also traveled 56 minutes right ascension, and Jupiter crawled along at the rate of 11 minutes right ascension during the first fifteen days of February 1975 (0.18° per day).

Since astrologers use orbs (i.e. allowable range for aspects) of 7° to 12°, the 1° inaccuracy involved in applying our local time sidereal horoscope to anybody born at 8:00 P.M. local time on February 1, 1975, can hardly show up in the final interpretation!

Local time horoscopy takes much of the mathematical gimmickry out of casting horoscopes and brings astrological techniques down to "local time earth," where it belongs. In addition, using local time horoscopy gives us a real sense of scale of our earth and its neighboring planets. Figure 7-4 illustrates our local time reference frame as it conceptually relates to the earth and the stars. Note that the local-time reference frame is attached to the stars and, hence, also is attached to the astronomer's right ascension reference frame and the astrologer's sidereal zodiac.

Because the planets move very slowly with respect to the earth, in the course of a day even the fastest planet will change position in our charts by barely more than a degree. So we can cast a local time horoscope for any particular local time and day and know we can apply that horoscope to essentially any point in the northern hemisphere for that day to within 1 degree of accuracy. Our only correction will be for latitude differences in the case of unequal house systems.

Why, then, do astrologers claim that they have to have the time of birth to the exact minute in order to be able to cast an accurate horoscope?

There are two answers to the question. First, in order to be able to use their tables of ephemerides, they must calculate Greenwich mean and local sidereal time. Their calculations look *so* much more "scientific" if they include a lot of decimal places. Second, astrologers place much stock in their system of houses which—unlike the signs—are attached to the earth and hence rotate one house every two hours.

HOUSES

In other words, the relative positions of the planets and signs don't change much as the earth rotates, but the houses *do* change, running through the entire set of twelve houses each day. With the relatively recent addition of refinements of their system of houses, astrologers have doubled the number of possible permutations available for interpretation. Ptolemy must be indeed jealous, for the term *house* meant an entirely different thing to him. In his *Tetrabiblos,* Ptolemy makes it clear that a planet's "house" is the sign ruled by that planet. For instance, the sun traditionally "rules" Leo, so Ptolemy considered Leo to be the house of the sun. Similarly, Cancer was designated the house of the moon, while Saturn had two houses, Aquarius and Capricorn. Needless to say, the planets were assigned to their houses according to the ubiquitous "principle of correspondences."

It's not known exactly when the modern concept of houses first arose. Since Ptolemy does not mention houses attached to the earth, it seems difficult to believe that the early Babylonians or Greeks invented the concept. Rome also seems an unlikely candidate for such an innovation in what was accepted by them as a given part of their magical world view.

This leaves only the Arabs or Renaissance scholars as responsible for the invention of the modern system of houses. Perhaps a germ of the idea first arose among the Arabs (it must be remembered that Al-Battan invented the equal signs division of 30° each), and this germ was then transmitted to medieval Europe, where it took root and grew into a number of different systems of houses.

During the fifteenth century, Regiomontanus, astrologer for Pope Sixtus IV, invented his system of houses based on equal divisions of the celestial equator.[1] It was also during the Renaissance that Campanus developed his system of houses based on divisions of the celestial vertical. However, the most popular system of houses still used today is the unequal house system invented by Placidus.

In the Placidean system, the houses are determined by the amount of time it takes the ecliptic (the path of the planets) to traverse the unequal portions of the noctural and diurnal arcs. At the equator, the Placidean system will be the same as the equal house system; as one approaches northern latitudes, the noctural and diurnal portions of the horoscope become more and more unequal. At far northern latitudes, the ecliptic may appear completely below the horizon, and the planets never appear in the upper half of the Placidean birth chart.

Most ephemerides are based on the Placidean house system. When one looks up the ascendancy, midheaven and other key points on the chart, the angular positions are usually given with respect to the Placidean unequal house system. This, of course, requires yet more calculations: trisecting to find cusps, adding and subtracting planetary positions to determine angular aspects, and on and on. In short, the result is a system so unnecessarily complex that just drawing up the chart requires the astrologer's undivided attention.

Modern astrological horoscopy leaves little time for the astrologer to focus on the magic in his "art."

We could apply a simple, equal house system to our simple system of local time horoscopy, thus removing all the mathematical complexity of calculating cusps and aspects. However, in the equal house system, the horizon in the horoscope no longer corresponds—as do the unequal house systems—to the real horizon viewed from the surface of the earth. The horizon in an equal house chart physically corresponds to an infinite plane passing through the center of the earth, extending out into space, and cutting the celestial sphere into equal halves.

Hence, it may be said that the unequal house systems give a "truer" picture of the sky from the viewpoint of the client. And astrology *is*, if nothing else, egocentric!

Sticking to tradition, we have based our local time sidereal horoscope in Figure 7-3 on an unequal house system. Thus the first house appears just below the horizon on the lefthand side of the chart. At 8:00 P.M., on February 1, 1975, the two constellations, Leo and Virgo, happened to share the first house. The houses are numbered counterclockwise, so we have Virgo and Libra in the second house, Libra and Scorpio in the third, etc.

Our sidereal horoscope in Figure 7-3, including the twelve houses, is accurate to within 1° for 8:00 P.M. anywhere on earth near 40° north latitude. We already know that within the space of a couple of hours the planets will scarcely have changed their relative positions to the stars.

Therefore, how will our local time horoscope of Figure 7-3 change if we were interested in a local time birth of 10:00 P.M.?

At any point on earth (i.e. any given local time), the rotation rate is 30° per two hours; therefore, the stars and planets will rotate 30° with the passage of two hours local time (this apparent movement of the stars becomes clear after a few minutes of watching through a telescope).

Thus two hours later, at 10:00 P.M. local time on February 1, 1975, our sidereal horoscope in Figure 7-3 will have rotated exactly one sign clockwise, giving us the local time sidereal horoscope found in Figure 7-5. The planets and signs haven't changed relative positions; only the houses have changed (along with the relative positions of ascendancy, midheaven, etc.).

Astrologers originally considered the astrological "effects" of the earth's rotation to be sufficiently accounted for in the placement of the ascendancy and midheaven points on the chart. No longer is Leo in Figure 7-3 considered just the ascendant sign. With the concept of houses, Leo now is also located in the twelfth and first houses, permitting twice the number of interpretations based on the same elements in the chart.

Table 7-1 gives the current astrological interpretations of the twelve houses (whether equal or otherwise). With Tables 6-1 and 6-2 and the new Table 7-1, we are now prepared to *interpret* our chart in Figure 7-3. Here, we will be able to see the magic of astrology at work.

Table 7-1   Current Astrological Meanings of the Twelve Houses

1st House	Outward personality; physical attributes; health; temperment; egocentric interests.
2nd House	Worldly possessions; money.
3rd House	Family; communications; relationship to environment.
4th House	Home; alpha and omega of life.
5th House	Recreation; creativity; children; new enterprises.
6th House	Work; health; competency.
7th House	Business and personal relationships.
8th House	Sexual feelings; attitudes toward death; big business; crime.
9th House	Travel; profound study; morals; languages.
10th House	Career; social status; ambitions.
11th House	Friends; social and fraternal groups; personal and intellectual pleasures.
12th House	Escapism; self-sacrifice; the unconscious.

INTERPRETATION

Before the astrologer can interpret a chart, he has to know what sort of interpretation he's aiming at. Most charts today are natal, or birth, horoscopes cast for the time, place, and date of the person's birth; therefore, most horoscope interpretations today are person-related character analyses and forecasts identifying events that might affect one's career or personal life. This type of chart and interpretation is called *natal,* or *genethlialic.*

As I demonstrated in Chapter 2, astrology originally was applied to the affairs of state, not to the lives of individuals. The relative positions of the planets and stars were noted and then interpreted in terms of what they signified for the future of the country and the king. This is called *mundane* astrology. While they didn't cast a chart quite as we know it, the Babylonians used methods of *mundane* interpretation that established the system of correspondences still used today (as modified by the Greeks) in interpreting *natal* charts.

Some contemporary astrologers—especially the more popular ones—still engage in mundane astrology. Whenever an astrology magazine gives the horoscope for the president of the United States or some other head of state and gives an interpretation of what this chart means for the nation and the world, it is practicing mundane astrology.

Very few modern astrologers, however, still practice the Renaissance's two most popular forms of astrology: *horary* and *electional.* In *horary* astrology, the client comes to the astrologer with a question—any question—and the precise time and date at which the question popped into his head. The horary astrologer then casts a chart for that time and gives an answer to the question based on his "interpretation" of the horoscope. A great many Renaissance clients came to astrologers with ready funds, asking questions about lost articles or missing spouses. And the astrologers, of course, were never at a loss for answers, either to the questions asked or for failures in the answers given.

The stars were never wrong. The astrologer just may not have "read" them accurately!

It seems impossible today that horary astrology, with all its potential for disproof via empirical test, could have survived during the Renaissance as long as it did. Perhaps this was because the scientific method had not filtered down to the common people, and statistics had not yet been invented for evaluating the data if anybody *had* tried to check. Writers on astrology, pro and con, continued to cite cases of astrological failures and successes, but statistics were not applied to astrology for several hundred years (see Chapter 10). By then, horary astrology was no longer practiced.

Neither was *electional* astrology, at least in the form it took during its Renaissance heyday.

Where horary astrology gave answers to specific questions, *electional* astrology merely provided the most favorable dates, astrologically speaking, for starting a new project or setting out on a journey. For instance, the electional client might be a sea captain whose ship was to set sail in a few days. The astrologer would cast a chart for the proposed day of sailing and weigh the relative "influences" of the various elements of the horoscope. If Saturn was located in Pisces, or Mercury in Scorpio, the astrologer advised the sea captain to wait until the malefic planet had "transited" safely into the next sign. Of course, if the astrologer's suggested date was wrong and the ship sank, he didn't have to worry about confronting a dissatisfied customer!

The current use of the term *transit* (to move across some particular part of the chart) in conjunction with the modern astrological concept of *progressions* hints strongly that electional astrology is still part of the modern astrologer's "art" (in *progressions,* the astrologer calculates where the planets will be located after a client's birth chart has been drawn up, using the formula: one day equals one year).

Clients still come to the astrologer asking when the stars say it will be best to get married or invest in the stock market. The modern astrologer, instead of casting an electional chart based on the proposed time, actually casts the client's natal chart, then uses the rather silly system of progressions to determine when transits favorable to the proposed project will occur.

Again, we see that modern astrologers have managed to further complicate their "art" in order to disguise its simple, magical methods. Modern clients would most likely find the old methods of *electiones* (charts drawn up for a future date) even more silly than progressions. The idea that planetary positions seven days after birth can "influence" events seven years later may seem silly enough, but once the idea is accepted, the much more complicated and "scientific" method of calculating progressions performs the same function as electional astrology while hiding its logical absurdities.

To illustrate the absurdities and magic in the process of astrological interpretation, I now will compare the interpretation of our sidereal chart in Figure 7-3 with its tropical counterpart (Figure 7-6).

First, we need a client. Let us suppose that a Broadway producer has a show due to open on the Great White Way in a couple of weeks, on February 1, 1975, at 8:00 P.M. The producer is concerned about the future of the show. How much money should he invest in advertising? Will it be a dud, and thus the extra advertising an unnecessary loss? Or will it be successful enough that the extra expenditure might turn a moderate success into a box office hit?

Moreover, our hypothetical producer has an additional reason for consulting an astrologer: this particular show happens to be *about* astrology. In fact, the show, which has been produced in total secrecy, is a spoof on the ancient "art." The producer, perhaps naturally, is a bit superstitious himself and is curious to see what the "stars" have to say about the upcoming opening. He decides to consult Jane Charles, the popular astrologer whose horoscopes appear daily in *The News.* For obvious reasons, the producer feels he shouldn't reveal the nature of the show to the astrologer. He just wants to see what the "stars" have to say for themselves—a "blind" experiment as the parapsychologists would call it.

Ms. Charles feels that for such an important client she should cast both the tropical and sidereal horoscopes; also, then she can charge twice as much!

First, she shows our producer the sidereal version, identical to the chart we have drawn up in Figure 7-3. "Leo is just rising into the ascendancy," she begins, "and the sun is in Capricorn, the tenacious sign. At the outset, this would seem to bode well for your venture. But when we look at the third house—communications—we find it occupied by Libra and shared with Scorpio, indicating the balance could swing either way for this upcoming play. You could well get bitten. This same uncertainty is reinforced in the fifth house—amusements, creativity, and new undertakings—whose cusp we find ruled by the airy, restless sign, Sagittarius, the archer."

"Do tell," replies the producer, still skeptical.

"Yesss . . . However, the show's chances are greatly enhanced by the position of Neptune, ruler of artistic creativeness, in the fourth house; your play will be at home in the theater. But—more importantly—the intellectual nature of the show may not appeal to the restless, aggressive audiences it may attract."

The producer is puzzled. "How do you know that?"

Ms. Charles explains, "Mercury is found in the seventh house, the house of business, imparting an intellectual elusiveness to the play. Mars, on the other hand, the aggressive planet, is found in the sign of Sagittarius which, as we have seen, occupies the fifth house of communications. While Mars and Sagittarius are reasonably compatible, you can expect their combined effects to produce an aggressively critical audience. The intellectual nature of your show just may not appeal to the audience."

The producer winces; that very same worry has been nagging him for weeks! "What else do you see in the chart, Jane?"

"As relates to your show? Quite a bit. The sun is found in the sixth house, casting a favorable influence over all work activities, but I don't have enough information to tell if this applies to your show. Then we turn to the aspects."

"Aspects?"

"The angles formed by the various planets. Conjunctions (0°) and trines (120°) are generally favorable, square (90°) and oppositions (180°) usually express negative aspects."

"I see . . . "

"First," says Ms. Charles, pointing to Figure 7-3, "we see Saturn is in opposition to Mars, thus balancing the two malefic planets, though enthusiasm for the play may soon wear off. Mercury is trine Uranus, imparting a dramatic flair to the show. Pluto is square both Mars and Saturn, forming a T-square obstacle which must be overcome, though this is balanced by Taurus at the midheaven."

"Why is that?"

"Taurus helps to stabilize . . . All in all, the sidereal chart looks quite favorable to your upcoming show. There's just one really disturbing element."

"What's that?"

"Uranus, often held responsible for communication breakdowns and mechanical failures, is near the cusp of the third house, the house of communications. There may be some interruption during your play's opening, a power failure or a labor strike, perhaps. I could tell you much more if I had the birthdate of your playwright."

"Why?"

"Then I could compare the key points of his chart with the chart for the show. I could also run progressions and tell you whether the time is ripe for your young playwright. If the transits are favorable . . . . "

"Assume he's a Capricorn."

"Sidereal?"

"No, tropical."

Then he's a sidereal Sagittarius. Ah, see how much difference that bit of knowledge makes"

"How so?"

"Sagittarius occupies the fifth house! This will be your playwright's night. Plus, Mars is found in Sagittarius, giving him drive and ambition. True, Neptune is square Jupiter within an 8° orb, indicating his finances are in need of advice, but I assume that's already taken care of."

"More or less."

"Then I see no reason why your show shouldn't be a huge success. All the positive elements are there, provided the negative aspects can be avoided."

"What about the traditional, tropical horoscope?"

Jane Charles pulls out the horoscope illustrated in Figure 7-6, drawn up from traditional astrological ephemerides. "Ah, an entirely different kettle of fish. Virgo's rising, the sun's in Aquarius, and Gemini is on the midheaven. This particular horoscope is based on an equal house system, so both houses and aspects are changed from our sidereal horoscope."

"There are two answers, actually. First, the horizon in an equal house system is located at the center of the earth, while in an unequal house system, the horizon is located on the surface of the earth at the place of birth; this, of course, shifts angles. Secondly, the ephemerides are not as accurate as they should be. Note the tremendous differences between the tropical and sidereal versions: the planets, Pluto, Neptune, Mars, the sun, Mercury and Venus are all found in different houses, a ridiculous state of affairs since planetary positions shouldn't change that much. The ephemerides are so inaccurate that angles between neighboring planets are not even close. For instance, the angle between Mercury and Venus is 22° in the tropical chart and 12° in the sidereal chart

"Which means?"

"Which means the ephemerides are at least 10° off, since the angles between planets that close together shouldn't change much more than 2 or 3°. So, you see the burdens we astrologers labor under: not only are there disagreements among different systems and interpretations, but our ephemerides are riddled with error!"

"You can still interpret the chart, can't you?"

"Oh, sure. A chart doesn't have to be accurate to be able to be interpreted! Some of the elements in the two charts are about the same—Saturn in the eleventh house, Jupiter in the seventh, etc. But now the rulers of the houses are different. Scorpio rules the third house, a much more ominous situation, and Capricorn occupies the fifth house."

"What's wrong with Capricorn?"

"Nothing. Your playwright's a Capricorn, and he still rules the fifth house of entertainment. But Capricorn is an entirely different sign from Sagittarius. Capricorn is the goat, tenacious, persevering; in order for your show to succeed, you must stick to it, weather the storms."

"What storms?"

"Well, in the tropical chart, the moon and sun are square, a rather dangerous situation where career matters are concerned. The trine between the sun and Pluto is generally favorable, but the now unbalanced square between Mars and Pluto is potentially dangerous, signifying a possible energy explosion. Uranus is now square the sun, and the moon has moved into trine with Mercury, which is a good sign for the third house, but probably not enough to offset the negative aspects."

Ms. Charles gives Figure 7-6 one last glance, "It's amazing, the difference between the sidereal and tropical charts; one is highly favorable to your show, the other indicates it may well flop."

The producer smiles; it sounds to him like the astrologer is covering all possible bets. "How do you explain such divergent interpretations?"

"I don't know, I'm really at a loss. Maybe if I knew what type of show it is . . ."

The producer chuckles, "What if I tell you the play deals with the occult?"

Ms. Charles brings down her ample fist onto the table. "That explains it! Naturally, only the traditional, tropical chart can apply to occult matters. And look," she cried triumphantly. "Neptune is square with Jupiter."

"I thought you said that meant financial advice was needed."

"It does. But it also indicates a disastrous attraction to occult affairs. Your show tries to delve into the occult, but your playwright's understanding of it is shallow. The audience will see through him; his short marriage with the occult will end in an embarrassing divorce."

A wry grin spreads over the producer's face, "Disastrous for whom? My playwright's a critic, a debunker. The play's a spoof!"

NOTES

1. Derek Parker and Julia Parker, *The Compleat Astrologer* (New York: McGraw-Hill, 1971), pp. 175 and 183.

8   The Astrological Debate

Throughout the ages, astrology has been the subject of intense controversy, far more than any other occult pseudo science. No doubt this controversy, this unending debate spanning millennia, has greatly contributed to astrology's survival and periodic popularity. What other field
offers the opportunity to debate such monumental thinkers as Aristotle,
Ptolemy, St. Augustine, Kepler, Jung—almost every brilliant mind our
culture has produced?

Needless to say, between the brilliant high points of the ongoing astrological debate, countless thousands of less-gifted voices have added
their two cents' worth. The debate ranges from warmed-over repetitions
to eloquent philosophical defenses and theorizing to downright ingenious charlatanism.

Few are original, and fewer yet are those who actually got down to
the nub of the matter: the *magic* in astrology.

MAGIC VERSUS SCIENCE

The Babylonians never questioned, as far as we can tell, the basic magical assumptions of astrology. The Greeks, steeped in their own forms of
magic, also accepted the Babylonian "principle of correspondences"

95

without question and added their own pantheon of gods and cor-respondences. The Greeks, however, performed a valuable service for the Inner Temple of astrology when they gave astrology's celestial "in-fluences" a theoretical physical basis. In so doing, they were setting the stage for later keepers of the temple to attach their "art" to each new and upcoming science.

The Greeks, for all their romantic mysticism, were the first civilized people truly interested in learning the "truth" about the world they lived in. Their methods of attacking the questions of reality and ultimate being were so unique, so original, that they served as standards for the next two thousands years. The Greek view of the world became ac-cepted in turn by the Romans, the Arabs, medieval Europe, and still contributes greatly to present-day civilization.

However, their methods for investigating the universe *were* pecu-liar—at their best, exercises in pure mental logic—far from what today is known as the scientific method. First of all, the Greeks accepted vir-tually without question not only their own ancestral superstitions but foreign myths and superstitions as well. They cleverly wove these theories and beliefs into what they saw as the physical world in which they lived.

The idea of experimentation hardly ever occurred to the Greeks; when it did, it crept in almost like an afterthought. In terms of their as-tronomy, the Greeks' two most valuable experiments were performed by Aristarchus, who was the first to attempt to measure the distances to the sun and moon, and by Hipparchus, who first discovered precession of the equinoxes.

Long before these important experimental observations, however, the Greeks had provided astrology with a theoretical physical frame-work with their famous "harmony of the spheres," those romantic musi-cal waves propagated through a mysterious "aether." The sixth century B.C. Greek mathematician and philosopher Pythagoras contributed greatly to this "music of the spheres," basing much of his school of phil-osophy upon this unity between the heavens and earth. It was the Py-thagoreans—to whom numbers represented the purest form of physical existence—who assigned harmonic numbers to the planetary spheres (see Figure 2-3).

By the fourth century B.C., Plato and his student Aristotle made astrology's new "physical basis" part of their teachings and writings. Plato's *Timaeus,* in particular, romanticized astrology and did much to popularize the Babylonian "art," both in his own times and fifteen hundred years later during the Renaissance. Aristotle's "scientific" works were in fact greatly responsible for the introduction of astrology into medieval Europe.

So it was the Greeks who first disguised astrology's magical roots by ascribing its celestial "influences" to a physical interaction between the earth and the universe, as if the cosmos were a single organic entity. It required religion—in the form of Christianity and in the person of St. Augustine—to put the magic *back* into astrology. Astrology, declared St. Augustine, is a form of evil magic, a temptation provided by the devil to lead men astray and entrap their souls. Astrology cannot possibly be true since God's will is all-powerful, and therefore the stars cannot be responsible for our actions. To follow the magical dictates of the stars is to abandon the long and tortuous route to God, a route of self-denial and abject religious piousness.

The ancient "science" just did not fit into the new Church's strict religious program for attaining that "mystic union with God." As St. Augustine preached, nothing must be allowed to lead the believer astray from the path of righteousness!

At the height of the Church's influence during the Middle Ages, astrology was officially classified as magic. In his important encyclopedic work *Etymologicae,* Isidore of Seville (sixth century A.D.) carefully separated magical astrology (*superstitiosa*) from the physical science of astronomy (*naturalis*). Superstitious astrology, wrote Isidore, "is that science which is practised by the mathematici who read prophecies in the heavens, and who place the twelve constellations as rulers over the members of man's body and soul, and who predict the nativities and dispositions of men by the courses of the stars."[1]

Other influential medieval theologians who classified astrology as magic include Rabanus Maurus, bishop of Fulda, who wrote *De Universo,* and Bishop George Carleton, whose *Astrologomania* discusses at great length the relation between astrology and magic. Carleton tried to prove that astrology is an inseparable adjunct of magic. Even Roger Bacon denounced the superstitious aspects of astrology in his *De Augmentis Scientiarum,* at the same time arguing for a "sane astrology."

By the twelfth century A.D., Hugh of St. Victor had changed Isidore's definition of natural astrology (astronomy) to include the "influence" of the stars over sickness and health. The medieval Church was beginning to open its doors to astrology.

Five centuries after Isidore carefully separated magical astrology from "natural" astronomy, Hugh of St. Victor's contemporary, Abelard, again united the two in *De Eadem et Diverso*. Church leaders had become convinced by the arguments of astrology's apologists that the stars were "signs" from God.

Perhaps recognizing the inevitable rise of the rediscovered "art," Church doctrine shifted to accept the popular new "science." No doubt, Church leaders felt, it would be wiser to admit astrology into its fold than to have a popular heresy tantalizing believers and challenging the power of the Church. Astrology, with its mystic vision of the universe and claims to reveal the future, represented a threat; the Church met the threat by slowly opening its doors wider and wider as astrology became more and more popular. Astrology was well on its way to becoming established as a Renaissance "science."

With Renaissance acceptance of the Greek physical celestial "influences," the magic was removed once again from astrology. And it never returned; Renaissance discovery of the scientific method would soon dispel the Greek notion that astrological "influences" can be due to physical causes.

First, the Polish Astronomer Copernicus overturned the Greek vision of an earth-centered universe in his *De Orbis Revolutionibus* (published posthumously). In the preface to his book (actually written by his friend, Osiander),[2] Copernicus tried to allay the opposition of the Church by stating that his theory of a sun-centered solar system should be considered as a suggestion only, not to be taken seriously. A few very important people, however, *did* take his "suggestion" seriously; one of the most outspoken "Copernicans" was none other than Johannes Kepler.

More than any other Renaissance figure, Kepler has been cited as a classic believer and researcher in astrology. Some writers have even gone so far as to suggest that Kepler stumbled upon his three famous planetary "laws" while attempting to uncover the "realities" behind astrology. Nothing could be further from the truth.

Kepler was born in 1571, not far from the Black Forest in Germany. Astrology was at the height of its Renaissance power; nearly every man, woman, and child believed in the "influences" of the stars; there were more university chairs of astrology than astronomy. Into this world seething with superstition and magic came young Kepler, brilliant, neurotic, and erratic; it was only natural that a person of his romantic and mystic bent should first look at the current theories and beliefs of his time, searching for the "baby in the bathwater."

But this does not mean that Kepler was trying to "prove" astrology. Kepler was one of the first true scientists; he was not looking for any "reality" within astrology but rather for reality itself. Kepler wanted to know what made the solar system "tick."

As a student at the Lutheran university of Tübingen, Kepler became fired with Copernicus's idea of a heliocentric solar system, with the earth revolving along with the other planets around a central sun. Somehow, the theory must have seemed intuitively more correct than the Greek system of epicycles within circular planetary orbits about the earth. If the center of the solar system were transplanted from the earth to the sun, perhaps that would explain why the planets moved so erratically across the sky as viewed from the earth.

Kepler became an ardent defender of the Copernican theory, essentially dedicating his life to proving its validity. Astrology merely provided Kepler with financial aid—and a "red herring" to lead him astray for several years.

To the modern, rational mind, Kepler appears as an impetuous mystic; his writings are eloquent, rambling mysteries. The terse, scientific writing style was just being developed by Kepler's contemporary, Galileo, the Italian astronomer who was the first to write about the new astronomical wonders to behold in his telescope. In contrast to Galileo's *Star Messenger,* Kepler's *Mysterium Cosmographicum* reads like philosophical science fiction, an excursion into a fantasy land composed of geometrical solids shaped by the harmonic "music of the spheres."

As we saw in Chapter 5, Kepler's flirtation with Greek "harmonies" and Pythagorean solids was an attempt to discover if there lay any reality at all within astrology's Inner Temple. He found none.

Nor can it be said that Kepler in any way misunderstood astrology; his mathematics position at the University of Gratz carried with it the duty of publishing an annual almanac. While most of the almanac was concerned with weather predictions and farming hints, Kepler apparently did hit the nail on the head with some of his more adventurous political predictions, including one of his first: that the Turks would invade and wreak havoc in the land.

Fifteen years later, Kepler would cast the chart for the German soldier, Albrecht von Wallenstein; he predicted "fearful disorders" to shake the country in March 1634. Wallenstein's assassination on February 25, 1634, caused political ferment to spread across Germany.[3] This famous "successful" political prediction by Kepler has been gleefully cited by astrologers for centuries. Far from demonstrating any validity to astrology, however, I would suggest that it illustrates two facts about the ancient "art":

> 1. Coincidence has played an important role in astrology's survival; a prediction that accidentally happens to "come true" will loom very large in the subjective mind of the believer.
>
> 2. There is a "secret" to making successful predictions and reading clients' characters from the horoscope chart, a knack that is learned unconsciously by most successful astrologers and consciously recognized only by a few.

We shall look further for this "secret" to successful astrology in this Chapter, Book IV (The Psychology of Astrology) and Book 0.

Kepler finally tossed out his "astrological bathwater" and turned to Tycho de Brahe's precise observational data for the final assault on the mathematical key to the solar system. With the publication of his three "laws" of planetary motion, Kepler nailed the lid on the coffin of the "harmony of the spheres."

Seventy-five years later, Isaac Newton would expand Kepler's early ideas concerning the forces that "drive the planets about the sun" into his own elegant mathematical "laws" of gravitation, inertia, and motion. Now, at long last, the actual physical influences of the planets upon life here on earth could be calculated and measured with scientific precision.

As Lee Ratzan has carefully demonstrated, the planetary gravitational tides acting on a new-born baby are fully compensated by a 100 kilogram doctor standing within half a foot of the child. Table 8-1 gives Ratzan's list of the gravitational forces exerted on a 3.4 kilogram baby for each of the nine planets and for a doctor standing 1 meter and ½ meter away.[4]

At the time of the Renaissance, of course, the scientific revolution initiated by Copernicus, Kepler, and Newton had a devastating effect on astrology, but not due to gravitational arguments as one might expect. Gravitation still allows for *some* effect, albeit extremely small. Strangely enough, it was Galileo's telescope and his short, terse *Star Messenger* that dealt astrology's physical "influences" theory a fatal blow, far more deadly than Copernicus's heliocentric theory or Kepler's planetary laws.

Galileo's telescope showed once and for all that the heavenly

Table 8.1 Force Exerted on 3.4kg Newborn

	mass	miles	meters	grav	tidal	accel(m)	dist(m)
Mercury	.320e+24	.930e+08	.139e+12	.373e−08	.267e−19	.110e−08	.548e−09
Venus	.480e+25	.930e+08	.139e+12	.559e−07	.401e−18	.165e−07	.823e−08
Mars	.636e+24	.140e+09	.210e+12	.324e−08	.154e−19	.953e−09	.476e−09
Jupiter	.189e+28	.480e+09	.720e+12	.827e−06	.115e−17	.243e−06	.122e−06
Saturn	.565e+27	.890e+09	.133e+13	.719e−07	.539e−19	.211e−07	.106e−07
Uranus	.865e+26	.180e+10	.270e+13	.269e−08	.997e−21	.791e−09	.396e−09
Neptune	.102e+27	.280e+10	.420e+13	.131e−08	.312e−21	.386e−09	.193e−09
Pluto	.530e+25	.370e+10	.555e+13	.390e−10	.703e−23	.115e−10	.574e−11
Moon	.730e+23	.250e+06	.375e+09	.118e−03	.314e−12	.346e−04	.173e−04
MD at 1m	.100e+03	.600e+03	.100e+01	.227e−07	.532e−07	.667e−08	.333e−08
MD at 0.5m	.100e+03	.300e−03	.500e+00	.907e−07	.459e−06	.267e−07	.133e−07

Source: Lee Ratzan, *The Humanist* (Nov.-Dec., 1975)

Note: 1 second for duration of force

bodies—the sun, moon, planets, and comets—lay far outside earth's atmosphere and were physical bodies possessing unique features. The moon had craters, the sun had spots, and Jupiter had satellites. No longer could Renaissance man look upon celestial objects as intimately linked to the earth. Furthermore, Tycho de Brahe's proof that comets are far more distant than the moon destroyed the old Greek distinction between "superlunary" bodies and "sublunary" bodies (above or below the moon's sphere).[5]

The earth and its "sphere of influence" had been physically disconnected from astrology's "celestial influences." The Babylonian magic and the Greek "harmony of the spheres" became relegated to their proper role of historical curiosity. Discredited, the Inner Temple of astrology lay in shambles; only the hulk of popular almanacs and astrological charlatanism remained.

THE CLASSICAL ARGUMENTS

Writers and thinkers who have wrestled with this great beast of astrology have left an impressive list of arguments and counterarguments, most of them far from the magical mark. Still, the arguments are interesting and tell us much about the historical development of rational thinking and logical disputation.

Outside of religion, astrology has probably been debated by more people over a far longer span of time than any other subject in the history of mankind. Astrology as a theory is totally invalid. It has nothing to do with physical reality; however, astrology as a subject for debate has certainly played a major role in the evolution of civilization. It has served as a mental foil for the imaginative and rational thinking powers of man throughout the ages.

In this sense, astrology's historical role has been far more important than generally recognized; however, we must keep this role as a foil-for-debate in perspective. The fact that Kepler, Newton, and Roger Bacon considered astrology important enough to discuss and investigate by no means implies that astrology contains any hidden germs of truth—that if we pound at the inner doors long enough we will find a gold key hidden in the lock or a gold nugget buried in the rubble. There may be a "secret" to successful astrological prediction, but that "secret" has nothing to do with planetary "influences!"

Of all the classical arguments for and against astrology, none have been more popular, more often repeated, than the ongoing debate over the question of twins.

When the Greeks began applying astrology to the lives of ordinary men, they noticed that astrological theory predicted that babies born at the same time and place should share the same horoscope and thus lead identical lives. Of course they noticed that identical twins look alike and often lead remarkably similar lives. But they also noticed that there was another type of twins: fraternal twins who neither looked alike nor possessed similar temperaments that would be likely to lead them to similar careers. Identical twins seemed to support astrological theory; fraternal twins tended to contradict it.

Then there are what the astrologers call "astral twins," people who are unrelated but happen to be born at the same time and place. Astrological theory says that these people too should lead very similar lives, their separate careers paralleling each other as much as in the case of identical twins.

As we have seen, St. Augustine rejected astrology after observing just such a case of "astral twins" who were destined by their widely differing parentages to lead vastly differing lives. It seemed reasonable to the Bishop of Hippo that a slave and a freedman could not possibly lead parallel lives and, hence, that the planets could not possibly establish their different careers at the moment of their simultaneous births.

Many modern astrologers would disagree with the good saint. They would say that it's quite possible for a slave and a noble to lead parallel lives *as far as permitted by their differing social positions.* Here we see the astrologer's great ability for splitting hairs and turning logic back upon itself.

For example, astrologers are quite fond of citing the famous case of the commoner, Samuel Hemming, who was born at the same time and place as the king of England, George III.[6] The parallels between their two lives at first seem remarkable: the commoner became an iron-monger on the same day the king took the throne; they got married on the same day and even died on the same day of the same causes!

How can this be? Can pure coincidence explain such parallelism, or must we admit that there may be something to the idea of astrological "time twins"? No, absolutely not; planetary "influences" need not be invoked at all to explain such phenomena. Where coincidence leaves off, psychology enters the picture!

Joseph Goodavage himself hints at the solution when he suggests that twins *"deliberately* synchronize their activities."' As the king's "time twin," Hemming gained much attention and publicity by synchronizing his life's activities to those of George III; it was socially and psychologically advantageous for the commoner to "ape" the king, even to the point of dying at the same time. Of course, after a lifetime of following in the king's footsteps, Hemming's entire psychological makeup would be dominated by this unnatural magical parallelism, so that even his voodoolike death becomes quite as probable as in the most primitive believer in magic.

Belief in magic—whether astrology or voodoo—can permit a dangerous psychological state of mind to develop in the believer, a little-recognized suggestive state of mind in which dangerous ideas and suggestions may be uncritically accepted. Belief in "astral twins," seemingly a harmless idea, turns out to be no exception.

The earliest writers against astrology, however, did not generally recognize the psychological dangers of such beliefs. They felt that there was no "truth" to astrology, and hence its followers were merely misguided, their money and time wasted on a "false art."

Both Cicero and Pliny the Elder discussed this question of astrological twins, noting that many such "astral" pairs did *not* lead similar lives and hence that the underlying astrological theory must be false. Yet examples of the psychological dangers of astrology were probably much more common during the Roman Empire than now. For instance, just thirty-five years after Cicero's death in 43 B.C., the poet Horace died two months after Maecenas because he believed that the "fatal" star he shared with his astrologer friend was destined to kill them both.

The question of "astrological twins" also leads us to the age-old questions of fate versus free will, and the time of conception versus the time of birth as the proper time for casting the horoscope. Pliny the Elder, the Roman naturalist of the first century A.D., is often credited with first presenting the argument that it is the time of conception, the moment when sperm meets egg, when life truly begins and thus when the horoscope should be cast. This argument has since appeared in nearly every discussion on astrology, from Ficino's unpublished "Disputationes," to Chamber's debate with Heydon, to present-day works.

As in the case of "astral twins," the conception versus birth argument completely misses the point that astrology's alleged "influences" are magical in origin and hence it doesn't matter whether the astrologer uses a rough time of birth, an "exact" moment of conception, or any other arbitrary time. What the argument *did* provide was yet another "excuse" by which astrologers could "explain" their failures and inaccuracies.

Needless to say, the moment of conception is even more difficult to determine than the moment of birth. As I shall demonstrate in Book III, this did not stop one modern researcher, the Hungarian astrological sex specialist Dr. Eugene Jonas: given the birth date, Dr. Jonas then calculated the time of conception by subtracting a fixed number of months and days based on the weight of the infant!

Apparently there is no end to the astrologers' ingenuity.

The astrological "twins" question also provides us with an introduction to the fate versus free will argument. If the "twins," argue the astrologers, do not lead exactly parallel lives, that's because the stars do not *necessarily* determine one's fate; there are full measures of environment, heredity, and *free will* to consider. By the time the astrologers get through explaining away all their failures due to outside "influences," there's little left to the stars but random chance. The free will argument is one of the fuzziest.

The entire fate versus free will controversy began when the Greeks revolted against the fatalistic shackles of Babylonian astrology and introduced a more moderate "catarchic" astrology (from the Greek word for beginning, *katarché*). The Greeks loved their freedom far too much to allot total determination to the stars. Astrology for the Greeks was essentially the same as the Renaissance *electiones:* "the learned choice of the right time at which to start."[8]

In other words, the stars could only "foretell" the right time for beginning certain projects. In modern astrological terms, one would say that astrology only indicates trends and does not absolutely determine one's fate. To quote an overworked cliché, "The stars do not compel; they only impel."

The fate versus free will arguments logically led to two further sources of debate. If there is a measure of free will in the stars' "influences," those "influences" must be due to *contingent* causes, as opposed to the *necessary* causes of fatalistic astrology. This argument, in corollary with the fate versus free will debate, played a major role in the Church's rejection and then later acceptance of astrology.

The religious arguments against astrology rested in the early centuries A.D. on the relative power of God and the stars. Christians declared that God's power was absolute and that any possible "influence" by the stars was thus ruled out. St. Augustine's observation concerning astrological "twins" clinched the matter; astrology was banned from the Christian world.

A thousand years later, at the dawn of the Renaissance, the Church would take another look at astrology, and this time the free will question would decide in the ancient "art's" favor. Both the public and certain Christian theologians were demanding that a measure of free will be allotted to man; God may have an overall, even ultimate, control but surely man must have a hand in deciding something!

Enter astrology: if the stars are considered only as "signs" of the will of God, then man still possesses the free will to follow or not follow those "signs." It was the perfect solution for the Renaissance Church.

Admitting astrology within the fold of the Church not only gave its followers more "freedom" to choose; it also insured that that "freedom" was controlled by the Church. Later, Martin Luther would condemn both the Church and astrology for being authoritarian workshops of the Devil. At the same time, Luther placed the blame for much of medieval Europe's ills upon the insidious work of witches, the same unfortunate scapegoats who were being so cruelly persecuted by the Inquisition.[9]

However, the Age of Enlightenment was dawning. When Copernicus and Kepler displaced the earth from the center of the universe and showed it was just another planet like Mars and Venus, the astrologer's geocentric and egocentric views of the world were displaced by the far more correct heliocentric picture of the solar system.

The astrologers soon recovered their footing, however, and were quick to point out that the horoscope is cast from the reference frame of the earth and, hence, the switch from a geocentric system to a heliocentric system affected astrology's calculations not a whit.

Nevertheless, discoveries like Galileo's and Kepler's did eventually upset astrology's hold upon the Renaissance mind. The realities of the modern world were rapidly becoming more fascinating than the fantasies of the ancients. By the twentieth century, science would confirm that the sun and moon *do* have obvious physical effects upon the earth: light, heat, tides, and the unending associated cycles of life—night and day, the seasons, the months, and the years.

Yet, as we shall see in Book III, none of these well-established physical effects of the sun and moon has anything to do with traditional astrology. But then, neither have any of the other arguments presented by astrologers in favor of their "science"; most arguments have tended to obscure the true magical nature of astrology, even many of the arguments presented by opponents.

Consider the question of mass tragedies.

Many opponents of astrology, including Cicero and Chamber, have pointed to wars and natural catastrophes as real events affecting all participants alike, be they Scorpios or Aries, ruled by Mars or Venus. How could the astrologers of Pompeii have predicted the thousands of simultaneous deaths when Vesuvius erupted on that fatal day in 79 A.D.? How could the court astrologer's horoscopes have separated the survivors from the hundreds of sailors lost during the disastrous voyage of the Spanish Armada? How could the charts of millions of Jews foretell each of their tragic deaths at the fanatical hands of Hitler in the space of a few years? How could the horoscopes of over a thousand unrelated people separate the survivors of the *Lusitania* from the 1,198 victims?

These are excellent questions, somehow emotionally stronger than the questions of "astral twins" and free will. Perhaps the fickleness of "fate," the arbitrariness of both personal and mass tragedies, strikes a deeper chord in twentieth-century man with his global, almost instantaneous, media and growing awareness of the limits of his home, the earth, once center of the universe and now a mere speck among billions.

Along with reality, of necessity, comes humility.

FAMOUS ASTROLOGERS AND THEIR PREDICTIONS

Astrologers have never been noted for their humility; the universe lies just within their grasp, within the circle of their charts. Their "art" was a "gift" of the gods, a royal, ancient "science" that gives them, alone, knowledge of the future and an understanding of the forces that shape our world and mankind within it.

Hence, astrologers' predictions have run the gamut from imminent world destruction to mild-mannered suggestions that one should pay attention to financial affairs. Nothing is too big or too small to fit on the astrologer's chart!

The astrologer's "art" is essentially an egotistical one, for both client and practitioner. Sometimes it results in dire consequences for both.

One of the first recorded tales of such astrological disasters comes from ancient China. Two astrologers under Emperor H'in were beheaded for being derelict in their duty to the stars; it is not clear whether they were put to death because they failed to predict an eclipse or because they were merely lax in performing the proper rituals to prevent the moon-god from being "eaten" up.[10]

Babylonian astrology was concerned strictly with mundane affairs of state, and its predictions were usually of weather and upcoming political situations. Unfortunately, Chaldean cuneiform tablets apparently give us little indication of their astrologers' "batting average." Likewise, we are left with few famous Greek astrological predictions; the Greeks were mainly interested in electional astrology and preferred more specific predictions to come from the beautiful mouths of oracle priestesses.

However, the Roman Empire has left us a wealth of astrologers' predictions and their batting averages. The most famous early Roman prediction was that of Sulla "predicting" Julius Caesar's death just before he entered the senate on that fateful Ides of March. Of course, the "prediction" was only Sulla's way of warning Caesar. As we saw in Chapter 2, it was the subsequent appearance of a comet and Octavius's "casterization of Caesar" that led to the tremendous popularity of astrology during the Roman Empire.

The crafty Roman astrologer Thrasyllus, along with his son, Balbillus, practically dominated Roman politics through their predictions after the turn of the millennia. Their collective predictions ranged from revealing conspiracies to "foretelling" future engineering projects and even to advising the marriages of emperors. Since many of the Roman "predictions" were self-fullfilling, the astrologers often scored very high batting averages, indeed. Thrasyllus and Balbillus were responsible for the murder of Seneca, the exhaustion of Caligula's imperial funds on the building of a pontoon bridge, and at least partly responsible for the ill-starred union between Nero and Octavia (ending in her death).

We do not see such a rash of astrological predictions and their outcomes for another thousand years. As astrology began creeping into medieval Europe via Arabian influences, a number of budding astrologers—notably John of Toledo—noticed that all the known planets would gather together in the same sign of Libra in the year 1186. Libra is a "fiery, airy sign"; hence this portentous conjunction naturally foretold of tremendous wind storms that would lay waste to the land.

All Europe awaited the year 1186 with great trepidation. Many people tried to prepare by digging tunnels and stocking caves with provisions. When the dread year arrived, the grand conjunction occurred in

Libra, all right, just as predicted (Arabian astronomy was at least *that* accurate). But 1186 passed by with no major storms or windy devastation. The significance of Libra had obviously been misinterpreted! Perhaps John of Toledo should have focused on Libra's "balanced" nature rather than its "airy" character.

Strange to say, the failure of the storm prediction for 1186 diminished the growing popularity of astrology not in the least. Apparently the populace had been so impressed by the astro*nomical* prediction of such a major conjunction that the subsequent failure of the astro*logical* part of the prediction soon became totally forgotten.

Astrology had gained entrée into the Middle Ages.

Medieval and Renaissance Europe provide us with endless examples of predictions, ranging from the mundane search for lost objects to grand disasters, usually storms, fires, or pestilence. These continuous predictions of widespread catastrophes are very popular among astrologers and their readers even today—anything to relieve the boredom of everyday life, one suspects.

Such predictions, however, fail to come true with monotonous regularity. Of course, tales of a few successes have come down to us; it would be quite surprising and contrary to the expectations of probability were there not a *few* successful predictions, whether due to trickery or chance (astrologers have been notoriously bold about publishing post factum predictions).

Again, even a chance "correct" prediction can get the astrologer in trouble. In 1651, William Lily published an astrological "hieroglyph" (see Figure 8-1) depicting the sign of Gemini (London's "ruling" sign) suspended upside down above a fire being quenched by a number of people with buckets. Fifteen years later, after the Great Fire of London had virtually wiped out the city, Lily claimed credit for having predicted the fire, and he was called before Parliament to explain his role in the catastrophe.[11]

Fortunately for Lily, he was able to convince the committee that he was blameless, that his "glyph" prediction was made according to the general principles of the "science" of astrology and had nothing to do with the *cause* of the fire. Perhaps Lily also pointed out that since his prediction included no date, *any* large London fire would have fit the prediction!

Needless to say, such grisly conflagrations were quite common back then, before pressured water systems and motorized fire departments existed. Predicting fires was nearly as safe as predicting California earthquakes today!

Even more successful than Lily in convincing people that his vaguest utterances were actually predictions was the famous Nostradamus, the sixteenth-century French astrologer and prophet. Nostradamus served as court astrologer to Catherine de Medici and became very unpopular for his correct "prediction" of the death of Henri II (another of those dangerous "coincidences"?). However, Nostradamus is today most famous for his "predictive" verses, obscure quatrains alleged by the seer to contain the future history of the entire world until the Day of Judgment in 7000 A.D.

No sign of humility here!

The most famous of Nostradamus's verses are no doubt those that supposedly foretold the rise to power of Napoleon:

> Pau, nay, loron, more in fire their blood shall be,
> Seen to swim, great ones shall run to their surreys,
> The aggassas shall refuse the entry,
> Pampon, Durance shall keep them enclosed.[12]

Napoleon's name is supposed to be contained in the first three nonsense words, slightly transposed, while the last three lines supposedly describe the flight of the French nobles after Napoleon seized power. While clever, the alleged "interpretations" of Nostradamus's verses cannot help but strike one as labored constructs. In fact, there's tremendous difference among translators as to the meaning and interpretation of the same verses and lines, each succeeding interpreter vying with his predecessors in the search for ever more clever hidden "meanings" and predictions. Obviously, Nostradamus was counting on his interpreters to be sufficiently intrigued and ingenious to construct prophesies from doggerel!

One also suspects that by keeping his verses vague and mysterious, Nostradamus took full advantage of Jung's principle of synchronicity (meaningful coincidences—see Chapter 13). Eventually, some world event that can be cleverly "explained" by Nostradamus's verses (i.e, "nay, pau, loron," in above quatrain sounding vaguely like the name, Napoleon) is bound to happen. Such post factum "predictions" are easy to make; now, if some Nostradamus scholar were to discover within his quatrains some *future* prediction that proved to be correct, then perhaps one might be inclined to lend more weight to Nostradamus's prophesies.

Some predictions are bound to come true; only the timing is in question. Consider the matter of death. If I predict that everybody now reading this book will be dead in a hundred years from the event, it's almost certain that my prediction will achieve 100 percent accuracy.

But if I were to predict correctly the death of a famous person even to within the month, my prediction would seem to take on much more meaning. I say, "seem to take on meaning" because coincidences *do* occur, in fact *must* occur. It would be a far more unnatural and boring world if coincidences didn't occur. Kepler's prediction within the month of "fearful disorders over the land," by reading Wallenstein's horoscope thirty years before he was assassinated, would seem to be such a "meaningful coincidence." The fact that Kepler did *not* predict Wallenstein's death seems to escape the serious astrological student; it was only because Wallenstein was such a notable German figure that his death brought about the "fearful disorders." One measure of a person's importance or noteworthiness is what happens during his absence.

Three hundred years later, Germany would again see several spectacularly "successful" predictions. In 1923 Frau Elspeth Ebertin predicted that Hitler's upcoming political putsch would be a disaster; when Hitler's grab for power failed and he was thrown into the jail where he wrote *Mein Kampf,* Frau Ebertin's prediction was hailed as a success and German astrology took a giant step forward.[13]

What most astrology books proclaiming the Ebertin prediction do not tell the reader is that the astrologist was fully aware of Hitler's political significance and had in fact lied about his sun sign, recognizing Aries as a far more dynamic sign that Hitler's own Taurus. Frau Ebertin, like many other German astrologers of the period, kept very close tabs on the political scene and was aware of the upcoming putsch and perhaps even the authorities' plans to handle the mistimed event.

With a little foreknowledge, it's far easier to make successful predictions!

Sixteen years after Ebertin's putsch prediction, the famous Swiss Nazi astrologer Karl Ernst Krafft predicted that an assassination attempt would be made on Hitler at the annual Munich beer hall celebration of the 1923 putsch. The year was 1939, Hitler was at the height of his power, and Krafft was anxious to display his talents to the S.S. On November 9, a bomb hidden in a column near the speaker's rostrum exploded, killing seven and wounding sixty-three.

However, Hitler, who had left the rostrum and beer hall just a few minutes earlier, escaped injury. Needless to say, when the S.S. learned of Krafft's prediction a couple of days later, they had much to discuss with the talented astrologer! Krafft, however, managed to talk the S.S. agents into believing his innocence. He even talked them into subsidizing his further astrological work; he was well on his way to infamy. Krafft's story will be picked up again in Chapter 10, when I discuss the many statistical studies which have been performed in futile attempts to "prove" astrology, and again in Chapter 12, "Astral Psychological Warfare."

For every "successful" prediction such as Krafft's, there are dozens of unsuccessful ones. Usually, only the successes get media attention; the failures must be really spectacular before the public learns about them. Recently, there was just such a spectacular astrological failure: in 1962, Indian astrologers predicted widespread calamity because of the upcoming conjunction of seven planets in Aquarius. There was no catastrophe. Instead, the prediction itself caused widespread panic and consternation; food prices rose due to hoarding and transportation became snarled.[14] Western astrologers, however, were not surprised by the failure of the prediction: in the Western systems of astrology, the conjunction did not figure nearly so prominent and dangerous as on the Indian charts. The system used, and the accuracy achieved, do not matter nearly so much as the method of interpretation; it is the magic in astrology that counts most!

This, then, is the Inner Temple of astrology: a mysterious, decadent structure with flimsy foundations and numerous abandoned chambers. Eastern keepers of the temple disagree highly with their Western counterparts, and both disagree among themselves. The priests have fought hard to maintain the Inner Temple and are struggling still to preserve something of the ancient structure.

But they struggle in vain, for the Inner Temple of astrology belongs to a different order, a different world: the magical world of our ancestors. As I will show in Book III, statistical studies and biological clocks do not belong in the Inner Temple: they belong to the modern world, a world of scientific reality far removed from the magical world of astrology.

There may be "secrets" to successful astrological prediction, but those "secrets" have nothing to do with planetary "influences" or magical correspondences. Chapter 14 Book 0 will delve further into these "secrets" of successful prediction. Again these "secrets" cannot be found in the Inner Temple; they are part of the real world, the psychological and mathematical facts of life. More than anything else, the Inner Temple was constructed to conceal such "secrets," a whole tin can of red herrings leading students astray and enmeshing them in mystic subterfuge.

In a way, we must tip our hats to the ingenuity and resourcefulness of the astrologers; their Inner Temple has stood for over two thousand years. It has withstood countless attacks and endless buffeting storms. One would be foolish to predict the ultimate fall and destruction of such a monolithic edifice.

The Inner Temple of astrology may well stand for yet another two thousand years despite this "disproof." Yet, I will be satisfied if the work finds its way into the cavernous Inner Temple itself.

NOTES

1. Theodore Otto Wedel, *The Mediaeval Attitude Toward Astrology* (New Haven, Conn.: Yale University Press, 1920) p. 27

2. Arthur Koestler, *The Watershed* (Garden City, N.Y.: Anchor Books, 1960), p. 50.

3. Derek Parker and Julia Parker, *The Compleat Astrologer* (New York: McGraw-Hill, 1971), p. 188.

4. Lee Ratzan, "The Astrology of the Delivery Room," *The Humanist* (Nov./Dec., 1975): 27.

5. Keith Vivian Thomas, *Religion and the Decline of Magic* (New York: Charles Scribner's Sons, 1971), p. 349.

6. John West and Jan Toonder, *The Case For Astrology* (New York: Coward-McCann, 1970), p. 257; and Joseph F. Goodavage, *Astrology: The Space Age Science* (New York: The New American Library, Signet, 1966), pp. 27-28.

7. Goodavage, *Astrology,* p. 27.

8. Jack Lindsay, *Origins of Astrology* (London: Frederick Muller, 1971), p. 123.

9. For a full discussion, see Marvin Harris, *Cows, Pigs, Wars and Witches: The Riddles of Culture* (New York: Random House, 1974), pp. 225-40.

10. P.I.H. Naylor, *Astrology, An Historical Examination* (North Hollywood, Cal.: Wilshire Book Co., 1967) p. 16.

11. Parker and Parker, *The Compleat Astrologer,* pp. 188-90.

12. *The Complete Prophecies of Nostradamus,* trans., ed. and interpreted by Henry C. Roberts (New York: Nostradamus, Inc., 1949), p. 242.

13. Ellic Howe, *Astrology and Psychological Warfare during World War II,* (London: Rider & Co., 1972), p. 29.

14. Christopher McIntosh, *The Astrologers and Their Creed: An Historical Outline* (London: Hutchinson, 1969), p. 103.

Book III   Biological versus "Cosmic" Clocks

The Copernican solar system and the Newtonian physical universe—in which there could be no "action at a distance" without a propagating medium—had thoroughly dispelled the astrological notion of planetary influences. Nineteenth-century science recognized gravitational and electromagnetic forces within the solar system, but had calculated that these forces were far too small to have any measurable effect except in the cases of the sun and moon.

Even the ancients had recognized that the sun provided the earth with heat and light and that the tides were generally attributable to the moon. However, these real physical influences played no part in astrology. Since the creators of astrology were trying to ascribe *all* earthly phenomena to the influences of the stars, they had to go far beyond such real physical effects and invent a full range of magical planetary and stellar correspondences.

In astrology today, the sun does remain the most important celestial object (e.g. sun signs), and the moon is considered a feminine, "watery" body, but that's about as close to reality as astrology has ever gotten. Everything else is pure magic. The scientific revolution has convincingly shown that reality differs almost totally from astrological fantasy. Following the Renaissance, astrology once again entered one of its "dark ages."

Then, in the latter half of the nineteenth century, Michaelson and Moreley began their classic light experiments to measure the speed of the earth through the aether. Much to their surprise, they detected no difference in the velocity of light when measured perpendicular, or parallel, to the direction of the earth's motion. The only possible conclusion was that the aether—a concept originally invented by the Greeks for transmitting the planetary "harmonies" and later taken over by the scientists as the propagating medium for light and gravity—did not exist.

Science was thrown into a tizzy. If the aether did not exist, then the forces of gravity and electromagnetism must be able to travel through empty space. Once again, man's notions of the universe were about to go through a traumatic change.

To what extent this challenge to the Newtonian universe contributed to the late-nineteenth-century growth of irrationalism and occult "sciences" cannot be judged. Astrology, as the leading occult "science," also began regaining adherents, particularly in Britain.

In 1905, Albert Einstein published his special theory of relativity, demonstrating that the constant velocity of light had immense consequences for our physical concepts of the universe. Both Max Planck and Einstein had worked on the important problem of the nature of light; since light could travel through empty space, it also had to have the nature of a particle because pure waves must have a transmitting medium.

This dual nature of the physical universe is tied together by the Heisenberg uncertainty principle, which states that particles can never be absolutely pinpointed but the probability of finding them is spread out over a finite (albeit very tiny) volume of space.

This new twentieth-century physics was further extended when Einstein added gravity to the force fields included in his general theory of relativity. According to this theory, empty space itself is curved by the forces of gravity—or, better put, the curvature of space *is* the force of gravity!

Finally, Einstein showed that if the mass of the universe were great enough and its rate of expansion slow enough, eventually the universe would stop expanding and collapse back in upon itself.

The world pondered these scientific discoveries with astonishment. All these discoveries seemed to have earth-shaking consequences for philosophy. Certainly, the nature of existence had been shown to be totally different from that previously expected, but what did the new physics mean? Did not relativity imply that man was more intimately linked to the universe than Newton's physics allowed? Were we not each composed of billions of unimaginably tiny particle/waves, atoms and molecules minute enough to be affected by electromagnetic radiation and even the weakest gravitational forces?

This new physics did cause elaborate and esoteric speculations to enter into philosophy on a legitimate level—and into the occult "sciences" on a much *less* legitimate level. Much of the new physics was misunderstood and misapplied: Einstein's theory of relativity was compared to the Hindu concept of the All-in-One universe; the "microcosm/macrocosm" relationship between atoms and man was compared to the magical "microcosm/macrocosm" astrological linkage between man and the stars.

However, Einstein's curved space is a far cry from the Hindu's All-in-One, and the nuclear and atomic forces acting between particles are far greater than any gravitational and electromagnetic fields.

The new physics only described reality; it provided no evidence in support of esoteric occult concepts. The two are a world apart: the first is based on physical observation, the other is based on magic.

During the first half of the twentieth century, however, both physical and biological scientists began finding evidence that certain *cyclic* phenomena on earth seem to correspond to periodic events and motions in the heavens.

First, in the 1920s, two Maryland biologists, W.W. Garner and H.A. Allard, tried to solve the problem of why tobacco plants north of Chesapeake Bay failed to flower before the frosts came. Nothing they tried seemed to make the plants flower earlier until they stumbled upon the idea of changing the *length* of the day.

By placing a light-tight box over several plants during the day and thus decreasing the amount of light the plants received, Garner and Allard learned they were able to make the tobacco plants flower at virtually any time during the summer. All they had to do was decrease the length of time the plants saw light to less than ten hours a day! Experimenting with several different species of plants, the biologists discovered that there are basically two types of flowering plants: long-day plants and short-day plants. Long-day plants bloom when the length of the day gets *longer* than a certain number of hours (those that bloom in spring), and short-day plants begin flowering when the length of the day gets *shorter* than the number of hours characteristic of the species.

So the sun does more than just provide light and heat; by means of the seasonal changes in the length of the day, it also provides the timing mechanism controlling the flowering of plants.

Soon, biologists were looking at all sorts of cyclic phenomena and comparing them with celestial cycles. Sunspots, especially, provided a very popular cycle for comparison; everything from animal population fluctuations to stock market changes to growth rings in redwood trees have been correlated with the sunspot cycle. As I will show in Chapters 9 and 10, most such correlations are completely coincidental and have nothing to do with cause and effect.

As always, the planets and stars turn with their various velocities, providing an almost endless number of cycles for correlation. Small wonder astrologers and scientists alike have been able to demonstrate *some* correlation between celestial cycles and periodic events here on earth!

In the realm of physics, scientists have claimed to find correlations between the quality of radio transmission and planetary positions, between the rate of chemical reaction and sunspot activity, and even between the process of solidification and phases of the moon.

Statistics, too, have entered the picture: where correlations have not been so obvious, elaborate statistical tests have been employed to uncover any slight correlation between earthly phenomena and celestial cycles. Scientists, pseudo scientists, and astrologers have tried to find statistical evidence of celestial influences. Such statistical studies run the gamut from linking diseases and lunacy to phases of the moon, to statistical studies of traditional astrology, to complex statistical evidence for a "new" cosmic astrology.

Where such statistical tests have been sufficiently large and properly conducted, researchers have found no evidence whatsoever to support traditional astrological aphorisms. Other statistical correlations (such as between lunacy and lunar phases) are most likely the accidental coinciding of two independent cycles. German and French studies into the new "cosmobiology" are plainly faulty and dangerously misleading. Chapter 10 ("Statistical Clocks") will take a look at these statistical studies purporting to demonstrate celestial influences on terrestrial cycles, carefully separating the valid from the invalid.

Book III will end with Chapter 11, "Known Physical Influences by Celestial Bodies," tying together the physical realities of life as we know them in the second half of the twentieth century. By that time, it should be obvious to the reader that the *known* planetary and stellar influences are of an entirely different order from the magical "influences" of astrology.

As complex and fascinating as astrology may be, I think the reader will find the scientific realities of biological clocks far more fascinating than the magical fantasies of astrology. In the field of biological clocks, with its ties to molecular biochemistry, genetics, and population dynamics, we are indeed stepping closer to solving the basic questions of life.

Bird migration, mysterious breeding cycles, the death march of the lemming, all these biological mysteries are fast yielding their secrets. In Chapter 9, I shall examine the general field of biological clocks, setting forth the two present competing scientific theories of how they operate and showing how important biological clocks are to the smooth and efficient running of the biological world.

Without biological clocks, life would soon be out of step with the daily and seasonal cycles that are so important for survival on this earth. The changing patterns of night and day, winter and summer, may provide the timing mechanisms for "running" the clocks, but the cycles themselves have nothing to do with the astrologer's "cycles and trends."

There's a great difference between discovering that the sun times our diurnal activities and claiming that the sun's magical influences in a particular sign will establish physical character and personality. The first is science, the second magical astrology.

9 The Science of Biological Clocks

When Garner and Allard discovered that the length of the day determines when plants begin to flower, it was a tremendous step forward for horticulturists and plant lovers around the world. With this new discovery nurseries could know how to induce plants to bloom artificially whenever they wished by merely increasing or decreasing the number of hours of light, either by shutting out the sun or by using artificial light. Now, too, farmers and gardeners around the world could know why certain plants bloom at certain times of the year, and thus why planting must take place well in advance to allow time for pure vegetative growth to produce plants of sufficient size.

In the next fifty years, the "budding" science of biological clocks would solve many age-old problems and answer many of biology's most perplexing questions.

It was not long before biologists discovered that plants were not the only organisms that possess clocks: animals, from the highest to the lowest orders, also possess timing mechanisms, internal clocks that permit their bodily activities to function with maximum efficiency by setting their cycles to match external environmental cycles. A nocturnal animal's metabolism must begin speeding up as the sun sets in order for the animal to be awake and alert as night comes on. Migrating birds must begin to store up energy-rich supplies of fat weeks before they set out on thousand-mile journeys, often across vast expanses of ocean or desert.

Without biological clocks, life could not exist on the face of the earth; the periodic environmental changes are far too great. Life forms that could not adjust to the environment would not last long unless they were extremely broad in their survival capabilities. Any competing organisms that *did* possess biological clocks would have a distinct adaptive and evolutionary advantage. As a result, every organism on the face of the earth, in fact, nearly every cell, nearly every bit of protoplasm, possesses the ability to keep time, to maintain its life-sustaining functions within accurate cyclic and periodic patterns.

How do they do this? How do certain plants know to open their leaves and flowers in the early morning hours (even when the sun is not visible)? How do the swallows know when to return to Capistrano? How do the grunion know when the highest tides will take them farthest up on the beach where their eggs can incubate in the warm, drying sun? How do the South Pacific palolo worms know when a particular last-quarter moon of spring will occur so they can accurately time their mass breeding nuptials?

How indeed?

At present, the science of biological clocks offers two hypotheses: the *endogenous* (internally run) clock theory and the *exogenous* (externally run) theory.

Most scientists in the field of biological clocks feel the evidence most strongly points toward the clocks being internally run and only *timed* or *entrained* by external environmental factors (which they call *zeitgebers,* or time-givers).[1] For instance, the changing hours of light acts as a *zeitgeber* for tobacco plants; when the hours of light decrease much below twelve, the plants begin to bloom. A few scientists, however, notably Frank Brown of Northwestern and his associates, feel that the biological clocks are run by external, "subtle" cosmic forces.

This controversy between the two hypotheses has been raging for years. At times, the controversy has gotten quite bitter, with opponents stooping to tactics not often seen in the annals of science.

The feud reached its peak in 1957 when a highly sarcastic article appeared in *Science,* "Biological Clock in the Unicorn," by LaMont C. Cole.[2] As its name implies, Cole's article presents statistical "evidence" that the mythical unicorn possesses a daily metabolic cycle, just as Brown's statistical evidence was demonstrating daily and lunar cycles in oysters and fiddler crabs. Cole never mentioned Professor Brown, but it was well known in the field where his article was aimed. How many recognized, however, that Cole's metabolic cycle of the unicorn (supposedly produced by statistically treating random data) was actually the result of a simple mathematical artifact? Cole merely imposed a periodic function upon his random numbers, assuring that his unicorn would have a cyclic metabolism. Unfortunately, while Cole's paper was clever and sarcastically amusing, it failed to shed any light on Brown's actual statistical methods or his claims of statistical evidence for the exogenous hypothesis.

For instance, Professor Brown had transported oysters from New Haven, Connecticut, to his laboratory in Evanston, Illinois, where he kept the oysters in total darkness and constant laboratory conditions, as far removed from the external world as he could get them. He kept very careful track of the timing of their activity—when they opened their shells to feed and when they closed them to rest. A thousand miles away in New Haven, the oysters had timed their activities with the tides, opening at high tide and closing at low tide. In Evanston, they maintained this same daily cycle for a couple of weeks; then suddenly, they began opening and closing their shells at the time the moon was overhead in Illinois, *as if they were responding to tides in the new time zone.*

Surely, claimed Dr. Brown, this was evidence that the oysters were able to respond to the gravitational forces of the moon passing overhead. However, as Lee Ratzan has shown (see Table 8-1), the moon only exerts a very minute force upon the oysters and their tanks, and they would have to be capable of detecting displacements on the order of the size of a single cell, or capable of detecting pressure changes far more minute than that caused by simply jiggling or bumping the tank!

We shall not look any further at Brown's statistical evidence supporting his exogenous hypothesis. Cole's sarcastic but contrived statistical criticism was countered many years later by Dr. A. Heusner in the book *Circadian Clocks,* where he shows that Cole's unicorn's periodicity is "an obvious statistical artifact which can be reproduced."[3]

However, the basic question—does Brown's statistical evidence actually indicate a cause and effect correlation between biological cycles and the motion of the moon and planets—remains to be answered. Brown himself—now Morrison Professor of Biology at Northwestern—feels that the electromagnetic responses presently so popularly demonstrated in many plants and animals provide a mechanism for his "subtle cosmic forces."[4]

In short, proponents of the externally run biological clock theory feel that the clocks are analogous to electrical clocks run by alternating household current, rather than by a self-contained timing mechanism (as in a windup clock). In Chapter 11, I will critically examine the theoretical mechanisms by which electromagnetic (E-M) fields within the solar system might conceivably do this.

Perhaps in the end, the controversy will be resolved by both hypotheses proving to be at least partially correct: while it's now clear that most organisms possess an internally run clock timed by obvious environmental factors, there may turn out to be a few cases where weak electromagnetic and gravitational forces provide the timing mechanism. Nature has a way of making use of all available factors; all that's needed is a mechanism and an evolutionary adaptive reason for making use of the factor.

Needless to say, if it is ever convincingly proven that oysters and potatoes can respond to the gravitational forces of the moon or the electromagnetic radiation from the sun and the planets, such "cosmic influences" still will be totally different from the "influences" of astrology. There is nothing in traditional astrology that implies that when the moon is overhead, oysters open their shells!

Professor Brown's statistical expertise also enters our story on another level: in 1967, he wrote the foreword to a book that claimed to present astonishing scientific evidence that the planets exert an "influence" on human life, in particular that rising and culminating planets "influence" one's choice of a *successful* career. The book was entitled *The Cosmic Clocks;* its author was Michel Gauquelin, a French statistician who had been trying to prove astrology statistically and in the process discovered what he now calls the new "astrobiology."

Chapter 10 will discuss some of the early statistical studies that form the foundations of astrobiology and touch briefly on the current controversy surrounding the statistical evidence for such planetary influences.

So much for the exogenous hypothesis, the concept that the biological clocks are run by "subtle cosmic forces" originating from celestial objects. The evidence is slim, the mechanism in doubt, and very few scientists in the field of biological clocks ascribe to the theory.

THE ENDOGENOUS CLOCK

What of the endogenous theory? How can both plants and animals—even the tiniest cells—possess internal clocks? By what possible mechanism do tobacco plants "know" that the number of hours of light has dwindled below ten? What possible internal organ or function could tell a rat to begin running on his wheel at precisely the same time each day, or a dog to run to the bus stop in time to meet his young mistress?

To be sure, the endogenous hypothesis is far more complex than Brown's exogenous hypothesis, at least at first sight, since it involves molecular biochemistry and rate of reaction theory. However, once the mechanism is more or less understood, the endogenous (internal) clock theory is actually quite simple, logical, and of immense utility to organisms possessing such a clock mechanism.

Figure 9-1 gives a schematic diagram of the endogenous clock hypothesis. It is felt that the basic clock mechanism—the encasement, if you will—is a single strand of DNA molecule, the basic protein building block of life. DNA contains a genetic code, all the molecular information needed to produce enzymes, hormones, proteins, and other molecular substances—in short, all the genetic information required for the functioning of life itself.

The genetic information contained in the DNA molecules is transferred throughout the organism via the process of RNA transcription. As pictured in Figure 9-1, RNA molecules are constructed right alongside the all-important DNA molecule, and the transcription proceeds at a *constant rate*. When the transcription is complete and the RNA molecule is an exact replica of the parent DNA molecule, the messenger RNA molecule pulls away and moves on to another functional site where protein or enzyme molecules might in turn be constructed via the information contained in the coded RNA molecule.

It is this constant rate of RNA transcription that the endogenous theorists feel provides the organism with a precise internal clock. Thus the organism, whether it be a plant producing chlorophyll or an animal producing the enzymes and hormones necessary for breeding, is continuously keeping time as it performs its normal functions.

Neat and logical, no?

Needless to say, we are talking here about the basic endogenous mechanism. Much yet remains to be learned: Which DNA-RNA transcriptions are the important rate-controlling ones? How is this timing information transmitted to the glands producing enzymes and hormones? How does the organism know which DNA "clock" to follow? Or are they all part of the timing mechanism?

Another important problem yet to be solved is how organisms can keep such accurate time in spite of great changes in temperature. All the evidence points toward biological clocks as being temperature-compensated. The clocks remain relatively constant in rate while the temperature fluctuates up and down. Yet the clock mechanism itself is thought to be a chemical rate of reaction, which normally doubles with every rise in temperature of 10°.

In order to introduce temperature compensation, the endogenous theorists have further complicated their model by introducing the concept of a chemical inhibitor (*I* in Figure 9-1), which controls the rate of DNA-RNA transcription; as the temperature rises, the amount of *I* increases and thus inhibits the reaction, keeping it more or less constant as temperature changes.

The endogenous biological clock hypothesis is not particularly simple, but it *is* elegant, and it helps to explain much about the biological world in which we live. Let's examine a few specific cases and learn precisely how. We shall begin with the lowly cockroach, one of the hardiest and evolutionarily one of earth's most successful productions.

The cockroach has been around for hundreds of millions of years with virtually no change; its internal clock still functions the same today as it did during the Paleozoic and Mesozoic Ages. Yet the first person to investigate the cockroach's internal chemical clock was a twentieth-century scientist, Dr. Janet Harker.

When Dr. Harker assumed her faculty position at Cambridge, she decided to attack the problem of biological clocks in a unique way. Everybody else in the field was trying to answer the question of *how* the clocks were run, internally or externally; nobody was trying to find *where* the clock might be located in a particular animal. Dr. Harker felt that if she could pinpoint the precise location of the clock and could demonstrate that this was indeed the clock responsible for the animal's cyclic behavior, then determining whether the clock is internal or not would be a relatively simple matter.

For seven long years Dr. Harker carefully dissected out minute portions from thousands of living cockroach brains; after each surgery she would watch the animal's rhythmic behavior to see if there was any change. When she discovered that, by removing the cockroach's tiny secondary brain (the subesophageal ganglion), the animal became totally arhythmic, its "clock" completely out of kilter, she knew she was on the right track. Then, by systematically cauterizing different areas of the subesophageal ganglion, she was able to trace the cockroach's biological clock down to four "neurosecretory cells that are necessary for the maintenance of the rhythm."[5]

The clock had been located.

Dr. Harker then went on to experiment with her new-found discovery. First, by transplanting the clock from a rhythmic cockroach to the bloodstream of an arhythmic one, she was able to demonstrate that the clock is essentially a biochemical one, its messages transmitted by hormones rather than by nerve connections. Then, by transplanting the clock from one cockroach to another living completely out of time phase (i.e., the donor's nighttime activity began just as the transplantee's own clock was telling him to go to sleep for the day), she showed that the stress induced by a malfunctioning biological clock resulted in stomach cancer.

Biological clocks were turning out to be very important, indeed!

So the clock has been located, at least in one species; it seems reasonable to suppose that similar biochemical clocks will be found in nearly every animal on earth. Perhaps even an analogous biochemical clock will even be found in plants, for certainly plants also rely on chemical reactions in order to function effectively within their environment. One suspects, however, that the clock in plants may be more generally located, perhaps found in large numbers of similar cells, such as those involved in the production of chlorophyll.

Evidence for the biological clock has popped up in unexpected avenues of biological research. In addition, scientists have been discovering that the clocks are used by animals to solve age-old problems of survival in unexpected and unique ways. The dance of the bees is a fascinating case in point.

THE CLOCK AND ANIMAL NAVIGATION

The famous biologist Karl von Frisch had long been interested in learning how bees managed to communicate the location—in terms of both distance and direction—of sources of nectar and food to other members of the colony. He began experimenting by training bees to find his sugared-water containers at specific locations and at specific times of the day. He noticed that when a single bee found his food offering and returned to the hive, the bee (identified by color coding) would perform a dance, a peculiar twisting and turning motion on the inside of the hive with large numbers of member bees clustered nervously around.

Could it be that bees communicate by means of movement?

And, if so, how? How could a bee, by means of a dance, tell other members of the colony the direction and distance to von Frisch's sugar water?

Only more experimentation and observation could provide the answers. Von Frisch varied the distance of his feeding stations from within thirty feet to more than three miles away. The first thing he noticed was that the bee's dance distinctly changed from the circular pattern, when the station was close, to a figure-8 pattern, when the feeding station was more than fifty to one hundred yards from the hive.

Figure 9-2 illustrates the two kinds of dances. When the food is near, the returning scout bee dances in a circle; then a swarm of bees will set out looking for food near the hive. Apparently, at close distances to the hive, the bees do not need to communicate direction or distance, but when the food is farther away than fifty or one hundred yards, the dance of the scout bee changes from a simple circling to a much more elaborate figure-8 pattern. So the figure-8 "wagging" dance communicates at least two kinds of information. The diagonal crossing of the 8 indicates the direction to the food with respect to the angle of the sun, and the rate of the dance tells the other bees how far away the food is (fast for close nectar, slow for food farther away).

How peculiar, thought von Frisch: bees not only can communicate, but they measure direction with respect to the sun! This, of course, meant that the bees changed the angle of their figure-8 dance as the sun moved across the sky throughout the day—and this in turn implied that they could tell time!

But not necessarily; the bees *could* be obtaining their knowledge of the sun's changing direction from some external factor. Von Frisch answered this question by flying his bees from Paris to New York. And, sure enough, three thousand miles from their home, the bees performed their dance and sought their food as if they were still on French time!

So bees, too, have internal clocks, delicate biochemical mechanisms that help them navigate from hive to food source.

Not surprisingly, then, the biological clock helps solve some of the mysteries of bird migration, for birds also have a very precise internal clock available for timing the movement of the sun and stars. Navigation, for man and beast alike, requires knowledge not only of the direction of celestial objects but also of the time. Otherwise, one tends to go in circles!

First, it was shown by the famous ornithologist Gustav Kramer that starlings and homing pigeons orient their migration flights by the light of the sun. In particular, he found that they could orient their migratory direction just by means of the *polarization* of sunlight. They did not need to see the sun itself; they could orient themselves even on cloudy days by means of the changing direction of polarization.

This sun compass of birds is very similar to the sun compass of bees; both orient by means of the direction of the sun and with the aid of an internal clock. How many other orders of animals possess such a sun compass can only be a matter of conjecture at this time. Certainly, it is one of the most important discoveries of modern biological science.

However, not all birds migrate during the day, when sunlight is available as a navigational guide. Many species, notably the tiny insect-feeding warblers, perform their migrations at night, leaving the day for rest and feeding. Perhaps not surprisingly to the reader at this point, these nighttime-migrating birds have been found to orient themselves by means of the stars: they use the same stellar patterns that man has been observing for thousands of years.

Strangely, it turns out that this stellar migration sense of birds does *not* require an internal clock. As Stephen Emlen has demonstrated in his excellent *Scientific American* article,[6] the indigo bunting can use groups of star patterns rather than individual stars which would require knowing the time to find direction (as warblers seem to do).

In other words, as pictured in Figure 9-3, there are two stellar orientation hypotheses. In the first, the bird flies at a particular angle to a certain star; this orientation requires an internal clock to inform the bird of its changing angle in relation to the star; in the second hypothesis, the bird flies at a particular angle with respect to the star groups around the North Pole, similar to how boy scouts are trained to find direction.

Here, again, we find real physical evidence that the sun and stars "influence" life on earth. But, again, as in the case of possible gravitational effects of the moon on oysters, the real physical effects are totally removed from the realm of astrological theory. Ptolemy had no idea that birds could navigate by means of the sun and stars; nor is there any hint of such a fact in astrological theory or literature.

BIOLOGICAL CLOCKS IN HUMANS

Yet, man too possesses a biological clock. Had ancient man been interested in basing his astrology on observation, there is a wealth of human cycles he could have related to the motions of the sun, moon, and planets. For instance, by taking his own temperature periodically throughout the day for a week or two, any ancient scientist could have discovered that his body temperature starts to rise approximately at the same time the sun rises in the east. As the sun climbed in the sky, his temperature would also climb until about midday when it would level off; then, as the sun set in the west, his temperature would likewise begin to drop to a low plateau well below the accepted "normal" of 98.6°F.

"Surely," our hypothetical ancient scientist would have cried, "this is proof that the sun directly influences life here on earth! As the god of heat and light approaches the zenith of heaven, our bodily temperature here on earth likewise rises; as the sun god sets, our temperature falls. Astrology is vindicated!"

And our ancient scientist would have been right—but for the *wrong* reason. Our body temperatures go up in the morning and fall during the evening hours because our biological clocks regulate our metabolic temperature so we will be most alert and efficient during the daylight hours, when the need is greatest.

And, of course, the sun *does* play a role, but not through any magical application of its "godlike" heat. It is the rising of the sun that starts the day, and in that sense the sun "affects" all life on earth every day. But, to the ancient astrologers, this was such an obvious effect that it was not even included in their magical system of astrological "effects." The traditional astrological "influences" of the sun—creativity, generosity, arrogance, extravagance—have nothing to do with its life-giving heat and light, nor with its other real physical effects such as timing biological clocks or serving as a navagational tool.

People, of course, vary considerably; their clocks are not all set to the same starting signal, as is true for most animals. Animal life is not nearly so elastic as human existence; the warbler who fails to rise with the sun may not find enough time in the day to feed his voracious appe-

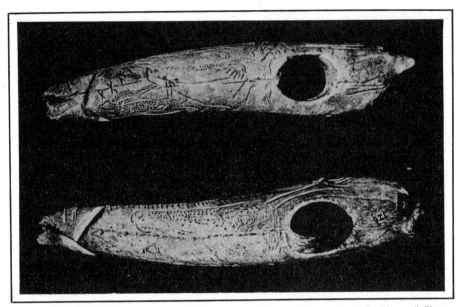

Figure 1.1: Prehistoric Notational Baton

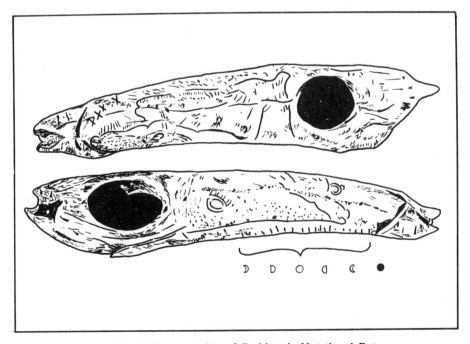

Figure 1.2: Lunar Model Interpretation of Prehistoric Notational Baton

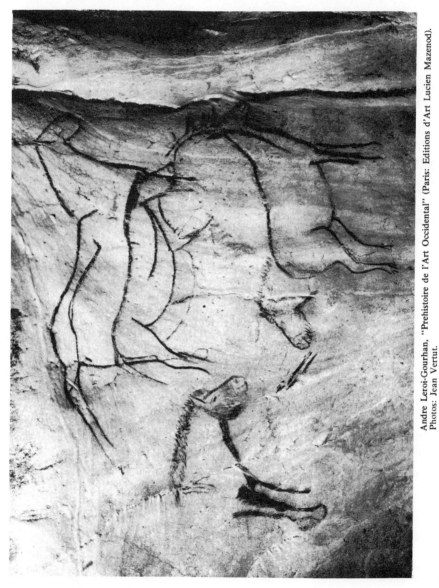

Andre Leroi-Gourhan, "Prehistoire de l'Art Occidental" (Paris: Editions d'Art Lucien Mazenod).
Photos: Jean Vertut.

Figure 2.1: Superimposed Prehistoric Cave Painting

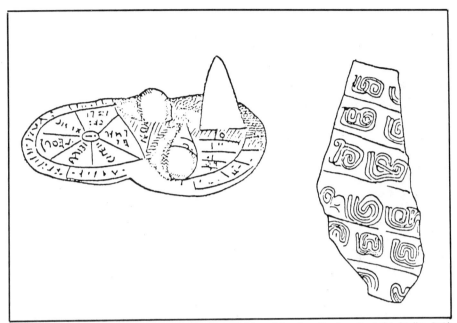

Jack Lindsay, *Origins of Astrology* (London: Frederick Muller, Ltd.).

Figure 2.2: Babylonian Liver Model

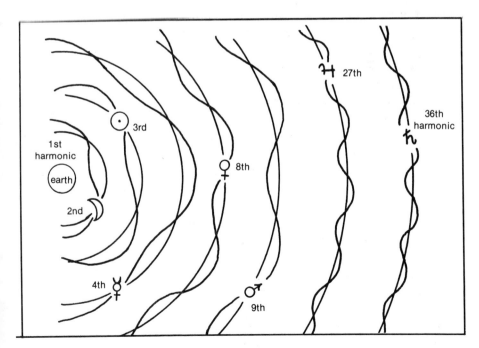

Figure 2.3: Greek "Harmony of the Spheres"

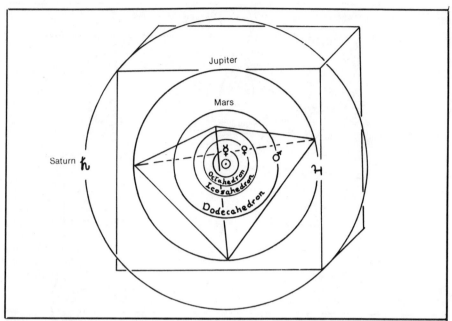

Figure 5.1: Kepler's First "Model of the Universe": A Chinese Box of Regular Solids

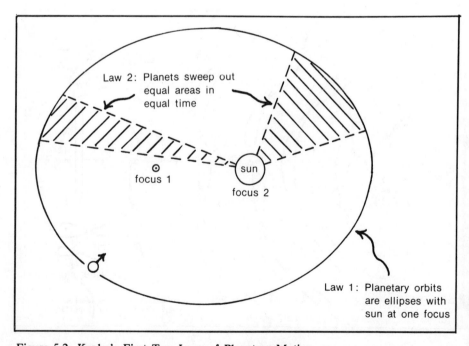

Figure 5.2: Kepler's First Two Laws of Planetary Motion

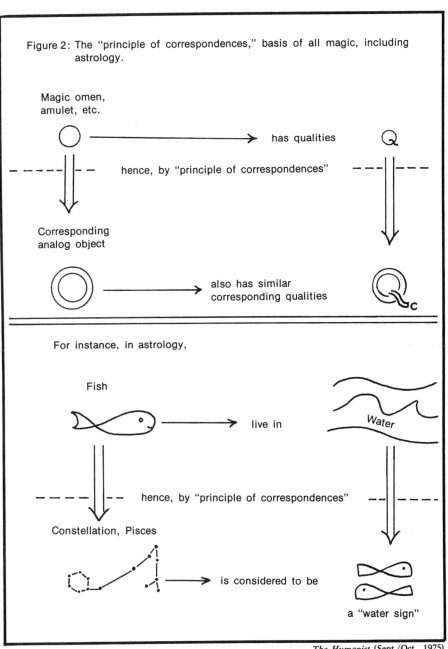

Figure 2: The "principle of correspondences," basis of all magic, including astrology.

Magic omen, amulet, etc.

has qualities

hence, by "principle of correspondences"

Corresponding analog object

also has similar corresponding qualities

For instance, in astrology,

Fish

live in

Water

hence, by "principle of correspondences"

Constellation, Pisces

is considered to be

a "water sign"

The Humanist (Sept./Oct., 1975).

Figure 6.1: "Principle of Correspondences"

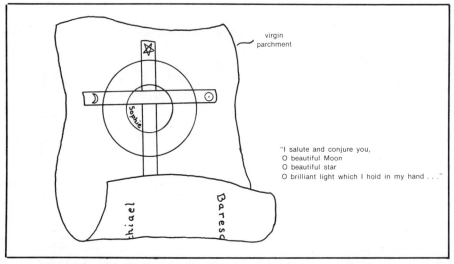

virgin
parchment

"I salute and conjure you,
O beautiful Moon
O beautiful star
O brilliant light which I hold in my hand . . ."

Richard Cavendish, *The Black Arts* (New York: G. P. Putnam's Sons). Copyright © Richard Cavendish, 1967.

Figure 6.2: Astrological Talisman and Its Magical Chant

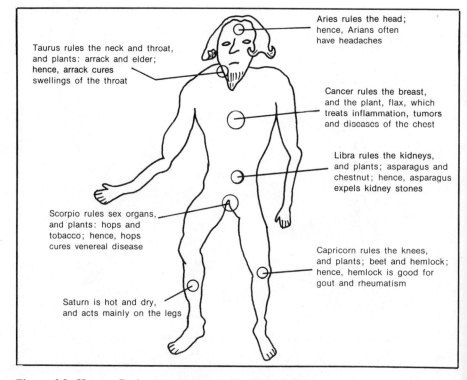

Aries rules the head; hence, Arians often have headaches

Taurus rules the neck and throat, and plants: arrack and elder; hence, arrack cures swellings of the throat

Cancer rules the breast, and the plant, flax, which treats inflammation, tumors and diseases of the chest

Libra rules the kidneys, and plants; asparagus and chestnut; hence, asparagus expels kidney stones

Scorpio rules sex organs, and plants: hops and tobacco; hence, hops cures venereal disease

Capricorn rules the knees, and plants; beet and hemlock; hence, hemlock is good for gout and rheumatism

Saturn is hot and dry, and acts mainly on the legs

Figure 6.3: Human Body, Astrology and Magical Medicine

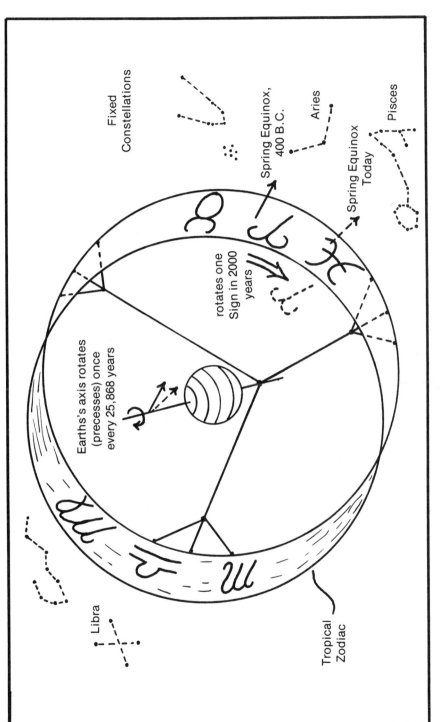

Figure 7.1: Precession of Earth's Axis Leads to Tropical Zodiac

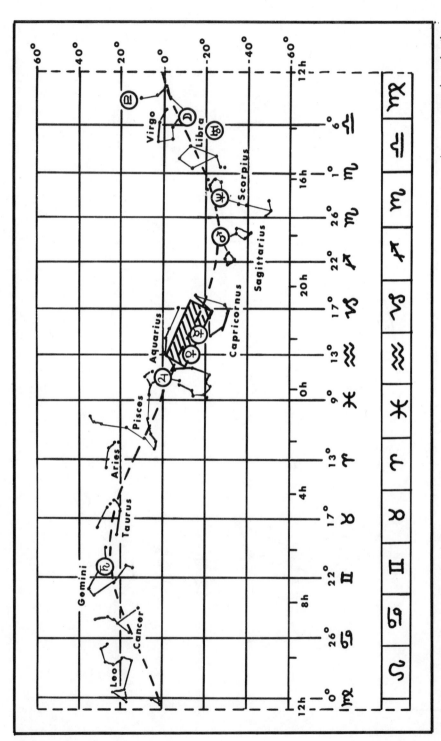

Figure 7.2: Sidereal Zodiac Superimposed on Planet-Finder Chart

Astronomy magazine and author.

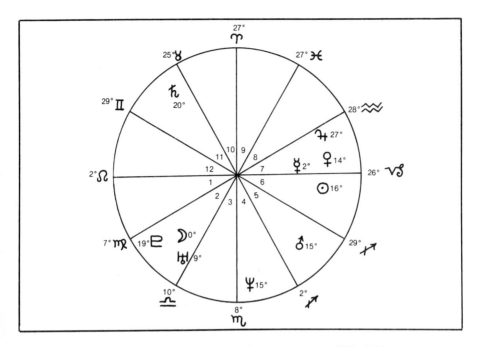

Figure 7.3: Local Time Sidereal Horoscope for February 1, 1975, 8:00 p.m.

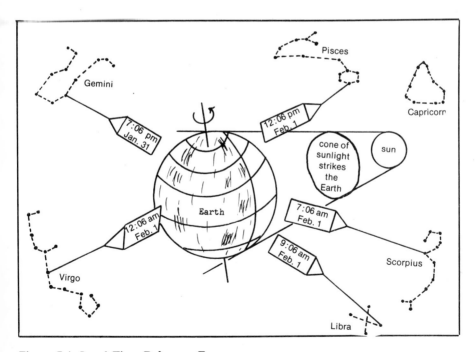

Figure 7.4: Local Time Reference Frame

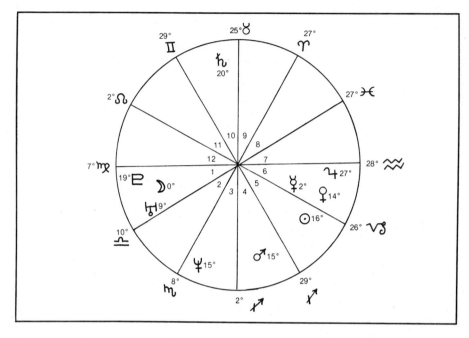

Figure 7.5: Local Time Sidereal Horoscope for February 1, 1975, 10:00 p.m.

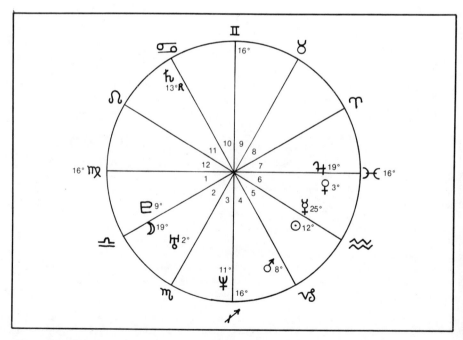

Figure 7.6: Tropical Horoscope for February 1, 1975, 8:00 p.m., New York City

From Derek Parker and Julia Parker, *The Compleat Astrologer.* Copyright © 1971, By Mitchell Beazley Limited. Used with permission of McGraw-Hill Book Co.

Figure 8.1; William Lily's "Hieroglyphic Prediction" of the Great Fire of London

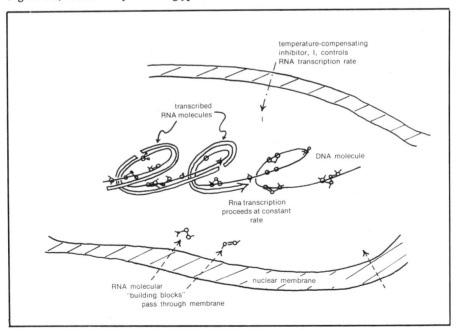

temperature-compensating
inhibitor, I, controls
RNA transcription rate

transcribed
RNA molecules

I

DNA molecule

Rna transcription
proceeds at constant
rate

RNA molecular
"building blocks"
pass through membrane

nuclear membrane

Figure 9.1: Endogenous Biological Clock Mechanism

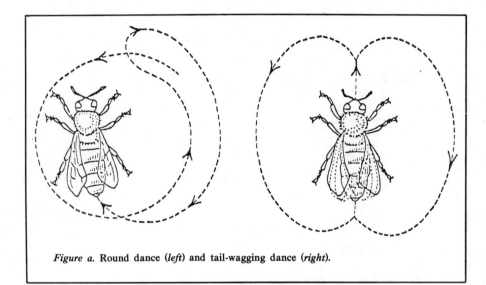

Figure a. Round dance (*left*) and tail-wagging dance (*right*).

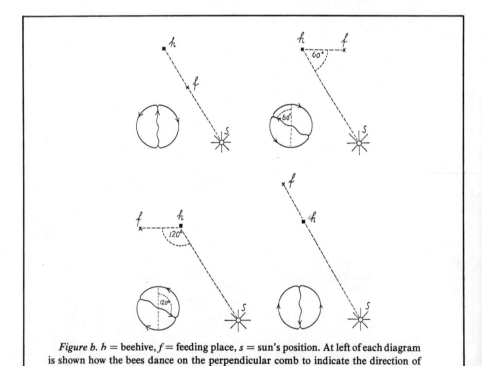

Figure b. h = beehive, f = feeding place, s = sun's position. At left of each diagram is shown how the bees dance on the perpendicular comb to indicate the direction of the feeding place with respect to the sun's position. Note that the bearing of the sun is transferred to the upward direction, perceived by means of gravity.

Figure 9.2: Dance of the Bees

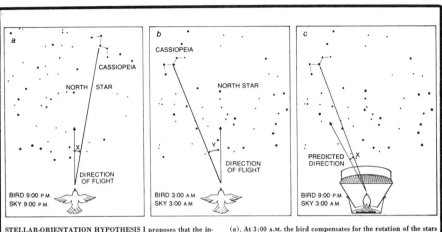

STELLAR-ORIENTATION HYPOTHESIS I proposes that the indigo bunting guides itself by flying at an angle to a particular star or group of stars. Since the positions of the stars change throughout the night, the bird would have to use an internal time sense to compensate for the motion of the stars. For example, a bunting going north at 9:00 P.M. would fly at angle X with respect to a critical star (a). At 3:00 A.M. the bird compensates for the rotation of the stars by flying at angle Y to the critical star (b). According to the hypothesis, when a bunting whose physiological time is at 9:00 P.M. is presented with a 3:00 A.M. star pattern in a planetarium, it should compensate in the wrong direction, that is, it should orient at angle X with respect to the critical star instead of at angle Y (c).

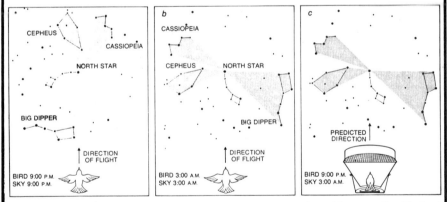

STELLAR-ORIENTATION HYPOTHESIS II states that the bunting obtains directional information from the configuration of the stars. The bird can determine a reference direction such as north from fixed geometric relation of the stars regardless of the time of night (a, b). When the bunting is exposed to a time-shifted sky in a planetarium, there should be no change in its orientation (c).

Figure 9.3: Steller Orientation Hypotheses in Bird Migration

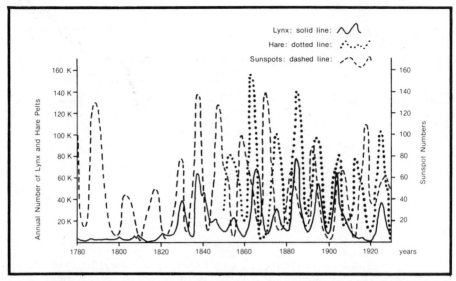

George L. Clark, *Elements of Ecology* (New York: John Wiley and Sons, Inc. 1954); D. A. MacLulich, Biological Series No. 43, (University of Toronto Studies, 1937), and Edward Kormondy, *Concepts of Ecology* (Englewood Cliffs, N.J.: Prentice-Hall, 1969).

Figure 10.1: Canadian Lynx/Varying Hare/Sunspot Cycles

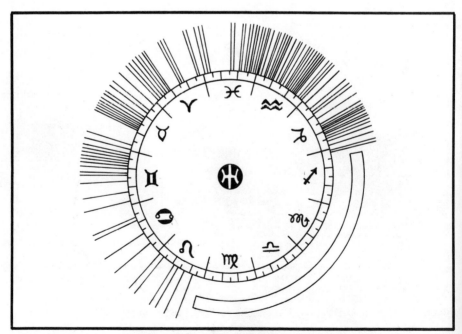

Karl Ernst Krafft, Traite d'Astrobiologie (Paris: Libraire Amedee Legrand, 1939).

Figure 10.2: Krafft's Plot of Moon-Uranus Conjunctions in Sun Sign of 115 Musicians

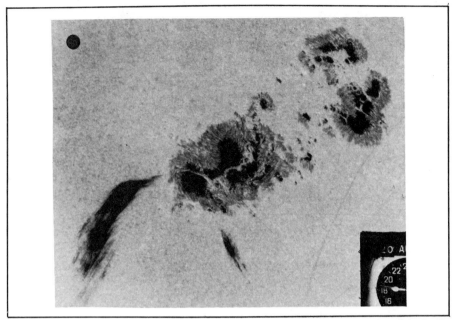

Courtesy, Astronomical Society of the Pacific.

Figure 11.1: Photo of a Solar Flare

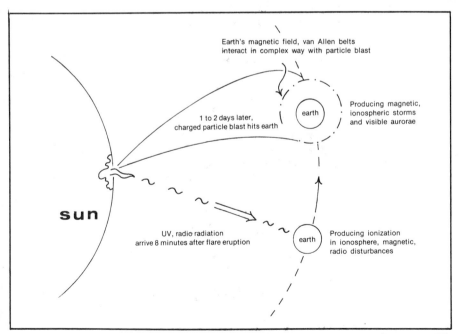

The Humanist (Sept./Oct., 1975).

Figure 11.2: Flare Emissions and their Effects

John Blofeld, *The Way of Power: A Practical Guide to the Tantric Mysticism of Tibet* (London: George Allen & Unwin Ltd).

Figure 13.1: Outline of a Mandala

tite *and* tend to all the details required to breed and genetically propagate his lazy habits. Civilization, with its artificial lights, heat, and shelter, permits man much more flexibility.

Thus we find some humans to be "morning people," their temperature curves rising even before the sun, while at the other extreme are "evening people," whose temperature curves do not start to rise until mid-morning or so. "Morning people" tend to be alert and cheerful in the morning; "evening people" tend to be grouchy and slow in the morning. Many people, particularly those who daily perform dull, routine tasks, have temperature curves that do not change very much: in the morning their temperatures rise to a low plateau that is maintained throughout the day and drops only a degree or two as night falls.

Thus, as Darrell Huff suggests,[7] there is evidence that one's "temperature type" is correlated with one's temperament and personality. "Morning people" tend to be conservatives; "evening people" tend to be arty, radical types. "Plateau people" are usually unimaginative average types—steady but dull.

This correlation between personality and "temperature types" will also enter into my discussion of the statistical evidence for planetary "influences" on people's career choices (see Chapter 10).

Scientific researchers have also found that our moods possess a cycle that is more or less independent of external events. Ranging from sixteen to sixty-three days, this mood cycle is governed by our hormonal secretions that in turn are controlled by our internal biological clocks.[8]

Note that the very large variability of the human mood cycle makes it impossible for it to be "influenced" by any celestial body. How could any cycle that varies from person to person over a range of sixteen to sixty-three days be governed by the relatively constant motions of the planets? To be sure, *some* statistician could find *some* combination of celestial cycles that will seem to statistically match *some* mood cycles. As we shall discover in Chapter 10, such coincidental matching of cycles is to be expected and is not evidence of any cause-and-effect relationship. The planets and stars go about their cycles, while life here on earth has evolved its own independent cycles, internally run but triggered by environmental changes and time-givers, none of which have anything to do with astrology or its theoretical aphorisms.

To modern man—if he would but pay attention—the real world cannot fail to be far more complex and fascinating than any of the magical and mystical fantasies of ancient astrology. The effort required to understand and appreciate the real world may be far greater than to grasp the concepts of simple magic, but ultimately the rewards are far greater.

NOTES

1. Ritchie R. Ward, *The Living Clocks* (New York: Alfred A. Knopf, 1971), p. 140.
2. LaMont C. Cole, "Biological Clock in the Unicorn," *Science* 125 (May 3, 1957), p. 874.
3. Jurgen Aschoff, ed., *Circadian Clocks* (Amsterdam: North-Holland Publishing Co., 1965), pp. 10-11.
4. Personal communication.
5. Ward, *The Living Clocks,* p. 235.
6. Stephen T. Emlen, "The Stellar-Orientation System of a Migratory Bird," *Scientific American* (August 1975): 102-11.
7. Darrell Huff, *Cycles in Your Life* (New York; W.W. Norton, 1964).
8. Ibid., p. 57.

10   Statistical Clocks

Cycles, both organic and inorganic, are an ever-present feature of life, so it's not surprising that researchers have turned to statistical methods of correlating and studying the various cycles that we see around us every day. But these are extremely complex problems, and unfortunately many of the early researchers into periodicities were not as well versed in mathematics and statistics as the complexity of these problems requires.

As a result, many of the early claims of statistical correlation between celestial and earthly phenomena are highly suspect. The real world is a very complex place, and it is all too easy to fall into a number of mathematical pitfalls when attempting to apply simple statistical tests to real physical experiments. The very nature of experimentation—collecting data under controlled conditions—permits the introduction of statistical errors, such as hidden biases and internal degrees of freedom.

Population variances in the real world—in layman's terms, deviations from the norm—can usually be expected to be fairly large, much larger, say, than in a simple die-tossing experiment. Why? A die has only six possible sides, and it can only land on one of them. Most real life experiments, on the other hand, involve a *continuum* of possibilities—in fact, several continuums if you look at all three dimensions of space as well as time.

Furthermore, we must expect a reasonable number of coincidences to occur in the real world, as Jung was so fond of pointing out. Coincidences between unrelated *cycles* can also be expected; all that's required is that their periods over time be approximately equal. Even cycles with widely differing periods will appear to coincide over a significant range. The famous case of the Canadian lynx/showshoe rabbit/sunspot correlation is a classic illustration.

SUNSPOTS AND LUNACY

The Canadian lynx is the northern relative of the American bobcat. The varying hare—also known as the showshoe rabbit—comprises a major portion of the lynx's diet. The Hudson Bay Company has been recording the number of pelts collected from the two species since 1735. Their records show that the populations of both the lynx and the hare fluctuate from year to year with a periodicity of approximately ten years.

Figure 10-1 illustrates these variations in the rabbit and lynx populations. The variations in the predatory lynx population tend to follow the ups and downs in the hare population. There is, of course, a time lag of a couple of years, as one might expect.

Looking for a cause for this cyclic behavior, one enterprising ecologist superimposed the lynx population curve on a similar curve representing the yearly number of sunspots (dashed line in Figure 10-1). Aha! The curves coincided over a good portion of their ranges, so the ecologist quite incorrectly concluded that sunspots must somehow regulate the population numbers of both hare and lynx. Thus was added yet another piece of statistical evidence to the growing number of studies into biological phenomena which have periodicities approaching that of the eleven-year sunspot cycle.

Growth rings in redwood trees have been found to be grouped in units of 11 and 22 corresponding to the 22-year sunspot reversal cycle (see Chapter 11). Both the redwood cicada and the long-haired rat of Australia possess 11-year cycles. Cinch bug outbreaks seem to occur at intervals of 9.6 years. And yet another study has shown that floods along the Ohio River valley are greatest every 23 years.

Indeed, a large number of periodic biological phenomena have been shown to have cycles at least approximately similar to the sunspot cycle. These similarities indicate that there may be a correlation between electromagnetic emissions from the sun and, say, weather cycles here on earth. The weather cycles, in turn, regulate animal populations and "influence" many other biological phenomena.

But is it a real correlation?

Close examination of the Canadian lynx and sunspot cycles in Figure 10-1 reveals that the correspondence is really not that great. The sunspot cycle is much more irregular. It varies from a periodicity of 7 to 17 years, while the periods between lynx maximums only range from 8 to 12 years. The two curves are often totally out of phase, sunspot maximums occurring during lynx minimums or vice versa for the years 1804, 1811, 1860, 1871, and 1923.

The first rule, then, when dealing with cyclic phenomena is to recognize that cycles with similar periods, whose peaks and troughs may appear closely associated over a length of time, may in fact turn out to be totally unrelated. For instance, the variations in the number of rabbits will obviously have some effect on their predators unless the latter are able to change their diet to some other source. Such an occurrence is much less likely in far northern climes, where the number and variety of species is not nearly as great as in temperate and tropical zones. Thus one may safely assign a significant cause-and-effect correlation between the lynx and hare cycles but *not* between the lynx and sunspot cycles.

Cause and effect requires much more than simple correlation over time. The scientific method also requires the demonstration of a mechanism, a means by which the cyclic phenomena can interact, as in lynx-eat-hare.

As we saw in the previous chapter, this question of an external celestial mechanism lies at the very root of the endogenous versus exogenous controversy in the field of biological clocks. Very little evidence for such a mechanism exists, but a number of writers have tried to show that modern science allows at least a *theoretical* interaction. They posit a connection between the sun's electromagnetic radiation and events here on earth via the earth's magnetic fields and radiation belts. (Chapter 11 will go into this theoretical sun-earth interaction mechanism in much greater detail.)

Suffice it to say that as long as such a mechanism is not positively and conclusively demonstrated, *all* correlations between sunspot cycles and events within the lower atmosphere of earth are highly suspect.

Yet sunspots, along with phases of the moon, remain the most popular celestial phenomena with which the statistical researcher can correlate his experimental data. A number of sincere, hard-working scientists have attempted to correlate sunspot cycles with biological and physical data. One of the most noted and energetic was Professor Tchijewsky, whose tireless research at Moscow University during the 1920s and 1930s pioneered the field of statistical sunspot correlations.

Professor Tchijewsky was, if nothing else, ambitious and far-ranging in his research goals. He wanted to apply his sunspot correlations to no less than the entire medical, political, and social history of his country and the rest of the world. Going over the cyclic history of the last two and a half millennia, he found that sunspots could be held responsible for epidemics, wars, and social revolutions. Likewise, Professor Tchijewsky found that the peak years for smallpox deaths coincided with peak years of sunspot activity between 1830 and 1930.[1] Unfortunately, Russia's staid leader, Josef Stalin, looked with considerable disfavor upon Tchijewsky's attempts to explain social events via "cosmic forces." The good professor was dispatched to the labor camps of Siberia.

Yet Tchijewsky's fall from grace did not deter later researchers from demonstrating many more "correlations" between sunspot activity and periodic events on earth. Heart attacks, tuberculosis, accidents, and unexplained sudden deaths are just a few of the "cyclic" phenomena that have been correlated with sunspot activity. Even fluctuations in blood counts have been ascribed to the sunspot cycle!

While the sun has been held responsible for a number of seemingly strange and unrelated cyclic phenomena, researchers have reserved their even more bizarre correlations for the moon. Cycles in crimes, births, and surgical hemorrhaging are only a few phenomena that have been alleged to increase with a full moon.[2]

The moon, of course, has had a long history of such associations, particularly with madness and the female menstrual cycle. Man had long been used to reckoning time by means of the moon's phases, so perhaps it was natural for the moon "god" to be blamed for periodic misfortunes, ranging from plagues to arthritis. In Italy, the moon was held responsible for the peculiar *chiodo lunare* (moon stroke), described by Henry Still as, "a neuralgic pain around the eye socket believed to occur when the moon rose. It would disappear as the moon set."[3]

Thus did madness come to be called "lunacy." Even today, there are psychiatrists ready to swear that our mental institutions become howling madhouses on the nights of a full moon. And, of course, the moon's ancient association with women is no doubt based on the biological fact (coincidence?) that the menstrual period is approximately a month long, though it can range from as little as two weeks to as much as two months.

While it is entirely too much for the scientific mind to seriously entertain the theory that the moon's tiny gravitational fluctuations upon the earth can have anything to do with breeding cycles and lunacy, there *is* evidence that the intensity of the full moon's light is sufficient to trigger biochemical and hormonal reactions. After all, a short flash from a dim red light is sufficient to reset the biological clocks of most plants (an unsuspected effect that led at least one early researcher astray). However, ever since the advent of the artificial lighting of modern civilization, one can be sure that any possible "influence" by the full moonlight upon human breeding cycles will be totally swamped by street lights and television!

So it is with nearly all possible theoretical "influences" of celestial objects. Their maximum possible intensity is so slight that the "effect" is easily lost in the background noise, the pressures and intensity of modern living, and the roar of trucks and glare of neon lights.

If the powerful planetary "effects" that the astrologers postulate actually existed, we would be able to measure them. We would be able to see clearly that Mars in certain signs and aspects causes aggressiveness, and that a significant number of people born under Pisces are uncontrollably attracted to sea and alcohol.

We do not. All properly conducted statistical tests of traditional astrology have come up blank. The observed data have always fit well within normally expected distributions. The important phrase here is "properly conducted." The number of *im*properly conducted statistical studies into astrology is legend. All too many budding astrological statisticians have poorly understood the real world and have devised statistical tests that underestimate the complexity of the physical problem.

One of the most common statistical errors made by "cosmic researchers" is underestimating the size of the sample needed to give significant results. It's statistically quite meaningless to say that 6 of America's astronauts are Libras or whatever, since the total number of astronauts is quite small. If there were 10,000 astronauts and 1,000 were Aries, then you *might* have a statistically significant result.

ASTROLOGICAL STATISTICS

Certainly, the earliest statistical studies into traditional astrology—both pro and con—can be faulted on the basis of sample size. Pico della Mirandola's fourteenth-century study of the success rate of astrologers' weather predictions (see page 45) was the first such improper statistical study. He followed their forecasts for only 130 days—barely enough time to get warmed up! Then, too, one must suspect that Pico's sampling and evaluating methods were highly biased since he found that the astrologers were right on only 7 of the 130 days, an incredible failure rate. As West and Toonder point out, one would only have to take the reciprocal of their predictions to attain a 95 percent level (assuming Pico used a binomial classification system, sunny or cloudy, success or failure).[4]

A much later researcher, Paul Choisnard, committed the same sample size error, though he was trying to prove astrology rather than disprove it. Choisnard studied 200 "death horoscopes" and found Mars in conjunction with the sun three times as often as expected, while Saturn was in conjunction with the sun at the moment of death twice as often as expected. However, as Michel Gauquelin correctly points out, such variations from the expected value are not unusual in a sample size of only 200.[5]

Gauquelin decided to test Choisnard's claims and collected 7,482 horoscopes, which he then analyzed for Choisnard's malefic planetary aspects. With a properly large sample, the results were well within chance level. Mars and Saturn were found conjunct the sun in 5.7 percent and 5.8 percent of the deaths, respectively, as compared to an expected rate of 5.5 percent.[6]

Even the great psychologist Carl Jung made a statistical study of astrology. He examined the relationships of the sun, moon, and ascendant in the horoscopes of married couples. At first, Jung seemed to find significant relationships, but as his sample size increased and results began to "tail off," so did his interest.

Jung did not study the occult sciences because of any "belief" in them. Rather, he was interested in their role as archetypical symbols of the unconscious. If Jung felt there was "anything to" the occult sciences, in particular the I Ching and astrology, it was because he felt that these arcane games might somehow express archetypical relationships within the unconscious. He realized that both astrology and the I Ching were systems by which people could be psychologically manipulated. Hence, their symbology had to lie closely rooted to the archetypes he felt were the inner mechanisms of the unconscious mind.

As the laws of statistics—particularly those regarding sample size—became better formulated and recognized, astrological statisticians began applying more sophisticated techniques using samples running into the thousands, or even tens of thousands. When traditional aspects and sun signs failed to yield significant results, the researchers turned to more complex astrological factors. For instance, if the tropical zodiac didn't seem to fit their data, they might try the sidereal one in hopes that it would work.

This methodology brings us to the American astrologer Donald Bradley. Gathering birth data for 2,492 clergymen from the annals of *Who's Who,* Bradley found that their distribution over sun signs was nonrandom (an expected result, by the way, since more people are born in January, February, and September). However, what bothered Bradley was that his curve (plotted in 5° increments) did not speak in the middle of signs (at 15°) as he expected until he shifted his birth data to the sidereal zodiac! Bradley did not bother with such complexities as statistical significance. On the evidence of his peak shifts alone, he became a staunch champion of the sidereal zodiac.[7]

The British astrologer John Addey got even more sophisticated in his statistical studies of polio victims and the aged. Looking at the charts of 1,000 ninety-year-olds, Addey was disappointed to find that the traditionally long-lived Capricorns actually survived into their nineties no more frequently than the traditionally short-lived Pisceans. As West and Toonder so poignantly stress, Addey was not satisfied with the failure of his astrological expectations. Instead, he began analyzing his data for hidden "cosmic correlations."

Since his subjects were more or less randomly distributed over sun signs, Addey decided to test his data for the truly esoteric astrological aspect called "separating" (when planets begin leaving important signs and angular aspects). Not surprisingly, Addey found what he was looking for: a "significant" number of his ninety-year-olds had a large percentage of "separating aspects" in their charts.

Of course, Addey's statistical discovery was new to astrologers. Once again, the traditional astrological magic failed to correspond to statistical "reality." Addey's results, then, really belong to the new "astrobiology," based on statistical studies such as pioneered by Karl Ernst Krafft and championed by Michel Gauquelin.

Not content with just a new astrological aphorism, Addey went on to collect polio victim birth data from the hospital where he taught and to submit it to wave analysis. Harking back to Pythagoras's "harmony of the spheres," Addey found that the 12th and 120th harmonics corresponded most closely to the birth "tendencies" of his polio victims.[8]

This is pure mathematical nonsense. As any mathematician who has performed Fourier analysis on real data realizes, only the first two or three harmonic coefficients can have any real physical meaning (unfortunately, Addey invented his own system of "wave analysis" and remained blissfully unaware of the properties of Fourier series). Higher-order Fourier coefficients—and thus higher-order sine and cosine curves—can only correspond to background noise or a necessary smoothing out between the approximations of the mathematical model and physical reality. Twelve and 120th harmonics cannot possibly, by themselves, correspond to any real physical effect.

For those astrologers who claim that astrology has not yet had a fair statistical test, I would point out that a number of believers and supporters of astrology have failed to find any statistical validity to traditional astrological aphorisms. Bradley's clergymen and Addey's ninety-year-olds were found to be remarkably randomly distributed over sun signs. Only by the most ingenious statistical manipulation of their data could they arrive at *any* significant findings.

More recently, the astrological economists Barth and Bennett tested the traditional astrological "influence" of Mars upon military careers. According to astrological theory, Mars "rules" Aries and Scorpio; hence, one should expect those seeking military careers to be born more often under these signs. Nobody can accuse Barth and Bennett of not dealing with a large enough sample. They analyzed a total of 154,500 entries into the U.S. Marine Corps during the years 1962 to 1970, comparing sun signs for reenlistments and initial long-timers with those who dropped out at the end of their first two-year stint.

Barth and Bennett found that Arians and Scorpios pursue military careers no more relentlessly than "peace-loving" Librans. In statistical terms, the deviations among military Arians, Scorpios, and Librans can be attributed to chance at the 5 percent confidence level.[9]

The god of war had been statistically stripped of his "power" over aggressive, warlike behavior.

An earlier statistical study headed by the renowned astronomer Bart J. Bok had stripped Mercury of his intellectual influence over the mind. Professor Bok's Harvard Committee on Astrology looked at the sun signs and Mercury aspects of 20,000 *American Men of Science* and found them randomly distributed quite according to chance. In their published report to the scientific community, Bok's committee also pointed to Farnsworth's study of the sun signs of over 2,000 musicians and painters in which he found the aesthetic influence of Libra conspicuously absent.[10]

Thus, contrary to the hopes and claims of astrologers, all statistical studies of traditional astrology—whether conducted by opponents *or* believers—have found absolutely no evidence of the alleged cosmic influences.

Even the leading researcher into the new astrobiology, Michel Gauquelin, was unable to find any significant distribution for the sun, moon, or ascendant in the horoscopes of 25,000 celebrities.[11] Yet, like Addey, Gauquelin was unable to accept the verdict of his own statistics and sought further for *some* significant correlation between the motions of the planets and human destiny.

To be strictly rigorous, these astrological statisticians have committed a basic statistical error in reexamining their data after their first astrological hypotheses were shown invalid. The rigorous statistician first formulates his hypothesis, then designs his experiment, and then collects his data in order to test his hypothesis. If he finds he cannot reject the *null* hypothesis (i.e. that the hypothesized effect does *not* exist and the data is distributed according to chance), the statistician must conclude that his test hypothesis is invalid and his experiment over.

To formulate a new hypothesis and retest using the same old data is *verboten*. To do so is to admit a very large possibility of bias. Once the data has been examined, the statistician cannot then select the most significant deviations to test. This is bias, pure and simple. Most, if not all, of the statisticians so far examined were themselves biased, either in favor of astrology or against it. And most retained their biases, not allowing themselves to be swayed by statistical results.

One early astrological statistician, however, *was* swayed by his results and became convinced that traditional astrology was false, nothing more than superstitious magic. This statistician then went on to become the unofficial founder of the new astrobiology; his name was Karl Ernst Krafft, the most famous of the Nazi astrologers, at one time reputed to be astrologer to Hitler himself. For much of Krafft's story, we are indebted to the brilliant "detective" work of Ellic Howe, whose minutely detailed and absorbing tale of Krafft's fatal attraction to both the occult and the Nazis has appeared under various titles.[12]

THE NEW ASTROBIOLOGY

Born in Switzerland, Krafft was brilliant, erratic, and driven by a demonic desire to "prove" astrology. Called by many a mathematical and statistical wizard, Krafft was also ambitious, egotistical, and hard to get along with. He seemingly would stop at nothing in his attempts to prove, first, traditional astrology and later, his own versions of astro- and cosmobiology.

While Krafft has been accused of deliberately stooping to statistical tricks to prove astrology, even his detractors recognized that he possessed a peculiar sense of ethics when it came to casting people's charts. He labored long days and nights over his clients' horoscopes, pouring over the endless aspects and transits. It was not unusual for Krafft's interpretations to run to fifty or sixty typewritten pages!

It is probably no exaggeration to say that Krafft was the most talented and gifted astrologer the world has ever known. His character assessments—almost always including handwriting analysis as well as astrology—very often startled clients with their accuracy and psychological insight. In his astrological predictions, unlike most astrologers, Krafft would not only specify time and place, but often his forecasts were alarmingly accurate. In Chapter 8, we mentioned his famous prediction of the 1939 assassination attempt on Hitler. Krafft also more or less correctly predicted a friend's sister's accident and generally upset his few other friends with forecasts of upcoming misfortunes.

How do we account for Krafft's startling talent as an astrologer? Chapter 14, "Astrological Dowsing," and the final Book 0 will provide a number of answers and suggestions. There have always been a few successful astrologers who seemed to be able to achieve well above chance results. Since there have no doubt been millions of astrologers throughout the history of the world, it's to be expected that a few should achieve high scores. Krafft, with his mathematical brilliance and psychological talents, was a natural.

It is Krafft's statistical genius that interests us most here. He provides the missing link between the simplicity of Choisnard's planetary "death aspects" and the mathematical sophistication of Gauquelin's planetary "influences" on one's choice of a successful career. It was Krafft, not Gauquelin, who first tried to duplicate Choisnard's statistical experiment. It was also Krafft who first investigated the "influence" of planets upon careers as well as upon heredity.

Krafft was certainly not modest about his mathematical abilities. He was convinced that he was destined for big things and devoted most of his time and energy to his astral researches, often getting into trouble with employers and his father because of his lackadaisical performance on the job. At every opportunity, Krafft imposed his astrological theories and analyses upon his fellow workers and friends. Krafft's reputation, for better or for worse, grew steadily.

Following the defeat and despair of World War I, astrology and the other occult sciences became enormously popular in Germany, so it was natural that Krafft should gravitate in that direction. He was well aware of Hitler's rising political fortunes and was anxious to hitch his astrological talents to Hitler's "star." Krafft had already amassed a tremendous amount of data from repeating Choisnard's experiment and performing several of his own. He realized that he had to deal with large samples, so he spent long hours in birth registrars' offices copying down birth data with which to test his theories. Krafft always operated on a grand scale.

Like most other astrological statisticians, Krafft was unwilling to accept the verdict of his own statistical experiments which convincingly proved that traditional astrology had no basis in statistical reality. He began searching for new celestial correlations in his masses of birth data, plotting up endless combinations of planetary aspects, mainly looking for celestial "influences" upon heredity and career choice.

For instance, Krafft studied the "effect" of the conjunction of the moon and Uranus for 115 famous musicians and showed that the musicians tended to be born more often when the conjunction occurred in certain signs. Figure 10-2 gives Krafft's plot of Uranus-moon conjunctions for the 115 musicians. Note that the births tend to be "bunched" in the signs of Capricorn, Aquarius and Pisces, although the small number of total births makes the "bunching" statistically insignificant.

However, contrary to published statements about Krafft's study of musicians,[13] Krafft was quite aware that the four signs of Virgo, Libra, Scorpio, and Sagittarius in Figure 10-2 are empty of the moon-Uranus conjunction for the simple astronomical reason that Uranus was never found in those signs during the years under study, 1820 to 1880.[14] While Krafft may have gone to great lengths to try to "prove" astrology and to establish a new astrobiology, he was not nearly so statistically and astronomically naive as elsewhere portrayed.

In another statistical study of 2,817 musicians, Krafft drew up a plot of their sun signs and noted that more were born under the sign of

Taurus (March 20 to April 20). But he fails to note that such seasonal variations are to be expected and that the deviation is not significantly large. While MacNeice points out that Krafft's study demonstrates a complete disagreement with traditional astrological theory (Taurus had never been associated with musical ability),[15] careful reading of Krafft's *Traité* reveals a surprising lack of similar comments. By the time he wrote the *Traité*, he had already become convinced that astrology was false, and in his introduction pokes fun at the superstitious magic in traditional astrology while proclaiming his intention to place the ancient study of celestial influences on a firm statistical footing.

Krafft was the first to institute studies into "planetary heredity" by casting charts for successive generations of the same family, a statistical technique used in modern versions of astrobiology. Like the modern researchers, Krafft felt that planetary positions and aspects could explain much of human behavior: career choice, personality, temperament, heredity, death, diseases, etc. In 1923, Krafft presented a Ph.D. dissertation entitled "Cosmic Influences on the Human Individual." While the professors at Geneva felt there was something "wrong" with Krafft's statistical evidence for planetary influences on career choice, they were unable to fault his statistical methodology. Krafft was thus encouraged to go on with his research, but he never received a degree.[16]

Following Krafft's failure to obtain a degree at Geneva, he became convinced that only in Germany could he find uncritical acceptance of his ideas. So he set up shop deep within the Black Forest. By the 1930s Krafft had graduated from cosmobiology to typocosmy, a truly esoteric philosophy based on the "general alphabet of the world of phenomena" and the "natural order of the planetary archetypes."[17]

Thus Krafft steered his statistical astrology into psychological waters, adding personality typology to his private form of astrology. Krafft made many efforts to get in touch with Jung, but he was snubbed each time. No doubt, his known liking for the Nazis made Krafft increasingly less acceptable to the scientific community, for by this time Krafft was actively working for the S.S.

Among all his other talents, Krafft was also an expert on Nostradamus. He wrote a number of pamphlets, papers, and eventually a book on the French seer's prophesies and their interpretation. The S.S. was interested in using Nostradamus for psychological warfare purposes. The theory ran that if they published interpretations of Nostradamus indicating that Germany was fated to win the war, the enemy would be demoralized and the German people would gain confidence. Chapter 12 will treat this World War II astral psychological warfare in further detail.

Krafft, however, did not appreciate the S.S.'s aims; he took Nostradamus seriously and put all his interpretative genius into his translations of quatrains. The S.S. then took Krafft's interpretations and twisted them to fit their own psychological warfare needs. Krafft complained of this misuse of his work, and his relations with the Nazis became strained. After Hess defected in 1941 and the Nazis rounded up all astrologers into their concentration camps, Krafft was thrown in jail and forced to work on Nostradamus and make astrological predictions for the S.S. Krafft became sullen, melancholy, and his health failed. He was never released by the Nazis and died in 1945 while being shunted between concentration camps.

But not before he had left behind a legacy of his work. In the late 1930s, when Krafft was at the height of his influence, both in astrology circles and with the S.S., he managed to put together a monumental book that ran to 351 pages and included all his statistical studies and astrological theories. This was *Traité d'Astro-biologie.* It was published in Paris in 1939; only 500 copies were printed. The book caused very little stir and lay in dusty oblivion in the publisher's bookstore on the Boulevard Saint-Germain.

Krafft's *Traité,* however, has not been unknown in astrological research circles. Krafft's statistical ideas have obviously contributed much to the current level of sophistication in astrobiological research. For instance, Ellic Howe details the continuity between Krafft and a leading astrobiological statistical researcher in a footnote to his exhaustive study of Krafft's life:

> After Krafft's death M. Michel Gauquelin, a French scientist with no astrological affiliations, attempted to repeat Krafft's work on the basis of indications and material published in the *Traité.* Apart from the fact that M. Gauquelin's findings were generally negative, he established that Krafft's statistical methods were at once primitive and misleading. Then, having "demolished" Krafft, he decided to repeat the experiment on more scientific lines. The results were surprising.[18]

Michel Gauquelin also tested traditional astrology and found it statistically invalid. He then became a critic of classical astrology and wrote a very critical book entitled, *Dreams and Illusions of Astrology,* now available in translation from Prometheus Press. On the basis of further, very complex statistical experiments, M. Gauquelin has cautiously proclaimed a new science of astrobiology[19] but stresses that his work provides no evidence whatsoever in favor of classical astrology and that his new astrobiology is not relevant to the question of whether or not astrology is valid.

There has been considerable controversy in recent years over the statistical evidence presented by M. Gauquelin's experiment.[20] A number of scientific experiments and investigations are currently being conducted into the various hypotheses presented by the modern astrobiologists, but it will no doubt be several years before the controversy is finally resolved to any degree of scientific satisfaction.

In the meantime, however, I would caution exponents of, and believers in, the new astrobiology to accept the final statistical verdict and not to go on looking for yet more planetary influences, or evidence that astrology might have *some* basis in fact. It cannot; astrology was born as magic. It can have no basis in science. There can be no scientific astrology, essentially by definition. The phrase is a contradiction in terms.

As we have seen repeatedly, the few real physical influences of the sun, moon, and planets are totally different from the magical influences of astrology. In the next chapter, we shall take a more complete look at the "Known Physical Influences by Celestial Bodies."

Again, I would caution the new statistical astrologers not to become too enamored of their "pet" theories. The real world is a very complex place, and very few theories turn out to correspond to reality. The true scientist cannot afford to become too attached to his theories. The odds are too good that they will become replaced by somebody else's theories.

Since the turn of the century, quite a few statistical researchers have attempted to establish a new astrobiology to replace the magical astrology they themselves have helped to disprove. In addition, many of the astrobiologists have tested and statistically disproved the theories of their predecessors. In time, I feel all their statistical claims for planetary influences upon human life will be understood by scientists and mathematicians as due to natural variations in human populations and planetary orbits.

COINCIDENCE VERSUS CAUSE AND EFFECT

Even if the astrobiologists' statistical correlations are borne out by future scientific investigation, the results would still be a far cry from demonstrating a cause-and-effect mechanism by which planets or stars can physically influence human heredity or career choice. Yet, astrobiological statistical claims are cited by astrologers around the world as providing proof that astrology does have a "scientific" basis. Here at last, astrologers claim, is "proof" that the heavens do have some effect on human behavior. How much these statistical "planetary influences" have contributed to the rise in popularity of astrology can only be guessed at, but there can be no doubt that such statistical research has given the ancient "art" of astrology a twentieth-century veneer of scientific respectability.

Astrology never had it so good.

Czechoslovakia recently had its own statistical researcher, Dr. Eugene Jonas. Dr. Jonas developed a method of "astrological birth control" based on the strange idea that women have a second fertility cycle independent of the menstrual cycle. According to Dr. Jonas, peak fertility occurs whenever the sun and moon realign at the same angle as the moment the woman was born. Dr. Jonas's research group, Astra, conducted tests with large numbers of couples and claimed a 98 percent success rate with their birth control "cosmograms."

However, Sheila Ostrander and Lynn Schroeder, authors of *Psychic Discoveries Behind the Iron Curtain,* have revealed the following almost unbelievable discrepancies in Jonas's research methods:

1. The astrological fertility cycle is used in conjunction with the usual "rhythm method."
2. The time of conception used by Jonas is an averaged value based on the *weight* of the infant.
3. The sex of the unborn child is determined by the masculinity or femininity of the astrological sign in which the moon is located (thus based on the old magic of astrology).
4. Test conditions were changed in the middle of Dr. Jonas's large-scale testing of women who answered his newspaper ads.
5. Dr. Jonas's astrological computations are riddled with errors.[21]

As in the case of the Russian scientist Dr. Tchijewsky, communist authorities did not appreciate Jonas's nonmaterialistic theories. Dr. Jonas was removed from his research position. His thousands of "cosmograms" and other research materials were confiscated, leaving the psychic world with rumors of his marvelous "birth control" methods.

Such rumors were enough. Interest in such statistical experiments into astrology is currently running at an all-time high. At least three other statistical studies, mainly dealing with sun signs, have recently been brought to my attention. Two are at the publication stage. How many more such astrological studies have been, or are being, conducted is anyone's guess. Certainly, they run into the dozens, probably into the hundreds.

To be blunt, it's all wasted time and effort: the physical problems are far too complex for such simplistic methods. Science just does not progress by means of broad, sweeping correlations between such complex systems as life on earth and the rest of the cosmos. The scientific method requires close, careful observation under as controlled conditions as possible. Variable factors in a scientific experiment are reduced to as low a level as practicable, preferably to a single set that can be controlled and varied by the experimenter. True, much valuable scientific insight has been gained through field observation alone, but it is only through the controlled experiment that the researcher can isolate variables and gain a true understanding of the inner mechanisms of the system under study.

None of the statistical studies of astrobiology has included controlled experiments. Most do not offer any experimental controls at all. Additional independent samples, varying sample sizes and ranges, varying sample periods and sampling points, control groups—all would help the statistical researcher understand the complexities of the problems he faces. A single unrepeated statistical study means nothing. The results must be confirmed again and again and again before the scientific community should accept any statistical evidence or claims for planetary influences—as it does for any hypothesis.

As astronomer Paul Couderc has said of modern astrobiological statistical evidence, "A chasm separates correlation from causality."[22] In order for a correlation to indicate cause and effect, the researcher must next demonstrate a mechanism, usually through controlled experimentation.

There is no quick and simple way of establishing new scientific "laws," much less a new science. One does not become a Mendel or Kepler without going through the painful process of testing and retesting one's theories until entirely convincing oneself, much less being ready to convince other scientists. And being convinced oneself is no guarantee against self-delusion. Hypotheses must be submitted to the fire of external criticism before they can become accepted theories.

Modern science continually finds reality far more complex and fascinating than previously expected. Theories are usually established only to be replaced or modified by new, more advanced theories. Science rarely returns to an old theory. Almost invariably, the old theory was based on insufficient evidence or a misunderstanding of the physical problem. For instance, of all the Greek astronomical and astrological theories, the only ones that modern science later vindicated were that the earth is round and that it revolves around the sun. Celestial spheres, planetary harmonies, and astrology have all been found invalid theories by modern science.

If modern science should find any celestial effects other than those discussed in the next chapter, the reader may rest assured that they will not resemble astrological theory in any way. Reality is just not as simple as tossing a die or waving a magic wand. The correlations shown by simple statistical tests merely tell us how complex the world really is.

While more difficult to conduct, true correlation studies would present much stronger evidence than the simple statistical tests that astrobiological researchers have used. Correlation experiments would remove much of the significance of coincidence, particularly in the case of overlapping unrelated cycles.

Coincidence is one of the most interesting of reality's complexities. As Jung's famous theory of synchronicity suggests, coincidences seem subjectively much more significant to the observer than normal chance would indicate. Perhaps in that sense, coincidences *do* have an effect—a psychological effect on the observer. But, as in the case of magic, the observer must see the coincidence and be aware of it, just as the victim of black magic must see or be told that the magician is sticking pins into his image.

Astrological coincidence, then, probably has an effect on the observer as well. No doubt, this is the source of the subjective "faith-through-experience" that astrologers talk about (see Book IV). Thus, statistical studies into traditional astrology come up with chance results, while the astrologer experiences the same chance results as subjective "proof" of his "art." While "faith" and "belief" are definitely part of reality, they are *not* part of statistical reality. Belief in astrology will not change the statistical results one whit.

If astrological "influences" exist at all, they exist only in the mind of the observer. Perhaps, if astrology ever becomes so popular that nearly everybody is following the "dictates of the stars," then, and only then, will researchers find any statistical evidence of celestial influences on human life!

NOTES

1. Michel Gauquelin, *The Cosmic Clocks* (New York: Avon Books, 1967), p. 140.
2. Darrell Huff, *Cycles in Your Life* (New York: Norton & Co., 1964), Ch. 10.
3. Henry Still, *Of Time, Tides, and Inner Clocks* (Harrisburg, Pa.: Stackpole Books, 1972), p. 134.
4. John Anthony West and Jan Gerhard Toonder, *The Case for Astrology* (New York: Coward-McCann, 1970), p. 149.
5. Michel Gauquelin, *The Scientific Basis of Astrology* (New York: Stein and Day, 1969), pp. 140-41.
6. Ibid.
7. West and Toonder, *The Case for Astrology*, p. 168.
8. Ibid., p. 167.
9. James R. Barth and James T. Bennett, "Astrology and Modern Science Revisited," *Leonardo* 7 (1974): 236-37.
10. Bart J. Bok and Margaret W. Mayall, "Scientists Look at Astrology," *Scientific Monthly* 52 (1941): 243.
11. Gauquelin, *The Scientific Basis of Astrology*, p. 143.
12. Ellic Howe, *Astrology: A Recent History Including the Untold Story of Its Role in World War II* (New York: Walker, 1968); *Astrology and Psychological Warfare During World War II* (London: Rider, 1972); and *Urania's Children*.
13. Gauquelin, *The Scientific Basis of Astrology*, pp. 142-43.
14. Karl Ernst Krafft, *Traité d'Astro-biologie* (Paris: Librairie Amedee Legrand, 1939), p. 41.
15. Louis MacNeice, *Astrology* (Garden City, N.Y.: Doubleday & Co., 1964), p. 24.
16. Ellic Howe, *Astrology and Psychological Warfare During World War II*, p. 78.
17. Ibid., p. 90.
18. Ibid., p. 78.
19. Michel Gauquelin, *The Scientific Basis of Astrology, The Cosmic Clocks,* and *Cosmic Influences on Human Behavior.*
20. *Leonardo,* 6 (1973): 128-30; 8 (1975): 228-31, 270; 9 (1976): 259; *The Humanist* (Sept./Oct., 1975): 15-16; (Jan./Feb., 1976): 29-36; (Mar./Apr., 1976): 52-53; *Nouvelles Brèves* du Comité Para, Numero 43, Sept. 1976, pp. 327-43.
21. These comments first appeared in my article, "Astrology: Magic or Science?" *The Humanist* (Sept./Oct. 1975): 16. See also Sheila Ostrander and Lynn Schroeder, *Astrological Birth Control* (Englewood Cliffs, N.J.: Prentice-Hall, 1972).
22. Paul Couderc, *L'Astrologie* (Paris: Presses Universitaires de France, 1974), p. 124.

11 Known Terrestrial Effects by Celestial Bodies

It was obvious to ancient man that the sun provided the earth with life-giving heat and light, yet the Babylonians relegated the sun to a lesser role in their astrology because they considered the moon-god more powerful. It was the Greeks who recognized the physical importance of the sun and made it foremost in their astrology. Still the sun's favorable astrological "influence" was based on magic, not on any real physical effects of the sun upon the earth.

It was almost as though the real solar effects were too obvious, too mundane, to be of any mystic value to the astrologers. Their system of astrology had to serve the immediate purpose of psychologically convincing the people that the priests—and only the priests—could read the stellar "signs of the gods."

There was no time for collecting data and performing statistical analyses. The astrologers stuck to their magic, ignored the real world as much as possible, and urged their clients to do likewise. Yet, two thousand years later, modern science has now found at least *some* evidence that the planets and stars produce real physical effects upon the earth, effects totally unexpected by both the scientists *and* the astrologers. Reality continues to grow in complexity and to confound man's attempts to limit it to simplistic theories.

While it's long been obvious that the sun is all-important, if only for its heat and light, almost all researchers have sought for the celestial/terrestrial interaction mechanism in the sun's other electromagnetic radiations, with planetary "influences" entering via magnetic disturbances upon the sun's emissions. Everybody missed the obvious: not only have the sun and planets affected life on earth, but so have the stars, for the simple reason that they are visible!

We have already seen in Chapter 9 that starlings and bees navigate via the sun's polarized light and that warblers and indigo buntings have been experimentally demonstrated to use the visible patterns of the stars for navigation in their long nighttime migration flights. Similarly, the South Pacific palolo worm times its breeding cycle to the last quarter of the spring moon, responding to failing moonlight or perhaps reacting to changes in the tides.

While science has found that the very visibility of the sun, moon, and stars has had an effect upon life on the earth, it seems doubtful that any animal but man has noticed and put to use the erratic wanderings of the planets, even though they are the brightest objects in the night sky. Planets change their patterns endlessly and it seems unlikely that there could be any adaptive advantage for any animal to time or base its activities on those motions. It was evolutionarily necessary for warblers to be able to migrate long distances at night while feeding and resting during the day. So they adapted by learning instinctively to navigate by means of visible stellar patterns, much in the same way man himself navigates.

VISIBILITY

Consider what the world would be like if the stars were *not* visible. If the earth's atmosphere was totally blanketed by a cloud layer like Venus's, thin enough to allow heat and light but thick enough to obscure any hint of the existence of the planets and stars, the sun would probably appear as a bright area in the clouds, while the moon's full light would only appear as a dim glow in the upper atmosphere. In essence, if the earth was covered by a cloud layer, there would be no way for living things on the surface to know of the universe outside. Daylight could be "easily" explained as an electrical discharge in the atmosphere high above the clouds; moonlight might then be interpreted as periodic residual discharges.

Starlings and bees could still manage to navigate by means of the polarization of sunlight, but warblers and buntings would have to learn some other way of navigating at night. Man himself would find navigation far more difficult without visible stars and would probably be loathe to sail far from the sight of land. Life without visible sun, moon, and stars would indeed be quite different. But the invisibility of the planets would most affect the astrologers. In fact, if the solar system consisted of only the earth, sun, and moon, it seems unlikely that the Babylonians would have ever invented astrology. It was the erratic motions of the planets that so intrigued the Babylonians; the motions of the sun, moon and stars are far too regular to be of any real interest in a system of magic. Without astrology, the Babylonian priests would have stuck to their entrails, the Greeks to their oracles, and the Romans to their own pagan theology. Without astrology, the Roman sun cult would never have been able to pave the way for monotheistic Christianity.[1]

Indeed, without astrology there can be no doubt that man's religious concepts would be totally different. The very concepts of afterlife, heaven, and gods above derive from ancient man's belief in "casterism," the ascent of man's "soul" to the stars after death. With a perpetual cloud cover and no visible sun, planets, or stars, pantheism—with its earthly spirits—would have no doubt dominated religious thinking. But a pantheistic god is far more immanent than an astral god, far closer and more accessible. Since death would still occur on a cloudy earth, the concept of an afterlife would probably still have arisen in response to the fear of death, but "heaven" would probably be situated on the earth itself, perhaps even within its center!

Life without visible stars and planets would be different enough; death would be even more different. Instead of the "soul" rising to the stars, it would probably sink to the center of a pantheistic earth. Where hell would be located is an interesting theological question, to say the least. In short, astrology itself is one of the most obvious "effects" of the visibility of the stars and planets. The residual effects upon religion and philosophy, not to mention politics, history, and medicine, can probably not be exaggerated. Science itself would have been greatly hindered were the planets and stars not visible; astronomy was one of the first of the physical sciences, and it was the astronomical discoveries concerning the solar system and the motions of the planets that led to the formulation of man's first physical laws.

Without visible sun, moon and planets, Newton would have been hard-pressed to come up with his theory of gravitation and laws of motion. Without the visible universe to provide a sense of scale, science would have progressed far slower. But imagine man's surprise upon building his first rocket and piercing the cloud layer—if he dared such a feat. The entire outside world would open up before him. The impact of such a momentous discovery would be staggering, perhaps even overwhelming. All of man's previous assumptions and concepts concerning the universe would have to be revamped; our hypothetical cloudy-earth inhabitants might not survive the impact of just simply discovering the existence of the sun and stars!

Can there be any doubt that their very visibility provides the stars' and planets' greatest real physical influence upon the earth?

The moon's gravitational fluctuations may cause the earth's tides, but it is the moon's visibly changing phases that helped prehistoric man keep track of the seasonal comings and goings of the plants and animals upon which he depended for food. And, certainly, any factor which aided the survival of early man has had an immense impact upon the earth today, far more impact than merely producing tides and timing the breeding cycles of obscure ocean worms.

The world in which we live is a very visual one, and it is there that researchers should first look for the physical influences of celestial objects. All other known physical effects pale into insignificance when compared to the effects of visibility (astrology, monotheism, astronomy, etc.). As in the case of the sun's heat and light, the visibility of the planets and stars was considered too mundane to be included in the magic of astrology.

ELECTROMAGNETIC INTERACTIONS

In their search for evidence of celestial "effects," modern astrologers have turned to the much more scientific-sounding theories concerning the interaction between earth's magnetic fields and sunspot emissions. On the whole, the sun is a remarkably stable nuclear furnace; its visible radiation does not vary by more than 1 percent, while eccentricities in the earth's orbit causes a yearly 7 percent variation in the amount of light that strikes the surface of the earth. In view of these facts, it's difficult to see how the sun—in and of itself—can have much overall effect on earth's weather conditions. Yet researchers have amassed mounds of statistical evidence suggesting that sunspots are somehow correlated with earth's weather cycles.

Again, we must raise the cause-and-effect versus correlation argument against any such sun-weather evidence. The earth may possess an eleven-year weather cycle, perhaps caused by minor wobbles and eccentricities in the earth's orbit and rotation. But this eleven-year pattern may be totally unrelated to the sunspot cycle. The earth's most important weather cycle is obviously that of the Ice Ages. Scientists generally accept four separate variations in the earth's motion as responsible for the Ice Ages:

1. precession of the axis of rotation (astrologers' precession of the equinoxes).
2. changes in the earth's angle of inclination to the plane of its orbit.
3. precession of the earth's orbit itself.
4. fluctuations in the eccentricity of the orbit (i.e. ellipse expands and flattens over a period of hundreds of thousands of years.[2]

With such strong cyclic variations in the earth's orbit itself, it seems superfluous to look for minor variations due to sunspots. In fifty thousand years, glaciers will return to the northern hemisphere as surely as the earth moves in its orbit. Any minor periodicities possibly induced by the sunspot cycle will then be totally swamped out. Even the majestic redwoods and their twenty-two-year growth rings will be dying out and migrating south before the press of ice.

But what are sunspots? How could they possibly affect the earth through an airless void of 93 million miles? Do sunspots have any *real* effects upon the earth, or is the evidence strictly limited to statistical correlations?

Sunspots are relatively cool areas on the sun's surface, the visual outer evidence of massive eddies within the sun's interior. These eddy currents bring "cooling" material from the sun's incredibly hot, dense center where the most basic fusion reactions take place. These "cool" materials are boiling hot gases that rise high above the sun's surface and then fall back toward the sun. The solar astronomer sees them as prominences. The larger, more powerful prominences throw off gases that escape the sun. They are called flares (see Figure 11-1). These escaping gases can reach the earth's orbit and beyond. As we shall see shortly, they provide the major source of interaction between sunspots and the earth's magnetic field.

The life span of a sunspot—or group of sunspots—varies from a few days to several months. Since the sun's rotation rate at its equator is twenty-five days, larger spots often appear, disappear for two weeks, and then reappear as the sun completes it rotation. The currents that produce the sunspots are composed of highly ionized material, atoms stripped of most of their outer electrons. These rapidly moving ions produce the magnetic fields associated with sunspots, each spot having either positive or negative magnetic polarity. Currents that have opposite polarity drift together, so that sunspots tend to be associated in pairs of opposite magnetic polarity, with the positive spot leading the negative counterpart in one hemisphere, while the reverse occurs in the sun's other hemisphere. At the end of the eleven-year sunspot cycle, this polarity switches signs, and the negative spots in the northern hemisphere will then lead the pairs for the next eleven years or so. Thus, solar astronomers speak of an overall twenty-two-year sunspot reversal cycle, in addition to the usual eleven-year cycle.

Both scientific researchers and astrological statisticians added the twenty-two-year cycle to their search for terrestrial correlations with sunspots. Of course, this expanded the range considerably. Now, twenty-three-year flood cycles and twenty-two-year growth ring groupings could be added to the growing body of evidence indicating that sunspots are responsible for variations in the earth's weather and climate.

But, before we can accept such statistical evidence for a correlation, we must establish a mechanism, a cause-and-effect mechanism, by which sunspots can physically influence weather conditions. And the physical evidence for such a mechanism essentially ends in the earth's upper atmosphere, mainly in the ionosphere 70 to 90 kilometers above the earth's surface.

The sunspot-ionosphere interaction mechanism runs as follows. When there is a flare eruption from an active sunspot, there are two basic types of emissions: electromagnetic radiations traveling at the speed of light (radio waves and ultraviolet light) and corpuscular radiation in the form of a blast of charged particles traveling at the much slower rate of 1,000 miles a second.

The radio waves and ultraviolet light strike the earth eight minutes after the flare eruption. The stream of charged particles begins arriving at the earth as early as 20.3 hours later and continues its bombardment for at least another day (particles with less energy are slower). The radio waves and ultraviolet radiation are caused mainly by collisions between charged particles as the flare erupts through the sun's atmosphere. These electromagnetic radiations cause a momentary radio outburst on the earth, but they are quickly swamped by the buildup of ions in the ionosphere, which lower the D-layer and increase long-wave radio refraction.[3]

A day after the flare eruption, the stream of fast-moving charged particles begins arriving at the earth's orbit. The surface of the earth has at least a triple layer of protection above it: the earth's magnetic field, the Van Allen radiation belts, and the layer of charged particles in the ionosphere. These serve to shield the surface of the earth from nearly all of the charged particle blast.

Figure 11-2 illustrates the two types of flare emissions and their physical effects upon the earth. The effects of the charged particle blast are limited to the upper atmosphere and the earth's magnetic field, which is in part produced by the Van Allen belts 3,000 to 10,000 miles above the earth.

When the stream of charged particles arrives near the earth, the interaction of its magnetic field with the earth's causes the stream to split into halves, positive on one side of the earth, negative on the other. On the far side of the earth, these two streams rejoin and form a ring of charged particles (this is called the Chapman-Ferarro theory). This ring of charged particles has its own magnetic field which adds to the earth's field. This activity causes magnetic storms to begin with a "sudden commencement," a buildup in magnetic components, and then a rapid drop and reversal.

Meanwhile, those charged particles that manage to make it through the earth's magnetic shields collide with the molecules and ions of the upper ionosphere, which causes ionospheric storms and the famous *aurorae borealis,* or northern lights. *Aurorae* are generally seen in the more northernly latitudes, though they have been seen as far south as Italy. There is also a southern version of the northern lights, *aurorae australis.* The ionospheric displays are concentrated near the Arctic and Antarctic because the earth's magnetic field guides the charged particles toward the poles.

This, then, is the sum total of the known physical effects upon the earth of sunspot flares and their emissions. First, there is a radio and ultraviolet radiation burst, followed by an ionization buildup in the upper atmosphere which causes long-wave radio reception to change. A day later, the corpuscular radiation stream arrives at the earth. This stream causes magnetic and ionospheric storms, and produces the beautiful *aurorae borealis.*

What about weather cycles and planetary "influences" upon radio reception? And what about all the other sunspot correlations, growth rings, and blood-count fluctuations?

Thus far, scientists have not found a mechanism that links effects in the high ionosphere with the movements of air masses in the much denser lower atmosphere, which are responsible for our weather. The tremendous amounts of heat absorbed and given off by oceans and continents exert a far stronger influence upon the movements of air masses than magnetic and ionospheric storms could possibly have. By their very nature these storms can exert only a limited influence on the earth. The ionosphere consists of a number of well-defined layers, and as a result these events are fairly well insulated from the lower atmosphere. Possibly, by affecting the jet stream, which lies between the upper and lower atmospheres, the ionosphere could conceivably impose a minor periodicity upon weather cycles, but it is difficult to see how sunspots and solar flares could cause any major changes in the weather.

Yet researchers still come up with statistical evidence that sunspots have had something to do with our weather. For instance, one solar astronomer, John Eddy, recently told an annual meeting of the American Geophysical Union that the lack of astronomical accounts of sunspots during the years 1645 to 1715—when Europe was plunged into one of the coldest spells in its history—indicated that minimum sunspot activity was correlated with cold weather on the earth. Eddy suggested that sunspots control the weather because they are related to increased output of the sun. I must hasten to add, however, that, unlike astrologers, Professor Eddy bases his interpretation on hard (though incomplete) evidence and states that it is one *possible* explanation. He doesn't use sunspots to predict the rise and fall of kings, when to invest in the stock market, or even when a farmer in the middle of Iowa should plant his corn crop!

In any event, the evidence for a sunspot-weather connection is not overwhelming.

Even less convincing is the evidence that the planets—Venus, Mars, Jupiter—interact with sunspot emissions via their own magnetic fields. The theory runs that the magnetic fields of the planets can either deflect or focus the stream of charged particles away, or toward, the earth. In other words, the theory runs, depending on the relative planetary positions and the resultant magnetic field, sunspot emissions will have a greater or lesser effect on the earth.

Thus, John Nelson, analyst for RCA Communications, claimed that he could use planetary aspects—square, opposition, conjunction—to calculate when active sunspot days would cause more radio interference than on days when the aspects were not present. Serious questions, however, have been raised concerning the validity and usefulness of Nelson's aspects. Again, questions must be asked of his statistical methodology and the value of any such correlation, if indeed one exists.

Certainly, any theories linking sunspot emissions, planetary motions and even minor radio events on earth are highly speculative. The lasting impact of clear transmission of "As the World Turns," or "All in the Family," or the Superbowl on the course of human events is hardly indisputable. By far, the major "effect" of the planets upon the earth remains the invention of astrology itself as a result of their erratic visible behavior.

Astrologers have to look no further than their own "art" for evidence of planetary "effects"!

There is one further theoretical mechanism for the interaction of the sun's electromagnetic radiation with events here on earth: the chemistry of water.

WATER, BLOOD, AND STATISTICS

Water, as we all know, freezes at somewhat below 32° F. However, as the temperature rises and ice begins to melt, liquid water molecules retain some of the structure of the solid ice, rather than becoming randomly distributed as expected of a "perfect" liquid. In crystallographic terms, some of the "long-range order" of the solid ice is retained as "short-range order" in the liquid phase.

Between the temperatures of 81° and 108° F (within the normal range of body temperatures), this short-range structure of water becomes unstable. A number of experiments have demonstrated that radiation, cosmic rays, and changes in the earth's electromagnetic field are capable of affecting water in this unstable condition. They can change both its physical and chemical properties.

This entire field of study into the anomalous properties of water began when Professor Piccardi examined the industrial operation known as "descaling boilers." Boilers, of course, get coated with mineral deposits that interfere with their efficiency. Traditionally, boilers have been "descaled" by using "activated" water (produced by swirling a vial containing mercury and neon through the water, causing static electricity and ionizing the water).[4]

However, the activated water did not always work, and Dr. Piccardi set out to learn why. He set up a series of simple experiments to compare the reaction rates of ordinary water and "activated" water. Using statistical techniques, Piccardi found that the reactions did not vary at random. He discovered, rather, that they varied in regular patterns in response to cosmic rays, sunspots, and magnetic disturbances. In addition, Piccardi found that the reaction rate of water varied annually, depending on the direction of motion of the earth through the galaxy!

Again, the same arguments against statistical correlation must be raised: there are too many variables here, too many unknown factors. First, it must be shown beyond all shadow of a doubt, by using carefully controlled experiments and man-made sources of radiation, that electromagnetic radiations control the reaction rate of water. Unless the reaction rate can be controlled by the experimenter, he is at a loss to demonstrate a physical mechanism.

This theoretical effect of the cosmos upon the reaction rate and physical structure of water is all-important to our discussion. Water is the liquid basis of life; plants, animals and humans alike contain large quantities of water, usually more than 50 percent of their total weight. If it could be shown that electromagnetic radiations from the sun directly affect the reaction rates and physical structure of the water within our cells, blood, and bodily fluids, such a finding would be of immense importance to the biological sciences. It would revamp our current concepts of life on earth and its relationship to the universe.

Thus, it's not surprising that certain properties and rates of reactions within the blood have been correlated with the sun's radiation and, in particular, with sunspot activity. The most frequently cited study is that of the Japanese doctor, Maki Takata. Takata had developed a chemical test for measuring the "index of flocculation" (i.e. how much blood curdles). But, in clinical use, doctors noticed that Takata's index varied much more than expected. Dr. Takata went back to the laboratory to find out why.

Interestingly enough, he found that the index of flocculation varied seasonally with sunspot activity. Far more surprisingly, however, Takata found that the amount of reagent required in his test increased greatly just before sunrise. Naturally, Dr. Takata leaped to the conclusion that there must be some radiation given off by the sun that affected his reaction. As the sun rose above the horizon, he reasoned, his patients, their blood, and his test tubes were immediately bombarded with solar radiation, which caused the morning rise in his flocculation index. This is equivalent to saying that our morning body temperatures rise because the sun's radiation warms our blood!

Of course, biological clocks were not a well-known phenomenon in the 1930s and 1940s, when Dr. Takata conducted his research. But it's now obvious that internal clocks and hormones are quite sufficient to explain daily variations in body chemistry. External forces and radiations other than visible sunlight are just simply not required. Dr. Takata did perform a few experiments using shielding, high altitude plane flights, and total solar eclipses to demonstrate his hypothesized physical effect, but his experiments were not controlled very well. Also, he tested only two or three subjects, a very small test sample.

Far more evidence is required before the evidence for electromagnetic "influence" upon blood can be accepted.

The evidence that living organisms can respond at all to electromagnetic fields is limited but interesting. For many years, magnetism was a favorite theory for explaining bird migrations. Now, magnetism is reserved as a last-resort theory, if at all, in a few cases of short-range flights (e.g. homing pigeons). However, there is some evidence that robins orient with respect to magnetic fields, and certain species of termites have long been known to orient themselves and their mounds with respect to the earth's magnetic field.[5] Electric fish and eels have been experimentally demonstrated to respond to and locate magnets by means of their electrical generating organs. These experiments suggest that electric fish locate their prey in muddy rivers and streams by means of this "electromagnetic sense," but as far as I know, there has been no scientific study of biorhythms in electric fish. Here would seem to be a fruitful field of study for the proponents of the exogenous hypothesis for biological clocks.

A large number of researchers have sought to demonstrate electromagnetic responses, first in the lower animals and, more recently, even in plants. Professor Brown found that slugs and flatworms tend to turn left more often in the afternoon and right in the morning, theoretically in response to daily variations in the earth's magnetic field.[6] He also found that his slugs and worms timed their directional preferences according to the phases of the moon, turning right at the full moon, left at the new.

Using magnets to "influence" the directional choices of flatworms was once a very popular pastime with experimental psychology students. Those with whom I was personally acquainted were bitterly disappointed by the almost abject randomness of their results. The flatworms stubbornly refused to follow the magnetic enticements, even of the strongest magnets. Quite a few watches got ruined, however!

In short, the statistical evidence for electromagnetic responses by living things—except those with electrical generating organs—is, if anything, less convincing than sunspot correlations. If the physically measurable forces of electricity and magnetism actually had a direct effect upon living things, we should be able to measure that effect fully as well as the electromagnetic fields themselves.

Minor statistical deviations just do not provide convincing evidence for a real physical mechanism. The cosmos—in the form of the physical universe—certainly exists, but science has found that earth protects its inhabitants from being overly bombarded and influenced by the outside universe.

Early astrologers had a much more limited view of the cosmos, a world encased within celestial spheres intimately connected to the earth. Early man thought the world was all "One" because it was the only world he knew. For him, there were no blazing suns forming countless galaxies, no expanding universe, no black holes. His world was a small, familiar place, and it seemed natural that he should be able to understand everything about it, almost intuitively.

Yet, modern science has proven over and over again that intuition is quite often far from the mark. It took the rationality of an Einstein to discover that energy and matter are dual aspects of the same interlinking equation, a finding quite contrary to intuition, yet all too real in the modern world.

For all its creative power, intuition can also be dangerously misleading. Intuition, in the form of analogical thinking, led to the concept of applying the magic of correspondences to the erratic motions of the planets, in turn leading to astrology.

Magical analogical thinking is appealing to the human mind because it appears intuitively correct. When Babylonian priests and Greek philosophers were developing and defending their astrology, they used pure intuition rather than collected data and tested hypotheses. And when individual people, from kings to peasant almanac readers, felt that their horoscopes were accurate and astrology valid, they were basing their decisions on intuition, on personal impressions based on inadequate data.

So, it is the client's intuition, his subjective experiences, that convinces him that the astrologer can "read" his character and foretell his future. As we shall see in the next section, this intuitive, subjective acceptance provided the astrological priests and shamans with a measure of psychological control over people. Whatever the astrologers said was uncritically accepted, almost as if their subjects were hypnotized.

In Chapter 12, "Astral Psychological Warfare," I will closely examine how such uncritical acceptance of fuzzy occult thinking paved the way in post–World War I Germany for Hitler's own brand of demagogery. Chapter 13 will take a brief look at the most recent innovation in astrological thinking: Dane Rudyhar's "humanistic astrology," which attempts to turn astrology into a psychological mental discipline.

Finally, in Chapter 14, "Astrological Dowsing," I will expand this idea of intuitive, analogical thinking to the subconscious level, where astrology can operate almost at will, influencing both client and astrologer alike. Unfortunately, very few recognize the true nature of this psychological influence and are thus being unconsciously—and hopefully randomly—manipulated.

Again, one cannot stress too strongly that the real physical "influences" of the stars lies mainly in the minds of believers in astrology. Statistical researchers are most likely searching in vain for additional physical evidence; their efforts might be better put to the task of exploring the psychology of astrology rather than correlating planetary motions and sunspots with the infinitely more complex events here on earth.

It requires far more than a simple parlor game to explain reality!

NOTES

1. Frederick H. Cramer, *Astrology in Roman Law and Politics* (Philadelphia: American Philosophical Society, 1954), p. 216 et seq.
2. George Gamow, *Biography of the Earth* (New York: Mentor Books, 1948), pp. 152-54, 183.
3. M.A. Ellison, *The Sun and its Influence* (New York: American Elsevier Pub. Co., 1968), pp. 91, 102.
4. Michel Gauquelin, *The Scientific Basis of Astrology* (New York: Stein & Day, 1969), p. 212.
5. Philip Street, *Animal Migration and Navigation* (New York: Charles Scribner's Sons, 1976), pp. 38-40, 138.
6. Michel Gauquelin, *The Cosmic Clocks* (New York: Avon Books, 1969), pp. 130-32.

Book IV: The Psychology of Magic and Astrology

Throughout this book, I have stressed the importance of magic as a psychological tool for manipulating large numbers of people. In Chapter 2, I suggested that magic played a valuable role in the rise of civilization and that it was the power wielded by the priests to entice, cajol, and terrorize the citizens to work for the good of the state.

Magic—with its implication of supernatural powers and forces—overpowers man's natural egotism and induces a fear of the unknown. As long as prehistoric man felt himself part of earth's natural ecology and the struggle to survive was personal and egocentric, he lived in small, related groups. Civilization, with its cooperative agriculture and city-states, required some cohesive power, some way of convincing individual members of the society to devote major time and effort to the common good.

Magic evolved in response to this need.

As I discussed in Chapter 1, the basic concept of magic arose along with language. To primitive man, there was "magic" in words, in the way they symbolically represented external objects and events and in the way they "magically" communicated inner thoughts and feelings. Words symbolized things and events; man learned that he could "think" with these symbolic thought forms, that words could be manipulated and juxtaposed to form new concepts and new symbolic objects.

In short, the development of language did not first lead to rational and logical thinking. It led to analogical thought processes, the very same sort of analogical thinking that forms the basis of magic. By the time language could be put down in recorded form, this analogical way of thinking had been codified as the magician's "principle of correspondences."

As above, so below; like attracts like; sympathetic natures align and mutually influence. . . . To the magician, there is power in words and symbols, much more than just the power to communicate. This is where magic parts company with reality: to modern man, words, thoughts and symbols are independent objects, totally unconnected to any external analogs. The magician would have us believe there is a magic link between a word and its analog, between magic omens and their corresponding external events (see Figure 6-2). Especially, he would have us believe that there is "magic" in names, written or spoken.

To the primitive mind steeped in magic, names are far more than just labels, a way of identifying people and things. To the magician, there exists a link between an object and its name, a sympathetic link which the magician can use to "influence" the object by performing ritual acts upon the name or other symbolic representation of the object. Thus the magician sticks pins in cloth dolls or clay images of his enemies, writes secret names for the devil in his own blood, circles to the left while chanting incantations, and performs endless other little rituals that are supposed to link his will magically between omen and analog.

Yet the only *real* effect of the magician's ritualistic acts is upon his own psyche—his own mind—and upon the minds of those who witness the performance. Magic operates not by any sympathetic linkages, but via the psychology of the human mind. All too little is known about the psychology of magic. That magic *does* have an effect upon the mind was not generally recognized by modern civilization until a few decades ago, when William Seabrook documented a number of real cases.[1]

Magic, in one form or another, was known to exist all over the globe, yet anthropologists and historians have, for the most part, ignored the role of magic in primitive societies and its potential importance to the rise of civilization. To the modern mind, magic appears to be a silly superstition; the magician's magic linkages and forces obviously have no objective existence in reality. So magic has generally been relegated to a minor role in history as an aberration in human thought and evolution. It just didn't seem possible that such an obviously incorrect theory and spurious body of knowledge could have any real influence upon the development of human societies.

But why, then, would an invalid concept such as magic arise simultaneously all over the globe? Why did the American Indians have their medicine men, the Babylonians their priests, and the Nordic nomads their shaman chiefs? If magic had no physical basis in reality, why did nearly every group of people on the face of the earth—from the tiniest tribes to the mightiest civilizations—develop similar magical theories and practices?

The answer, I think, is deceptively obvious. Magic arose because it had evolutionary and adaptive value for the societies that developed it. If increasingly larger numbers of people were to live and work together in cooperative harmony, there had to be some cohesive force welding the people together. Promising greater individual rewards as the result of cooperative work just isn't a sufficiently strong motivation for people to give up their freedom and egotistical desires.

Society, whether primitive or civilized, requires that individual wants be supressed or modified in the face of community needs. In terms of survival, adaptation, and evolution, it doesn't matter *what* kind of mechanism serves society's purpose of convincing the people to abandon their egotistic desires for the common good. All that counts is that the mechanism works!

In his provocative book, *Cows, Pigs, Wars and Witches: The Riddles of Culture,*[2] Marvin Harris presents a number of such societal mechanisms for drawing people together into a coherent group and maintaining the necessary hierarchal structure. Of particular interest is Harris's suggested evolutionary sequence for the mainstream of human societies: reciprocity (humble sharing) develops first, then evolves into competitive feasting (potlatch), which in turn leads to the establishment of a monarchy.

Harris's general thesis is an excellent one: he attempts to explain the riddles of human culture—the taboos, the strange rituals, the wars—as ecological and evolutionary adaptations aiding the survival of the societies. Unfortunately, while Harris does treat the question of witchcraft and the origin of some of its myths (pointing out with Thomas Szasz[3] that "scapegoat" persecution of witches during the Inquisition helped the Catholic Church combat the Reformation), he does not go into the evolutionary aspects of magic itself.

In short, the theory of evolution predicts that only those societal practices that have adaptive value—that they increase the chances of survival—will themselves survive.

Thus war has adaptive value because it limits population growth; in primitive societies, war prevents populations from exceeding the resources of their land. Then, too, it is possible that the loose hierarchic structure of primitive societies would become unstable and unmanageable with unrestrained population growth. (Interestingly enough, Harris claims that war limits populations in primitive societies *not* because of the number of men killed. Rather women limit the number of babies by birth control and even infanticide. This might explain why war fails to limit population growth in civilized societies).

Magic has probably been a part of human society for nearly as long as war; like war, magic must have had some evolutionary adaptive value.

My thesis simply is this: magic—both the theory and the practice—provided the group's leader with a means by which he could impress other members and win their admiration, fear, and support. The rituals, symbols, drugs, and other magical trappings increased the impressiveness of the magician's performance, lending far more credence to his supernatural claims. In essence, magic played an adaptive role analogous to Harris's competitive feasting in which the chief/big man throws a huge party just to impress his neighbors and get their cooperation in the joint productive effort.[4] Instead of throwing a feast, the magician/priest hold a ritualistic ceremony that impresses his subjects with his ability to drive off the beast eating the moon or to make weather forecasts from entrails pulled from sacrificial animals.

Small wonder, then, that the language and claims of magic are so grandiose and romantic; they are meant strictly to impress, to convince people that the magician/priest is in contact with supernatural beings and forces and that he is all-important to the group if they are to appease such beings and to bend magic forces to society's ends.

To be blunt, magic is another of society's con games. The priest used the myth of magic to populate the world with nonexistent forces and beings, instilling fear and devotion among his subjects. Since only the magician himself could communicate with these magical beings and make them do his will, the magician/priest necessarily became society's go-between. Once the myth of magic had become accepted by the people, the magician/priest became a necessary function in order to forewarn of impending disasters and wars and to gain the help of the gods in protecting the state.

Any society that did *not* have a magician/priest would logically appear to be at a considerable disadvantage. The myth of magic no doubt imparted much greater confidence to the societies developing and propagating it. As long as people believed that their priests had enlisted the gods on their side and that their predictions of victory were based on a "true" knowledge of future events, such belief undoubtedly added tremendous moral support.

In terms of evolution and survival, all that matters is that the societal mechanisms work. Rationality, logic, and "truth" need not be involved. There was no "logic" to Hitler's condemnation of the Jews, yet by offering a persecuted minority as scapegoats, he was able to draw the dispirited German people together and weld them into one of the most powerful and dangerous societies the earth has yet produced. As we shall see in Chapter 12, Hitler's Third Reich was not adverse to using the old myths of magic and astrology as tools of psychological warfare to encourage the German people and to demoralize the enemy.

The psychological mechanism of magic still operates today; it is still capable of affecting large numbers of people and influencing the course of historical events. "Modern" man still has a long way to go before he finds true freedom, before he is free from manipulation by society's mechanisms.

How, then, does the psychology of magic operate? How does the doll stuck through with pins "kill" its victim? How did the Babylonian astrologer/priests control the masses with their simple magic of sky omens? How did the Mayans' "cosmological handball game" help keep the priests in power and the people in line? And, finally, how could a simple horoscope have any psychological impact upon sophisticated, intelligent people today?

In a sense, to ask, What is the psychology of magic? is to beg the question. Magic first arose, in part, *due to* the vagaries of human psychology; evolutionary mechanisms must have *some* trigger, *some* basis in reality (e.g. warblers do not navigate by means of magnetic lines of force because their evolutionary ancestors were not able to *detect* magnetic forces).

The psychology of the human animal is just now beginning to be understood by modern science. Unique experimental techniques have disclosed that there are many psychological phenomena previously unsuspected and even now little understood. "Out-of-body" experiences, hypnotic suggestion, hysteria, and visual and aural hallucinations are just some of the common psychological phenomena that have helped keep magical myths in the mainstream of human society.

D. H. Rawcliffe, in his excellent book on the *Psychology of the Occult,*[5] offers the following basic physiological phenomena as sources of mystic myths: (1) hypnosis and suggestion; (2) dissociation; (3) hallucinations, imagery, and delusions; (4) unconscious sensory inputs; and (5) involuntary muscular reactions.

By experiencing, inducing, and/or drawing on these physiological oddities, the early shaman/priests were able to impress both themselves and their followers with this seeming connection with supernatural "forces."

Consider, for instance, what is commonly known as the "out-of-body" experience, what medical psychologists call autoscopic hallucination.[6] This phenomenon can be induced by many physiological conditions: pain, drugs, religious fervor, hunger, and a host of other human states that have regularly recurred billions of times over in the course of human history. If anything, the phenomenon is more common today as a result of medical anesthetics and drugs, so common that the *National Enquirer* regularly runs reports by readers of such "out-of-body" experiences (usually occurring on the operating table).

In the "out-of-body" experience, the subject feels as if his consciousness is "breaking loose" of its physical shell and rising upward, usually coming to rest near the ceiling, from where the person often "watches" his physical body below. When the subject's consciousness returns, he usually describes the experience as "very real" and goes on to describe what he "saw" while "out" of his body.

However, contrary to the claims of some parapsychologists, such spontaneous experiences are *not* evidence of psychic forces and extrasensory perception. Rather, they merely illustrate how complex the human mind is and how poorly we understand it. The mind, in maintaining an integrative personality, regularly creates a facade of illusions and delusions, regularly fooling us with *its* interpretation of events, both internal and external. The mind can create dreams that seem perfectly real at the time and later may even get confused with real events, so it's not surprising that the mind can create illusions of reality under more abnormal physiological conditions. Imagine the effect upon an apprentice shaman who, told by his tutor that he will travel out of his body by fasting and ingesting certain drugs, actually experiences the promised phenomenon first hand!

Small wonder that shamanism and shamanistic myths spread across the prehistoric globe. The out-of-body experience no doubt greatly contributed to a number of early myths, particularly the idea that humans possess a "soul" or "spirit" that departs the earth upon death and takes up residence on the moon, sun, or even among the multitude of stars.[7] This same idea of "casterism" later increased the acceptance of astrology during the Roman Empire and paved the way for the monotheistic sun cult that preceeded the establishment of the Holy Roman Empire.

Without the psychological existence of the out-of-body experience, both astrology and religion might well have taken different turns. Certainly, magic has heavily depended on such physiological and psychological phenomena for the source of its myths and mysticism.

While the *theory* of magic is based on the analogical thinking processes summarized as the principle of correspondences, its actual practical application relies heavily on the psychology of the human animal, mainly on the power of suggestion. Of course, hallucinations, delusions, fear, faith, and fraud have all played their parts. Without fear of and faith in the efficacy of the magician's pin-stuck doll, the victim cannot be affected by this psychological warfare.

William Seabrook has described how magic operates on the physical plane as "induced autosuggestion."[8] In short, the magician suggests that his doll image of the victim will soon kill; the victim himself, in his own mind, completes the act through self-suggestion. There are a number of documented cases of such victims of black magic dying within twenty-four hours or a few days of being informed of the magical attack.

Seabrook carefully documents and explains that, for the magic to work, "The intended victim must *know,* i.e., must literally have been informed of what is being done against him."[9]

Astrology, while rarely used for such black magical purposes, has also been known to psychologically kill in the same way (see the tale of Emperor Titus dying at his horoscope's appointed time in spite of good health, page 32). If astrology has had such a strong psychological effect upon a few people, is it not reasonable to expect that the ancient "art" has had at least *some* psychological effect upon its billions of only slightly less devoted adherents?

It is impossible for us to even guess at the psychological impact of astrology on its practitioners and believers over the ages. It would be very interesting to see a modern study of astrology's psychological impact among believers today, particularly within America's "counterculture," whose philosophical theories are mostly derived from the mysticism and magic of Eastern thought.

It's also difficult to ascertain the depths of people's beliefs in astrology in today's societies. The Indian peasant may regularly consult astrologers regarding questions of money and marriage, but such consultations may be performed due more to tradition than belief in the "dictates of the stars." In America, the vast majority of the Gallup poll's 32 million believers actually look upon astrology more as a parlor game, a fun topic of discussion, rather than as a serious theory upon which to base one's conduct. To these people, astrology does not hold the psychological dangers that it does for dedicated believers.

The deeper one's belief in magic theories, the more likely one is to be psychologically influenced. As we shall see in Chapter 12, there is also a group psychology to such magical practices. As the German people's interest and belief in astrology and occultism grew, so too grew the power and influence of Hitler's own brand of psychological mysticism. While astrologers today will strenuously object to the inclusion of astrology with the other occult "sciences," there can be no doubt that belief in astrology has greatly aided and spread the more esoteric forms of occult magic.

Thus, we cannot safely separate the psychology of astrology from the psychology of magic in general. As the Rosicrusians, Atherius, and other occult societies amply demonstrate, people today tend to take their occultism as a "whole" package, drawing not only on the Western traditions of astrology, alchemy, and witchcraft, but also on the Eastern concepts of "All-in-One," reincarnation, and transcendental self-attainment to Buddhahood.

Dane Rudhyar, in particular, has been quite successful in welding astrology to the up-and-coming popular Eastern ideas. Chapter 13, "Humanistic Astrology," will look closer at Rudhyar's new astrology, which combines the holism of Eastern wisdom with the psychology of Jung.

Eastern ideas are at once fascinating, sweeping, and based on "internal" observations as opposed to the Western tradition of external observations. Since these Eastern concepts arise from "inward-looking" mental exercises, they are in reality based on the physiology and psychology of the human mind. When the Yogi says he has "centered his consciousness," he is describing a particular mental and psychological state; when the Zen master claims to have achieved *satori,* he is describing yet another physiological state, what is known to the Western world as the "religious experience."

Eastern thought does have much to teach the Western mind, but these lessons are much more psychological than philosophical. As in the cases of astrology, magic, and competitive feasting, Eastern religion and occultism must be viewed in their cultural milieu and as an adaptive societal mechanism. Even at the time Eastern mysticism first arose, Eastern countries were mostly poor and overpopulated. Without some mechanism for directing people's attention inward, away from their poverty and suffering, there may well have been far more unrest and rebellion then did occur.

In a sense, *all* occult "sciences" have this goal and effect: to direct people's attention away from external reality toward spurious parlor games and "inner" tranquility. A busy, contented citizenry is an orderly, well-behaved citizenry. As Charles MacKay documents in his delightful classic work, *Extraordinary Popular Delusions and the Madness of Crowds,*[10] there is a "mob psychology" to myths and their effects. The myths may be as mundane as sudden economic wealth or as esoteric as Pythagoras's "harmony of the spheres."

Occultists have no monopoly on the spread of myths.

Unfortunately, the psychology of myths is virtually unexplored if not totally unrecognized territory. Westerners are too used to thinking of myths as fictitious tales of super-humans and super-beings. Our concept of myth needs to be broadened to include the spread of *any* false belief, occult, religious, or mundane.

For the nonce, we must be content with examining the psychology of the myth of astrology.

NOTES

1. William Seabrook, *Witchcraft: Its Power in the World Today* (New York: Lancer/Harcourt Brace, 1940).
2. Marvin Harris, *Cows, Pigs, Wars, and Witches: The Riddles of Culture* (New York: Random House, 1974).
3. Thomas S. Szasz, *The Manufacture of Madness* (New York: Harper & Row, 1970), pp. 7-8; 105-7.
4. Harris, *Cows, Pigs, Wars, and Witches,* p. 118.
5. Reprinted as *Illusions and Delusions of the Supernatural and the Occult* (New York: Dover, 1959).
6. Ibid, p. 115-23.

7. Franz Cumont, *Astrology and Religion Among the Greeks and Romans* (New York: Dover, 1960), p. 95.

8. Seabrook, (New York: Harcourt, Brace, 1940), pp. 7-10.

9. Ibid.

10. Charles MacKay, *Extraordinary Popular Delusions and the Madness of Crowds* (1841, 1852, and L.C. Page, 1932).

12 Astral Psychological Warfare

If Babylonian priests were employing their sky omens for the purposes of impressing, manipulating, and controlling their subjects, then it's no exaggeration to say that they were using astrology for psychological warfare. As long as the people believed that their astrologer-priests were really in communication with the celestial gods and were obtaining fore-knowledge of the future, the stars provided them with moral support. Also, a shared, common belief unifies and strengthens a nation, welding its people into a coherent whole that would be difficult to achieve by merely appealing to their "better natures." Concern for the state would soon be lost in a welter of egotistical desires if there weren't mechanisms for limiting the scope of individual wants and needs. It's very difficult to maintain control of slaves once they get a whiff of freedom; the "psychology of the mob" causes any hint of the release of repressed desires to spread like wildfire, often ending in confrontation and violence. Of such social phenomena are rebellions and revolutions built.

To what extent astrology as a psychological warfare tool has contributed to social revolution can be guessed from the overwhelming success of the Babylonians, Chaldeans, Assyrians, and Persians. Each inherited astrology, and as we've already seen, the Romans and their Provincial subjects were particularly adept at using astrology for causing social foment and instituting revolutions. To combat this astral psychological warfare by their enemies, Roman emperors continually issued edicts against the Chaldean "art," published their own horoscopes, and employed astrologers as countermeasures. During the Roman Empire, astrology truly came into its own in its rightful role as a mechanism of psychological warfare.

However, by the time astrology was revived during the Renaissance, it seems to have lost at least some of its psychological impact. People were still psychologically influenced—kings had their court astrologers and people built arks when astrologers predicted storms—but revolutions were not hatched or nations toppled due to the "dictates of the stars."

Perhaps the dawning rationality, the birth of the scientific method, prevented Renaissance believers from taking their astrology *too* seriously. The dawn of the Renaissance (thirteenth-century Italy) saw armies launched by the clang of an astrologer's bell at the most propitious astrological moment,[1] but by the fifteenth and sixteenth centuries, astrological doctrine and practice had been watered down and "corrupted" for popular consumption. Few intellectuals and fewer politicians would permit astrologers to dictate their actions. As I showed in Chapter 8, "The Astrological Debate," astrology was already under heavy attack by the fifteenth century, and heavily satirized by the seventeenth. At the height of the Renaissance, astrology could no longer attract such fervent and fanatic believers as the Roman sun cultists, or the Gnostics who wove astrology into their own version of Christianity.

While astrology was almost universally popular during the Renaissance, its magic psychological power over people seemed lessened—as if humans were truly emerging from the Dark Ages of mysticism. Astrology was already well on its way to becoming the amusing parlor game, the diversionary "mirror for the self," that it mostly is today.

Following its monumental decline during the eighteenth and nineteenth centuries, astrology nearly disappeared from the Western world. Only in Great Britain did the ancient "art" continue to have followers into the late 1800s, mainly due to the continued existence of popular almanacs. Yet this slender thread of continuity was enough to insure a significant role for astrology during and between both world wars, not to mention its tremendous rise in popularity today.

After 1890, British astrology was greatly stimulated by Madam Blavatsky and her Theosophical Society, forerunner of the neo-Rosicrucians and a major promoter and source of modern occultism. The Theosophists began the modern trend of combining all occult "sciences" into a single, coherent philosophy and body of belief. The Rosicrucians, America's counterculture, the various UFO societies, Dane Rudhyar's "humanistic astrology," even the Scientologists in their own bizarre way, epitomize this trend. Aleister Crowley, Gurdjieff and Karl Ernst Krafft each in their teachings promoted this all-encompassing brand of occultism.

The fuzzier and more romantic the thinking, the greater the success of the mystic!

In the 1890s Britain's Theosophical Society soon spread to France, where cabalism and the Rosicrucians flourished through the misery of both world wars. But it was in Germany that Theosophy and astrology gained their greatest following, particularly after the defeat and humiliation of World War I.

THE GERMAN ASTROLOGICAL CRAZE

As Wilhelm Wulff notes, periods of economic and political unrest often see large numbers of people turning to "hypnosis, mesmerism, clairvoyance, and every form of occultism . . . ."[2] Wulff, a German astrologer who was a witness to and a leader of the German astrological movement, goes on to point out that sections of American society were struck by a similar craze during and after the Civil War. In their despair, people turn to whatever promises help and relief from their misery and suffering. Astrology, like all occultism, offers almost instant relief, instant "cosmic" knowledge to lead people out of their mundane plight. The same magical promises that lured the Babylonian people into the hands and control of their priests still hold immense attraction for people today.

Hitler knew this and was willing to put his knowledge to work.

So, astrology became immensely popular in Germany during the 1920s and 1930s. Astrological literature during this period was enormous; dozens of periodicals appeared, thousands of articles were written, and a number of astrological organizations were formed. To the Germans, astrology and the other occult "sciences" were much more like abstract philosophical systems than practical ways of learning the future or influencing events on the "physical plane." The abstract, non-material quality of German thought has always been strong; in the nineteenth century, German philosophers such as Nietzsche, Schopenhauer, and Hegel had left the intellectual Western world spinning with the detached abstractness of their philosophies. In comparison, astrology and other occultisms must have appeared attractively simplistic while still retaining sweeping generalities of abstract thought. Even Aleister Crowley and Abu Ma'shar are easy reading compared to Hegel and Nietzsche.

It was this German love for abstract philosophical thought that—more than the popularity of astrology—attracted Karl Ernst Krafft to Germany where he felt his theories of cosmobiology and typocosmy would be more readily accepted. In part, Krafft was right; he did win tremendous renown and prestige for his astrological prowess and theories. By the late 1930s, Krafft was considered the foremost astrologer in Germany, no mean feat for an unpersonable foreigner.

But what Krafft did *not* foresee was that astrology would not fit in with the fuzzy-minded occultism espoused by the Nazis.

At first, it seemed that astrology and Hitler's brown shirts were destined for each other. Following the defeat of World War I, many obscure political groups discussed and plotted Germany's future. For instance, astrologer Baron Rudolph von Sebottendorff, editor of the periodicals *Astrologische Rundschau* and *Volkischer Beobachter,* was associated with the Munich political groups from which the Nazi party emerged in 1920.[3] The Baron's *Volkischer Beobachter* would later become the Nazi's official newspaper organ.

Another astrologer and psychic with whom the young Hitler was connected was Dr. Wilhelm Gutberlet, believer in the "sidereal pendulum" and an array of other occult absurdities. Hitler had many racial discussions with Gutberlet and often availed himself of Gutberlet's mystic power to "sense the presence of any Jews."[4]

Yet, when Hitler came to power ten years later, he frowned upon astrology and its practitioners. Any theory—however rational or bizarre—that did not distinguish between Aryans, Jews, and Negroes could not possibly be valid to Hitler's demented mind. Only those theories—and Hitler ascribed to some of the most bizarre—that fitted his scheme of Aryan supremacy and made "scapegoats" out of the Jews could possibly be acceptable to the Nazi party line.

So astrology was "out," except for its usefulness as a tool of psychological warfare. Perhaps the world is lucky that no ingenious astrologer convinced Hitler that astrological theory according to Ptolemy *did* attempt to account for racial differences. German astrology was already highly organized and popular, and the moral support that the ancient "art" would have given the Nazi movement might well have been enough to tip the scales of victory in World War II.

As it was, astrology had its role to play.

Not only did Hitler's Nazi party have its roots in obscure astrological/political organizations, but top German astrologers went out of their way to link themselves and their "art" with Hitler's political destiny. Chapter 8 told the tale of Frau Ebertin's "correct" prediction that Hitler's 1923 putsch would be a failure; we also saw that, sixteen years later, Krafft "correctly" predicted an assassination attempt on Hitler's life at the Munich beer hall celebration of the 1923 putsch.

This propensity for German astrologers to involve themselves in politics was soon to get them in trouble, both individually and collectively. Any "predictions" of Germany's future could only safely come out of Hitler's own propaganda machinery. The astrologers were seen as a threat, and Hitler was determined to keep them under his control.

While Hitler sat in jail penning *Mein Kampf,* the German astrological movement became the most organized and successful in history. There were several astrological societies, and a National Astrologers' Congress was held yearly from 1923 to 1936. The annual congresses actually accomplished very little other than set up Central Statistical and Astrological Offices for the collection and analysis of data to support astrology. Both the leaders and the membership were split on policies, and many of the meetings were taken up with internal squabbles.[5]

During this period, astrology was given an additional veneer of respectability by the Academic Society for Astrological Research, which boasted a membership of over 100 *Doctoren* who professed belief in astrology. While the Academic Society did even less than the Congress, it did add prestige and greatly influenced popular interest in astrology.[6]

It was also during this peak period before Hitler took power that the Germans openly began to discuss "psychological astrology." Lord Northcliffe had used astrology in his propaganda to influence British public opinion during World War I, and his efforts did not go unnoticed in Germany.[7] Wilhelm Wulff cited Northcliffe's work in selling the idea of using astrology for psychological warfare purposes to S.S. Officer Schellenberg.

Most of the German astrologers, of course, were merely interested in the psychological aspects of astrology in analyzing their clients. Psychology, as a science, had originated in nearby Austria and Switzerland. Both Freud and Jung's work fascinated the German passion for classification, and at the time psychology was, if anything, more popular in Germany than astrology. Psychology became grafted onto a number of bizarre occult systems: typology, handwriting analysis, and Krafft's typocosmy, to name a few.

Only the more daring astrologers—Wulff, Krafft, Ebertin, Haushofer—were willing to compete with the S.S. in the realm of psychological warfare.

When Hitler came to power in 1933, he rapidly began placing restrictions on astrologers and their organizations. All leading astrologers were taken into custody, questioned, and released with the warning that they restrict their predictions to individual clients and not attempt national or political forecasts. A few astrologers failed to convince the S.S. of their harmlessness, and several fell victim to S.S. interrogation techniques; the first such hapless astrological victim was named Heimsoth; he died early in June 1934.[8]

Krafft, as one of Germany's up-and-coming "scientific" astrologers, eventually fell under S.S. scrutiny and was detained and interrogated. Much of his manuscript material was confiscated, particularly his Nostradamus work. Krafft, of course, wanted nothing better than to demonstrate his prowess to the Nazi regime. Finally, after enduring innumerable insults and disappointments, Krafft was recommended as an expert on Nostradamus to Goebbel's Propaganda Ministry; the Nazis had already experimented with bogus versions of Nostradamus prophesies of German victory and wanted a real expert to turn out similar interpretations. Krafft agreed to the S.S. offer to work on Nostradamus and was placed on retainer. This was Krafft's most active period; he was feverishly trying to get his *Traité d'Astro-biologie* published, delivering series of lectures, and working long hours at night on horoscope interpretations.

In October of 1939, Krafft made his famous prediction in a letter to Dr. Fesel that an assassination attempt would be made on Hitler's life between November 7 and 10. On November 9, his prediction came "true" when a bomb exploded at the Burgerbrau beer hall celebration. Within a few days Krafft was again under S.S. detention.

For the next year and a half, Krafft was in and out of trouble and

S.S. jails almost continually, and his life and his health began the down-hill slide that eventually ended in tragedy. He found his work for the S.S. increasingly onerous, and his relationship with the dread Nazi Secret Police was becoming perilous. German astrological movements had been smashed by 1939; Krafft found himself alone in a field being rapidly abandoned by his more judicious fellow astrologers.

Small wonder, then, that the British High Command mistakenly thought Krafft was Hitler's personal astrologer! Actually, they had been so convinced by Louis de Wohl, a huge walrus of a man who sincerely felt he could help the Allied cause by using his astrological abilities to combat the advice and predictions supposedly given by Krafft to Hitler and his war machine. By knowing what the stars "foretold," the theory ran, de Wohl would know what Krafft's next move would be, and the British would be able to take appropriate countermeasures.

THE BRITISH COUNTERATTACK

Astrological psychological warfare was about to see its first major skirmish of World War II.

In actuality, of course, neither Hitler nor Goebbels believed in astrology. But they were quite willing to use it toward their own ends. In fact, Goebbels had his men watch for astrological predictions of assassination attempts against Hitler, and he encouraged predictions of German victory.

On the British side Ellic Howe was assigned to help Louis de Wohl on a related project: putting out counterpropaganda material based on Nostradamus. As Howe states, the British Political Warfare Executive had been putting out both "white" and "black" propaganda to be distributed in Germany, the "white" material obviously British propaganda dropped by planes, the "black" material forgeries made to look as if originating in Germany, and distributed via underground channels.[9]

With the help of Howe and others, de Wohl produced faked issues of *Zenit* (mistakenly named, *Der Zenit*) which played back Nostradamus quatrains to the Germans as part of the ongoing British program of "black" propaganda. What effect these "black" propaganda had on the German people is impossible to know. At least one of the fake *Der Zenit* issues was detected early by the S.S. and confiscated. It was this confiscated issue that later involved Wilhelm Wulff, author of *Zodiac and Swastika,* in the Nostradamus propaganda campaign after Krafft proved unwilling to cooperate.

Of course, the astrological warfare aspects of World War II pales in significance to modern weapons, gas chambers, and atomic bombs. Astrology did not make or break World War II, though it might have played a much bigger role. Hitler ignored its possibilities for the most part, and the British command gave very little support to de Wohl, whose efforts were mainly lost in a welter of red tape and confusion.

De Wohl had been sent to America to counter the astrological surge predicting eventual German victory. Popular astrology magazines in the U.S. were almost to a page—letters, articles and editorials—solidly behind the Germans. The situation was so one-sided that Ellic Howe goes so far as to suggest that the Nazis had infiltrated the astrological publications, though Wulff's version from the German side would seem to rule out such a possibility. British command felt it might speed America's entry into the war if de Wohl went on a speaking tour to counter the German propaganda by claiming that the stars "predicted" Allied victory. However, there was a mixup in the bureaucratic exchange between England and the U.S., and de Wohl's tour was limited to a few talks in Canada.

Perhaps it's just too much for the modern mind to accept that the ancient magic of astrology still has any psychological effect today. Yet, astrology obviously *did* highly influence a number of people during World War II. In 1941, Rudolph Hess defected to the British side in a Messerschmitt. An occultist and mystic himself, Hess had received astrological advice from Professor Haushofer that Hitler's "stars" indicated disaster after May 1941. Hess's flight to Scotland was an attempt to "save" Hitler from his fate. The official Nazi story at the time was that Hess had been weakened and confused by his associations with astrologers and occultists.

Following Hess's defection, the remaining astrologers at large were rounded up and detained in concentration camps. Krafft and Wulff were among them. Krafft's astrological delusions had led directly to his incarceration and later his death.

Astrologers were not the only ones so affected by the ancient "art." Near the war's end, a number of Hitler's henchmen (Himmler, Nebe, Schellenberg, and Kersten) turned in their desperation to their prisoner, Wilhelm Wulff, for his astrological counsel and advice. At least one of Wulff's war-end predictions led directly to the downfall and death of one of his Nazi clients. He had predicted violent death for Nebe, head of the Kriminalpolizei, causing the S.S. officer to become nervous and depressed. This psychological condition caused Nebe to lose his conspiratoral nerve and go underground after the assassination attempt on Hitler on July 20, 1944, naturally leading to Nebe's capture and death several months later.[10] According to Wulff, he and his astrological horoscopes played a major role in some of the war-end intrigues against Hitler.

German fortunes had taken a tail spin in 1943, and the Nazis thrashed about desperately for solutions to their problems. They began organizing "research" institutes looking into both natural and supernatural ways of aiding the German cause. Thus, when the British began sinking large numbers of U-boats by means of their new invention, radar, the Germans illogically thought that the British were sitting around in their War Games Room "dowsing" for submarines by swinging pendulums over maps. So, naturally, they set up their own "Pendulum Institute!"

Much to his dismay, the ubiquitous Wulff was summoned to participate in the map-dowsing for Allied convoys, but he took a dim view of such "occultism." Later, his astrological talents were put to use in the search for the captured Mussolini.

The German war machine had been ground to a halt and was rapidly becoming mired in political intrigues and occultism.

Mussolini was eventually found, but not through map-dowsing or Wulff's horoscopes. For a short time there was rejoicing among Hitler's General Staff, but it proved to be a short-lived victory: Mussolini was obviously confused and defeated. Hitler and his men soon fell back into the well of despair from which they never emerged.

Hitler's bizarre racial occultism had enflamed a nation, thrown the world into bitter war, and cost many millions of lives. The fuzzy thinking, the irrationality of Hitler's brand of occultism, should serve to warn us of the dangers of such beliefs.

Astrology may seem like a harmless diversion, but belief in astrology can lead to interest in other forms of occultism, and the resulting loss of rationality can only be considered dangerous in our modern, complex society. In America, the recent rise in occult popularity has given birth to a number of bizarre and dangerous occult groups: satanists, the Manson Family, and a host of other cultists ranging from minor-league con artists to dangerous revolutionaries.

It is time to face squarely the psychological dangers of occultism in general and of astrology in particular.

ASTROLOGER AND CLIENT

Even the most dedicated and serious astrological "counselor" may be dangerously misguiding his clients. While it's true, as I will show in Chapter 14, that many astrologers seem to give their clients "successful" character evaluations and predictions, such successes are due to the astrologer's unconscious assessments (as well as astrology's mathematical setup) and are not due to any planetary "influences."

It's like the blind leading the blind: the astrologer doesn't understand how he unconsciously arrives at his results, and the client doesn't understand that he is being psychologically evaluated and manipulated. Just as Wulff did not really understand why he predicted violent death for Nebe, so Nebe had no inkling that he was being psychologically manipulated. Such tales suggest that astrologers and their clients are actually engaged in battles of psychological warfare.

The client comes to the astrologer with a given set of problems, usually looking for a given set of answers. The astrologer, on the other hand, wants to "help" his client while "making a buck." The resulting compromise gives the client no assurance that he has been well served. The astrological advice may by chance be quite good (*any* random advice might be better than the client's own indecision), but on the other hand, the astrologer's advice may psychologically launch the client on the road to disaster.

One wonders how astrologers can take such responsibility upon themselves, how they can in all good conscience give such life-and-death advice to people for pay. Surely, any astrologer who advises on a lifetime career, marriage, and health is likely to influence people's lives for good or ill. Such psychological responsibility must weigh heavy, yet one searches astrologers' writings almost in vain for any evidence indicating that they feel the weight of their counseling burden. For instance, Wulff proudly documents the fact that his astrological advice led to Nebe's nervous breakdown and death. Krafft shows a similar coldness to the results of his predictions. When his scathing analysis causes a fellow employee to become dispirited and lose his job, Krafft merely notes that he was incompetent and undeserving anyway. When his prediction of a friend's sister's injury comes "true," Krafft gloats over his success and scarcely notices the resulting loss of friendship.

Of course, Wulff and Krafft were not ordinary astrological counselors; they were supremely dedicated to their "art," in Krafft's case, almost to the point of total delusion.

What of average, run-of-the-mill astrologers? Are they, too, engaged in psychological warfare with their clients? Can ordinary astrological advice psychologically influence people to such an extent that perhaps their lives, careers, and health are destroyed? The evidence is sparse. Astrologers are notoriously good at remembering their successes and conveniently inept at recalling their failures. Clients, on the other hand, rarely admit to seeking astrological advice. If the outcome is good, they naturally want the credit for themselves; if it is bad, they are hesitant to admit seeking and following such poor counsel.

Again, I strongly suggest that a modern psychological study of astrology and its effects on believers and followers would be of great interest. Without such information, I can only suggest a few areas where astrology might be causing psychological damage to the average client and believer today.

First of all, we must realize that the majority of clients are women seeking marriage and family counseling, and it is here that the astrologers no doubt have their major influence. Myra Kingsley, a career astrologist who has made a lifelong living from astrological counseling, provides us with an insight into the profession in her book, *Outrageous Fortune.*[11] Mrs. Kingsley is a conscientious counselor, quite aware of her potential impact upon clients and always insists on a personal consultation. The latter is very important: with only the birth information to go on, the astrologer is really operating in the dark, and any advice is liable to be far from the mark. At least a personal meeting permits discussion and gives the astrological counselor a chance to pick up conscious and unconscious clues (see Chapter 14, "Astrological Dowsing").

Most of Mrs. Kingsley's clients have been women, their problems usually related to love, marriage, and family. The few men who came to Mrs. Kingsley (J.P. Morgan was one of her steady customers) were mostly concerned with business and finances. Since most of her clients' problems and her advice dealt with major questions of marriage and career, there can be no doubt that Mrs. Kingsley has had considerable influence upon her clients' lives.

Mrs. Kingsley advises many women *not* to get married, that "this is not the man." She claims to be able to tell whether or not a woman has the "right man" and she certainly put her ideas into action! She also often uses astrology to help couples plan the birth of their children, claiming thereby to eliminate virtually all possibility of the baby turning out "spastic, Mongoloid, or otherwise tragically deficient."[12] Unfortunately, Mrs. Kingsley is woefully misinformed about genetics and breeding: she suggests that if people were bred as carefully as race horses, we could produce a "super-race," ignoring the fact that thoroughbred race horses are not necessarily better, stronger, or healthier—they just run faster! One hopes she doesn't apply her racial breeding theories to her astrological counseling.

In reading Mrs. Kingsley's book, one is also struck by her frequent fatalistic advice to clients. She often tells unhappy people that their suffering and misery is predetermined by the "stars" and that there is nothing they can do but accept their fate.[13] Interpretations on this may vary, depending on one's outlook on life, but it certainly seems that such fatalistic advice can only serve to further depress the person, closing off avenues of positive action and possibly convincing the client that he is not to blame, when in some cases, remedial change could alleviate his depression. While many of life's problems and suffering *are* due to uncontrollable external events, taking no action, no positive steps, can neither improve the situation nor one's approach to it. Quite the contrary: abjectly accepting one's unhappy lot in life without trying to improve it smacks of defeatism and self-humiliation.

Mrs. Kingsley may well have done tremendous psychological damage to her unhappy clients by telling them their emotional suffering is predetermined by the "stars." If so, she never hints of any such cases in her book, nor indicates that she felt any special burden when issuing her advice. Such confidence in one's ability to guide the lives of others must be the product of years of experience, or require the cold fanaticism of a Krafft. However, one cannot envy their burden of responsibility, nor feel nearly as confident of their abilities.

Mrs. Kingsley's unhappy customers suggest yet another type of client who could very easily be psychologically damaged by astrological advice: the client whom the astrologer doesn't happen to like.

It's impossible for the astrologer to warm to every client, every person coming to seek advice. There are bound to be those clients who are obnoxious, overbearing, disgusting in appearance, or incompatible on a personal level. As psychiatrists well know, it's very difficult if not impossible to give as much attention and care to a client who is personally unattractive.

What further psychological effects could accrue from astrological counseling today? What of the various sun signs, ascendants, and people "ruled" by malefic planets? What of Geminis, Scorpios, and Cancers? Do the magic characteristics of the signs and planets themselves impart psychological damage?

Consider the case of Geminis, people who happen to be born between May 21 and June 21. These people are constantly reminded that they are supposed to have "split personalities" and an agile, vacillating mind. Does it not seem likely that *some* Geminis, perhaps those who take astrology most seriously, are edged closer to the brink of schizophrenia through such constant reminders?

Then, too, consider the case of Scorpios. People born between October 23 and November 22 are told by astrologers that they are secretive and calculating, possessing all the fine, human attributes of a scorpion! Not only are Scorpios themselves told they are suspicious and reserved, but all the other sun signs are told to beware of Scorpios and their secretive, back-biting machinations. Scorpios who spend much time around astrologers and their followers must feel that somebody's out to get them! One might even suggest the term *induced paranoia*.

One popular British astrologer of the 1930s even included autosuggestion as part of his astrological methods. In his book, *Your Next Ten Years and After,* Edward Lyndoe provided a different slogan/suggestion for every day of the year for each sun sign. The daily astrological "suggestion" was to be repeated over and over throughout the day, so that it would provide the reader with the proper mental attitude to match the day's astrological "aspects."

Astrological autosuggestion, indeed! Unwittingly, Lyndoe was using virtually the same terminology used five years later by William Seabrook in describing the psychological effects of magic as "induced autosuggestion."[14]

We have nearly come full circle. We began by linking the origins of astrology and magic in prehistoric man's developing use of language, seasonal time-keeping, and the need for a societal mechanism to maintain hierarchic control. Astrology and magic arose together as part and parcel of ancient man's magical world view, and just as the two cannot be separated in theory, so they cannot be separated in practice.

Now we have shown that the psychology of astrology is very similar to the psychological mechanisms of magic in general (unconscious suggestion).

And magic seems to hold a special appeal for the human psyche.

Jung even talked of the archetype of the "miracle" or "magic effect."[15] He realized that when people witness some "unexplainable" event, the experience has a special "magic effect" upon the person, often a much more profound effect than any corresponding explainable event could possibly have. Stage magicians well recognize this facet of the human personality. While they are careful to explain that their "magic" is simply tricks, illusions, and sleight of hand, they are also careful not to reveal how they perform their best tricks. As long as the trick remains unexplained, the audience will be far more impressed and awed by their "magic." For this reason, the "secret" of a good magical stage trick can demand a very high price. The stage magician who fails to come up with new "unexplainable" tricks soon becomes "old hat"; his livelihood depends on his ability to induce a new "magic effect" among each audience.

Similarly, the astrologer induces the "magic effect" upon his client each time he looks at a mystical chart of the client's birth and produces out of the hat, as it were, a magical interpretation of the client's character, personality, and future. This astrological "magic effect" further prepares the client psychologically to accept unquestioningly the advice and "dictates of the stars." No doubt it also provides the basis for the astrologers' oft-cited subjective "faith-through-experience." Since, as I will show in Book 0, the client's horoscope will be 50 percent "accurate" by chance alone, it's quite easy for the astrologer to provide the client with sufficiently close character assessments to induce the "magic effect." To be blunt, the client is hoodwinked into believing that the astrologer's quite ordinary performance is "supernatural" and marvelous. Thus, modern astrologers are combining the talents of ancient magician-priests, employing the subterfuge of stage magicians, and using the psychology of magic to impress clients while taking their money. A fine "art," indeed!

Edward Lyndoe's astrologial autosuggestion combined Jung's "magic effect' with the power of suggestion. One modern astrologer has gone a step further and attempted to include Jung's psychology of archetypes into his astrological system. In Chapter 13, we shall take a look at how Dane Rudyhar has combined astrology, Jungian psychology, and the "wisdom of the East" in his "humanistic astrology." Here again, we will see the trend toward all-encompassing occultism and have a chance to examine the attendant fuzzy cliché thinking it engenders.

Occultism is definitely on the rise. One need look no farther than

World War II's Germany for evidence of the psychological dangers such a phenomenon presages, yet one looks almost in vain for signs of any attempts to stem the tide. While 192 leading scientists were speaking out in *The Humanist* against astrology, there was a bill before the California legislature to license astrologers!

Once again, magic and the state are about to be wed.

America will not be the first modern country to flirt with magic and occultism. Argentina's politics was dominated during 1974 and 1975 by Colonel Lopez Rega, a mystic and astrologer who believes deeply in witchcraft. Like many mystics, Rega has an exalted view of himself and his role; he tried to seize total power from Isabel Peron through infiltration and deceit and was only barely stopped in his machinations.

It's especially disturbing to once again find occultists gaining power and moving into politics. Believers in occultism are not noted for their rationality, nor for their humanity, despite all their protestations to the contrary. Somehow the higher spiritual plane always seems to require even more barbarous means than the physical plane.

And once occultists gain power and are able to propagate their theories, evaluations and predictions, the old psychology of magic will begin to operate. Once people are drawn into their mystic fold, it will be difficult for them to see out, to comprehend what is actually going on. Yet, as I will show in Book 0, it's very easy for an astrologer to appear to be accurate, to somehow seem to be in touch with the "stars" and the mystic universe.

NOTES

1. Louis MacNeice, *Astrology* (Garden City, N.Y.: Doubleday & Co., 1964), pp. 143-44.
2. Wilhelm Wulff, *Zodiac and Swastika: How Astrology Guided Hitler's Germany* (New York: Coward, McCann & Geoghegan, 1973), p. 29.
3. Ellic Howe, *Astrology and Psychological Warfare during World War II* (London: Rider & Co., 1972), pp. 23-25.
4. Ibid.
5. Ibid, pp. 34-36.
6. Ibid.
7. Wulff, *Zodiac and Swastika,* p. 94.
8. Howe, *Astrology and Psychological Warfare,* p. 50.
9. Ibid., p. 11.
10. Wulff, *Zodiac and Swastika,* pp. 86-87.
11. Myra Kingsley, *Outrageous Fortune* (New York: Duell, Sloan, and Pearce, 1951).
12. Ibid., p. 72.
13. Kingsley, Ibid., p. 46.
14. William Seabrook, *Witchcraft: Its Power in the World Today* (New York: Harcourt, Brace & Co., 1940), p. 7.
15. Ira Progoff, *Jung, Synchronicity, and Human Destiny* (New York: Julian Press, Inc., 1973), p. 105.

13 "Humanistic" Astrology

The entire field of the occult—magic, spiritualism, psychic phenomena—is rife with myth, delusion, and downright deception. As researchers such as Houdini, D. H. Rawcliffe, Martin Gardner, C. E. M. Hansel, Milbourne Christopher, and the Amazing Randi have repeatedly shown, one must be constantly on the watch for fraud and/or unconscious manipulation when investigating occult phenomena.

Conjury is an extremely well-developed art; any good stage magician can, with practice, duplicate virtually any of the entire range of "psychic" phenomena, from the spiritualistic tricks of the seance room to the mind-bending-metal feats of Uri Geller. Conjury has heavily contributed to the occult "arts," providing physical illusion where "psychic" forces failed to work in time to convince the breathless audience. Also, the rhetoric and ritual of occult ceremonies conveniently provided the magician/priest with precisely the visual subterfuge that good stage magic requires.

It's not so much that the hand is quicker than the eye. It's just that the hand being watched is not necessarily the hand doing the performing! Fortunately, such deception and stage trickery rarely play a role in astrology, at least in astrology today. The rhetoric of astrology is so well developed that such conscious deception is not required. Also the astro-

logical rhetoric is attached to a system designed (as we shall see in Book
0) to nearly always attain an accuracy of over 50 percent, a rate of success that must make the other occultists envious indeed. Thus, astrology
has usually been the first occult "science" to gain acceptance and adherents, paving the way for the less convincing varieties such as witchcraft,
alchemy, astral projection and other esoteric Eastern theories and
myths.

The "astral plane" appears far more real to people who believe in
the "influences"—whether magical or physical—of the stars.

Any number of physiological conditions can induce peculiar sensa-
tions, hallucinations, and delusions in the human mind. As I have
shown, the concept of astral projection and spirits dwelling among the
stars is a very old shamanistic myth, common to almost all peoples and
lands. It probably arose long before civilization, within the depths
of Paleolithic caves where anthropomorphic fears of death caused imaginations to soar. The peculiarities of human physiology particularly interested and fascinated the Eastern cultures. From the river valleys of
India to the mountain steppes of Tibet, special exercises and lengthy
physiological conditioning procedures were developed and used to induce, emphasize, and capitalize on these vagaries of the human mind.

So, when the Easterner says his wisdom comes from "within," he's
not kidding. The only bone of contention is his interpretation. The
Hindu and the Buddhist would have us believe that their internal revelations are proof of a cosmic unity, of a "spiritual plane" linking the entire
universe into "One." "One what?" is never quite made clear; they only
say that It[1] must be experienced firsthand by the Self and that the experience is indescribable. For an indescribable experience, however, It
certainly has evoked some of the world's most amazing rhetoric. Hindu
literature is replete with terrifying visions of multiheaded gods, auras,
astral webs, and white lights. While both the Buddhist and Zen litera-
tures emphasize spiritual enlightenment here on earth, visions of nirvana are still held up as enticements to followers. Spiritual enlightenment here on earth is all well and good, but nothing compared to eternal
bliss upon reaching the highest "astral plane."

Thus several Eastern disciplines were developed for attaining the
promised physiological states to achieve It and to put one in contact
with the "One." Yoga provided a series of physical and mental exercises
that, combined with fasting, would eventually lead to the desired states.
Zen Buddhism, on the other hand, offered an alternative method, an

emotional and psychological technique swamping the conscious mind and inducing a druglike sensation of joy and understanding. Yoga and Zen have provided enough fresh revelations and spiritual enlightenments to maintain and revitalize Eastern religion and mysticism for many millennia. By contrast, the corresponding Western traditions appear prosaic and mundane, lacking in spiritual discipline and mysticism. Small wonder, then, Eastern thought has been taking the Western world by storm.

The Theosophists and Rosicrucians started the invasion by looking to the Near East and drawing on Egyptian myths, Arabian magic, Semetic cabalism, and a full measure of Western astrology. Madam Blavatsky, Gurdjieff, and Aleister Crowley devoted their lives to making their neo–Near East philosophies popular, but they were still too close to Western tradition, and the novelty of their ideas soon wore off.

EAST MEETS WEST

Following World War II, a restless generation found itself caught between the existential realities of the horrors just experienced and the materialistic straitjackets provided by Western society. The search was on for some "meaning" to life, some new wind-blown straw to grasp. In America's cultural center—New York City—young intellectuals renounced the "straight" Western life and began a new approach, a new, open lifestyle that eschewed the rigidity of society around them. They would become known as the Beat Generation.

While this new Western phenomenon was brewing in New York, the seed of Far Eastern thought had already taken root in the West, brought over by the Oriental scholar D. T. Suzuki, the philosopher Alan Watts, and the young mystic poet Gary Snyder. When the restless energy of New York, led by Jack Kerouac and Alan Ginsberg, ran headlong into the cool fountainhead of Eastern thought, the result was an explosive mixture that has grown and mushroomed into staggering proportions during the twenty-five years between 1950 and 1975.

Today, Eastern philosophies and disciplines are commonplace in the West. Zen, Transcendental Meditation, Yoga, vegetarianism and even the Oriental martial arts have become immensely popular and gained wide followings. Gurus are making fortunes, and ashrams are sprouting. And along with the more legitimate disciplines have come the quacks and the charlatans: "psychic" surgeons and an endless stream of world-savers asking only for your money and your life. It was inevitable that some enterprising astrologer would hop on the Eastern bandwagon and combine the astrological macrocosm/microcosm with Eastern holism.

But before we examine this new "All-is-One" astrology, let us take a closer look at these Eastern disciplines and see if there's any validity, any real bits of wisdom for the Western mind.

The first influx of Eastern wisdom was through the peculiar mental and emotional discipline known as Zen. The despair and abject acceptance of Western existentialism matched very well the personal surrender and meaninglessness of Zen philosophy. Here was a body of thought the Beats could relate to in their restless search for "meaning."

Only in the complete acceptance of the meaninglessness of life does the Zen adept find "meaning." Yet, for most Westerners, such an esoteric discipline, almost a nondiscipline, could not long hold their interest, not long contain the Western drive and energy. Kerouac's Beat Zen ended in alcoholic death, Ginsberg's and Snyder's in poetic expression and ecological concern, and Alan Watts's in teaching and writing. For them, the ectasy of Zen meaninglessness—and only Watts hinted at attaining *satori*—was alone not sufficient to quiet their Western energies. Zen may provide a psychological tool for discovering the self amid the surreality of life, but it obviously did not satisfy the Western quest for answers to questions poorly formulated.

In Yoga, we find a different situation. Basically, there are two major systems of Yoga: Hatha Yoga, which is strictly physical, and Raja Yoga, which is a series of mental exercises. The two systems are not unrelated, but go hand-in-hand. Contrary to popular opinion, Hatha Yoga has nothing at all to do with the "spiritual plane" but is a rather sophisticated system of isometric exercises designed to teach the Yogi maximum control of his voluntary muscular system. Raja Yoga, on the other hand, is a series of mental exercises designed to teach the Yogi control of his *in*voluntary bodily functions.

As anyone who has performed a regular program of Hatha Yoga exercises can testify, it limbers and tones the body unlike any other program of exercises. Hatha Yoga involves every muscle, every tendon, from the abdominal region to the tip of the tongue and toes. First, the body is stretched one way, then the other; tensions are balanced by contractions. The end result is body tone and mental relaxation: nothing more, nothing less.

Raja Yoga is an entirely different matter. The Yogi attempts to do what the conscious human mind *cannot* ordinarily do: induce abnormal psychological and physiological states, teaching control of autonomic functions such as slowing down the heart, constricting blood vessels, and interfering with the digestive system. The physiological states induced by Raja Yoga range from maintaining hypnogogic ("eyes-closed") imagery for long periods of time (for example, the standard candle concentration technique) to falling into trance states with minimal brain wave activity.

At first, Western doctors and scientists refused to believe that Yogis could control their autonomic functions, yet carefully controlled experiments demonstrated that they could indeed control involuntary functions that ordinary humans could not. While no Yogi has yet been seen levitating as claimed in *The Yoga Aphorisms of Patanjali,*[2] Yogis have been recorded as virtually stopping their heartbeat and breathing, increasing their skin-galvanic response, and controlling their brain wave patterns to a remarkable extent. There is even a fairly well documented case of a Yogi "willing" himself to death (not unlike a voodoo victim).

To Western medicine, such feats verged on the supernatural until the medical world discovered biofeedback! Suddenly, *anybody* could teach himself how to increase his alpha brain waves, to interfere with his digestive system, and to constrict his blood vessels. All that's required is a mechanical system to inform the subject that he has succeeded in altering the desired bodily function.

For instance, a simple version of the doctor's electroencephalogram can tell him when his alpha brain waves are strongest. By "willing" the alpha buzzer to stay on, the subject learns to maintain the blissful physiological state known in biofeedback lingo as the "alpha state." Similarly, a blood-pressure gauge can be used to teach the patient to "will" his blood pressure lower.

Modern science had discovered that the interface between mind and body is far stronger than previously suspected. The mind could do more than will a finger lifted. It could also "will" the heartbeat slowed and induce strangely pleasant mental states. Eastern discipline had beat Western science to the reality of biofeedback by a couple of thousand years.

Yet, there is a vast gulf between the strong mind-body interface uncovered by biofeedback and the Eastern myth of "All-is-One." If anything, such a strong connection between mind and body makes it even *more* unlikely that there exists a "spiritual plane" separate from the physical plane."

Reality is rapidly coming down to earth. Unfortunately, not rapidly enough. While stage magicians and biofeedback scientists uncover the "secrets" of Eastern mystics, fakirs, and Yogis, the old Eastern myths of "All-is-One," opposing Yin/Yang forces, spiritual enlightenment, nirvana, and "astral planes" are being spread and assimilated into our indigenous Western myths and culture. The technology and media of the twentieth century are at last seeing to it that "East meets West."

ASTROLOGY AND OCCULT MYSTICISM

As the West's leading occult "science," astrology has naturally been near the forefront in assimilating and disseminating Eastern thought and ideas to the Westen public. But no modern astrologer has been more caught up in the Eastern "wave" than Dane Rudhyar, founder of "humanistic astrology," and certainly the most innovative and prolific writer in astrology today.

Born in Paris in 1895, Rudhyar immigrated to the United States in 1917 and, establishing himself as a mystic author, began writing on astrology fifteen years later. His more than a dozen books on astrology show a definite progression from traditional astrology to an "organic, holistic" astrology to "humanistic astrology," and finally to "galactic astrology."

Like all good mystics, Dane Rudhyar attempts to correlate no less than the entire universe to everybody and everything here on earth. His most recent "galactic" vision of the universe, man, and their astrological interrelationships[3] would have made even Krafft envious. Rudhyar's "cosmic psychology" combines the holism of the East with astrology and Jungian psychology in a way very reminiscent of Krafft's "cosmobiologie" and "typocosmie."

Krafft tried several times to get in touch with Jung (see Chapter 12) to discuss his astrological typology, but he was rebuked. However, Jung later studied Krafft's *Traité d' Astrobiologie* and cites it in his *Synchronicity: An Acausal Connecting Principle.*[4] Jung also conducted a few experiments of his own into the possible relationship between the psychology of personality and the symbology of astrology, introducing the idea that the planets and zodiacal signs might represent archetypes within man's unconcious.

Dane Rudhyar began combining astrology and psychology in the 1930s. Before even Jung and Krafft had published their influential works, Rudhyar first published his *The Astrology of Personality* in 1936, which was followed by *The Pulse of Life*[5] and supported by a steady stream of articles appearing in the popular astrological press. Even in his early works, Rudhyar's approach is a novel combination of common sense, astrology, and practical psychology that seems to focus more on helping people than in determining one's astrological destiny. No doubt, Rudhyar's emphasis on the person and his personality greatly appealed to clients and readers whose interest in astrology was principally egotistical in the first place.

Following a hiatus of fifteen years, Rudhyar began expanding his psychological astrology in the late 1960s with *The Lunation Cycle* (1967), *The Practice of Astrology* (1968), and *An Astrological Study of Psychological Complexes and Emotional Problems* (1969).[6] Perhaps sensing that Eastern mysticism had made sufficient gains in popularity, Rudhyar had already begun adding the myths and "holistic wisdom" of the East to his psychological, "person-centered" astrology. For instance, in *An Astrological Study of Psychological Complexes*, Rudhyar speaks of the astrological universe as an organism, invoking the Yin/Yang polarity between pairs of planets, between the sun and male sperm, between "Mother-principle" and "Father-principle." In invoking Eastern "holism," Rudhyar merely extends the astrological "influence" of each planet into all spheres of activity. In his search for an all-embracing "holism," Rudhyar descends in nearly all his later books to frequently citing the all-too-popular cliché, "Everything is everything," or variations on the theme.

In 1969, Dane Rudhyar established the International Committee for Humanistic Astrology and stepped up his already prodigious publishing rate. In rapid succession followed *The Astrological Houses: The Spectrum of Individual Experience, Astrological Timing, An Astrological Mandala,*[7] and a number of others. As the last title suggests, Rudhyar and his following of "humanistic" astrologers now view the horoscope as a mandala, a personal symbolic chart of the archetypical forces of the universe at the time of a person's birth. Mandalas are Eastern geometric forms upon which mystics and Yogis often meditate and concentrate their mental "energies" (see Figure 13-1 for an illustration of a mandala).

Without a doubt, Dane Rudhyar has done an impressive job of incorporating nearly every Eastern myth into his astrological system; only nirvana and satori seem to have escaped Rudhyar's all-encompassing vision. That is not to say that "spiritual enlightenment" does not play a role in humanistic astrology. In fact, Rudhyar's much younger followers see his system of astrology as a "mental discipline," a way of "centering one's energies" and discovering the Self through astrological symbology.[8]

How, exactly, astrology is to serve as a "mental discipline" remains a bit vague, to say the least. Certainly, the humanistic astrologers are not referring to the same sort of mental discipline as taught in Raja Yoga, Zen, or even Transcendental Meditation. One is almost reminded of Edward Lyndoe's "astrological autosuggestion." The horoscope is supposed to serve as a "holistic" symbol of the individual's potentiality, a chart of the universe's "cosmic imprint" upon the psyche and personality. By studying one's natal chart and its "progressions," the humanistic astrologer claims to be able to understand both the nature and timing of the "cosmic forces" that "interpenetrate" everything and everywhere. "Everything is everything"—every chart contains all planetary "principles"—all is "One."

Such is the beauty of rhetoric.

It's hard to believe that such mind-staggering vagueness could mean something to people in the twentieth century. Yet, the Eastern myths seem to mesh with and support Western beliefs sufficiently well that even the most logically absurd Eastern tautology can appeal to large and varied segments of the Western world. This is not to say that the "mental discipline" of humanistic astrology cannot yield at least *some* results or have some real effect—whether positive or negative. However, not for the "cosmic" reasons they cite. *Any* attention by the individual to his own condition, to his own situation, can provide the person with some enlightenment as to the sources of his problems.

Like the "psychic" or stage magician who "repairs" stopped watches by warming them in his hand and stroking them, any personal attention can start clogged mechanisms working again. No magic is required—just a little attention to detail and realization of personal realities.

As I will show in Chapter 14, astrology—whether "humanistic" or traditional—can serve as an unconscious foil, a "witching stick," triggering unconscious desires and knowledge. Just as the crystal ball or tea leaves serve to "crystallize" the medium's unconscious thoughts, the astrological horoscope can guide the astrologer and client into the depths of their unconscious, encouraging them to explore areas that would otherwise be left alone.

In short, humanistic astrology—as many other forms of occultism—is nothing more nor less than a psychological tool, an arbitrary way of discovering the "self." And herein lies the danger: amateurs wind up psychoanalyzing themselves and each other, blithely offering analyses and advice based on astrological interpretations that are psychologically naive and potentially dangerous. It's difficult enough for a professional psychiatrist or psychologist to analyze and advise the vagaries of the human mind. To expect to be able to do so by means of the simple-minded magic of astrology and the horoscope is to totally ignore the complexities of human personality, and to jeopardize its delicate inner balance. Such "cosmic insights" as Rudhyar and his followers claim have a long history of clouding the mind to reality and inducing permanent psychological impairment. Martin Gardner's *Fads and Fallacies in the Name of Science*[9] is replete with tragic tales of such deluded "cosmic researchers." It's dangerous enough to be taken in by existing occult myths and nonsense. But when the "researcher" begins inventing his own occult theories and systems, he's treading on thin ice indeed.

In the case of Rudhyar, one strongly fears that his "person-centered" astrology has cosmically stretched and expanded reality beyond all recognition. True, there is at least *some* physical evidence that the sun, moon, and stars, if not the planets, have some effect upon life here on earth (as we saw in Chapter 11), but when Rudhyar begins talking about "interpenetration" as a fourth dimension, describes the universe as a "mirror-image" of ourselves, and then announces plans to reformulate the old astrology in terms of the new "symbols" of physics (black holes and galactic centers),[10] one can only feel that he has overstepped the bounds of human potentiality and reality.

The earth is a very large place, with a hundred-mile thick protective atmosphere, within which biosphere millions of species, thousands of chemicals, and dozens of different kinds of forces interact to shape the physical and biological world as we know it. Rudhyar's "interpenetrating galactic forces" just cannot hope to compete with such a plethora of real interactions. And, when Rudhyar talks about "unperceived entities" (angels and nature spirits) coexisting among us to guide these "interpenetrating" cosmic energies, there can be no doubt that East *has* met West! Not only is everything everything else, but apparently no myth—whether Eastern or Western—is too silly or bizarre for Rudhyar's new galactic astrology.

The holism of the East, rather than providing us with any true wisdom, is sufficiently vague and all-encompassing to accommodate any idea, any theory. This type of holism no doubt was an exciting and romantic concept to the ancients, who were already steeped in a magical world view. As long as the earth was thought to be small, flat, and surrounded by transparent celestial spheres, the universe did appear homey and understandable, the sort of world likely to be interconnected via the magical "principle of correspondences." But such holism is totally meaningless in light of the discoveries of modern science. Far from being the center of the universe, the earth is a tiny speck of a globe circling a tiny pin-prick of light stuck off in one corner of a monstrous galaxy, one of thousands in the now-known universe.

Any attempt to apply the ancient Eastern concept of holism to the vast universe now known to exist is absurd in the extreme! If the vast distances to the planets caused seventeenth- and eighteenth-century astronomers to declare astrology's planetary "influences" impossible, how much more impossible must be Rudhyar's "interpenetrating" forces from the far-more distant stars and even galaxies!

For those who feel that the complexities and confusion of the twentieth century call for some holistic approach, I can only suggest that modern science *does* provide a number of quite valid holistic approaches. Ecology, systems analysis, field theory, information and hierarchic theories, cosmology, relativity—these are just some of the scientific disciplines that spring to mind.

With so many valid modern holistic approaches, I fail to see how returning to the holistic wisdom of the East can be anything but a step back into magic and mysticism.

NOTES

1. Capitalized, It here refers to the experience described by Alan Watts in *This Is It* (New York: Collier Books, 1967).

2. Lin Yutang, *The Wisdom of China and India* (New York: The Modern Library, 1942), pp. 129-30.

3. Dane Rudhyar, *The Sun Is Also a Star: The Galactic Dimension of Astrology* (New York: E. P. Dutton, 1975).

4. Bollinger Series, volume 20 (Princeton, N.J.: Princeton University Press, 1973).

5. *The Astrology of Personality* (New York: Lucis Press, 1936); *The Pulse of Life* (New York: David McKay, 1943).

6. All of these works were published in the Netherlands by Servire N.V.

7. *The Astrological Houses: The Spectrum of Individual Experience* (Garden City, N.Y.: Doubleday, 1972); *Astrological Timing* (New York: Harper & Row, 1972); and *An Astrological Mandala* (New York: Random House, 1973).

8. Michael R. Meyer, *A Handbook for the Humanistic Astrologer* (New York: Anchor Press, 1974), pp. 7-9.

9. Martin Gardner, *Fads and Fallacies in the Name of Science* (New York: Dover, 1957).

10. Dane Rudhyar, *The Sun is Also a Star,* Ch. 1.

14   Astrological Dowsing

Shamans, magician-priests, and mystics had been performing seemingly supernatural feats of character analysis and prediction for millennia before science finally got an inkling of what they were doing. Strangely enough, the "psychic" who finally gave away the "secret" was not even a person, but a horse!

UNCONSCIOUS TRIGGERING

During the early 1900s, Wilhelm Von Osten, a mathematician, became intrigued by animal acts in which dogs and horses seemed to be able to learn to add numbers and answer questions, so he decided to experiment on his own. He bought a horse and began training him to answer questions by tapping his hoof or moving his head. The horse—to be named Clever Hans—soon displayed an amazing ability to give yes and no answers and perform simple additions. One nod of the head was yes, and a shake of the head was no, and numerical answers were given by tapping out the appropriate number with his front leg.[1] In addition, Clever Hans was almost incredibly accurate. After only a couple of years' training, he showed nearly a fourth-grade intelligence.

His trainer was both mystified and delighted. He began giving public performances with his "thinking horse," and soon Clever Hans's reputation spread across Holland. Clever Hans's repertoire became increasingly complex. He could answer virtually any question, provided it was couched in yes or no terms. But it was his mathematics that truly astounded audiences. Here was a horse that could not only add and subtract but could also multiply and divide! And he nearly always got the right answer, even in the case of fractions, where he would first tap out the numerator, then the denominator.

At the height of Clever Hans's fame, a psychologist came to investigate the marvelous horse. Dr. Oskar Pfungst quite naturally suspected trickery on the part of the trainer; in this, both he and the trainer were to be surprised. At first, Dr. Pfungst watched the trainer and horse in action. Von Osten would write a question on a placard, then stand back and watch Hans tap out the correct answer. Dr. Pfungst couldn't see any way in which the trainer was signaling the horse; the psychologist instructed the trainer to remain perfectly motionless, and still the "thinking horse" managed to tap out, "Two times three equals six." The phenomenon was becoming quite perplexing.

In fact, it was to become even more perplexing before Dr. Pfungst finally stumbled upon the answer. The psychologist took over the handling of the horse himself and, much to his surprise, found that Clever Hans could answer questions when his trainer wasn't even around! Now here was a phenomenon indeed: a horse that could read German and perform arithmetic virtually by himself. All he needed was somebody to write down the questions and. . . And know the answer! Dr. Pfungst found that when Clever Hans could not see the person who wrote the question and knew the answer, he simply tapped away endlessly with his hoof, almost like a Friden calculator dividing by zero. Somehow, Clever Hans was getting the information from someone the horse knew, his trainer or someone else who knew the answer.

Herein lay the key: the horse had to be able to *see* someone who knew the answer, and since vision was involved, ESP was not. At least the "thinking horse" was not telepathic!

In order to learn Hans's secret, Dr. Pfungst devised a series of ingenious experiments. By hiding various parts of the trainer's body behind a canvas shield, Dr. Pfungst found that the horse focused attention on the trainer's head as he began tapping. When Hans reached the correct number of taps, somehow the trainer's seemingly immobile figure signaled the horse to stop tapping. But when the horse could not see the trainer's head, he went on tapping well past the correct answer.

Then Dr. Pfungst knew the answer: it had been known since Darwin that our mouth, eyes, and face are all subject to involuntary movement. We communicate our thoughts through tiny muscular flections and reactions to whatever we are thinking or experiencing at the moment. Hans's trainers could no more think of the answer yes and not give it away by flinching than they could talk without thinking. Whatever thought, whatever action, is contemplated by the mind, the muscles of the body automatically react appropriately. Almost fifty years later, this automatic response was traced back to the brain's E-wave (E for expectancy). Before the body can act, the mind must first prepare the necessary channels by producing the electrical discharge brain scientists call the E-wave.[2] With the E-wave coursing through the frontal lobe, the brain is prepared for synchronous activity such as reading, adding, or walking.

Dr. Pfungst knew nothing about brain waves, of course, but he was able to recognize and even measure the involuntary muscular reactions that resulted. Clever Hans had been doing simply what magicians and "mentalists" have known for eons: that people cannot avoid giving unconscious and involuntary clues to what they are thinking. When asked to multiply three times two, the "thinking horse" would watch his trainer and begin tapping. After he tapped "six," his trainer would involuntarily flinch, a slight movement of the head that only the horse could see. This signaled Hans to stop tapping.

The answer was that the horse did not think and the trainer did not consciously deceive. The physiology of the two species—the horse's acute vision and the human's involuntary reactions—fully accounted for the phenomenon. Unfortunately, Hans's trainer, Von Osten, refused to accept Dr. Pfungst's solution and went on exhibiting the "thinking horse." Van Osten was convinced to the end that his horse was actually thinking out the answers he tapped to questions written on his placards.

Such is the power of delusion, especially where psychic phenomena are concerned!

Unconscious triggering, involuntary muscular reactions—these are just some of the aspects of human physiology that have been exploited by "spiritualists" and "psychics" to convince audiences of their paranormal abilities or that "spirits" are conveying information from "the other side." Clever Hans would have made an incredibly convincing "spiritualist." Who would have suspected *he* was getting his information from involuntary clues rather than from his spirit "guide?" Yet, "spiritualist" and "psychic" audiences are lucky if they get even so clever a performance as Hans's. Most "psychics" resort to cheap tricks and paid accomplices in order to accomplish the same feats. Mind-reading acts based strictly on involuntary reactions are much more difficult to set up or control. But "muscle-reading," as it's known in the trade, often does play a part. Some performers have gotten quite skilled at picking up such involuntary clues.

However—and this is a crucial point often missed by researchers—such involuntary clues do not have to be seen consciously, but they can also be picked up *un*consciously. The person may not even be aware that there has been an information transfer. Needless to say, such unconscious triggering has greatly contributed to the myths of "mind-reading" or "thought-transfer." No doubt many of the "spontaneous" events cited by parapsychologists are manifestations of what we might call the "Clever Hans phenomenon." So, when the "spiritualist" gazes into her crystal ball and begins asking questions about loved ones on "the other side," we can be sure she is fishing for clues, involuntary reactions that let her know she is on the right path, that the "spirit" she has gotten "in contact with" is the right one.

While shamans and priests have claimed to commune with the "spirits" for millennia, the modern forms of spiritualism and talking to the dead began in the 1840s with the Fox sisters' mysterious raps (actually produced by cracking their toe-joints).[3] Since the Fox sisters, "spiritualist" mediums have shown an amazing ingenuity in devising ways of convincing their audiences that messages and manifestations from "the other side" are getting through. And their ingenuity has been surpassed only by their audiences' credulity! Spiritualist audiences are compelled to sit in the dark, while the medium sits safely hidden in a cabinet producing raps, knocks, strained voices, and gauze-bandage "ectoplasm." Such is the will-to-believe that audiences will accept almost anything, from strumming guitars to overturned tables, as "evidence" of survival after death. Even when mediums' tawdry tricks are exposed, believers often retort by saying she was "pressured" into resorting to trickery!

There are two basic types of mediums: the "physical mediums," who produce knocks, raps, and ectoplasm as physical evidence, and the "mental mediums," who rely on trance states, voices, and writings from "the other side." In a way, "mentalists" produce the most interesting phenomena because their "communications" are usually trancelike ramblings from the depths of their unconscious. Their "spirit voices" are much like split personalities developing within the medium's unconscious mind. Often, mediums who go into trances will not remember their performance upon waking. They are actually somnambulists—sleep walkers—who have learned to self-hypnotize their conscious minds, permitting aspects of the unconscious to come to the fore.

So, when the mental medium lets a "spirit" take over his voice and begins sounding strangely like somebody's long-dead uncle, he may be consciously producing the effect, or it may actually be some portion of his unconscious speaking. "Automatic writers"—mediums who write while "possessed by spirits"—are particularly well-developed somnambulists; many people are able to teach themselves to write while in a trance or semi-trance state.

However, as the reader may suspect, such self-hypnosis and induction of trance states that encourage the unconscious to "take over" is not exactly good for one's mental health. Psychiatrists feel that the more advanced mental mediums suffer from the mental disease known as "dissociation," which is a prelude to full-blown split- or multiple-personalities, such as the famous cases of Bridey Murphy or *The Three Faces of Eve* or Sybil and her sixteen distinct personalities.

As in all fields of the occult, there are dangers involved in communicating with "the other side," which may in fact be nothing more than the other side of the coin—the dark, repressed side of one's personality. The same may be true of the astrologer who is relying on his unconscious to pick up involuntary clues from his clients.

Most astrologers do not fall into trances, so their degree of dissociation is not very great. In this sense, astrologers are much more like water dowsers, who unconsciously pick up environmental clues to the presence of water. Water dowsers are best known for their use of a forked stick to indicate where water should be found. However, the water dowser's stick serves the same role in finding water that the Ouija board serves in producing "spirit" messages or that the astrologer's horoscope serves in providing predictions. The dowser's stick, the medium's Ouija board, and the astrologer's chart only serve as indicators for the unconscious, a means by which the unconscious can "talk" without giving away its presence to the conscious mind.

Dowsers are *not* psychically gifted with the ability to "sniff out" water. They usually have a good knowledge of the local topography and hydrology and know which areas are likely to produce water and which are not. They can tell from the color of vegetation, the slope of the land, and the types of rock outcroppings, where the underground water flows are located. When the dowser grasps his forked stick in both hands and begins walking, he is both consciously and unconsciously evaluating all the various signs and indications of water. Then, when the stick suddenly begins to quiver and twists toward the ground as if controlled by some "mysterious force," it is actually just the dowser's subconscious muscular response to unconsciously observed clues.[4] While the dowser is consciously seeking out the most likely looking areas, his unconscious is registering the more subtle variations in the environment. When his unconscious decides all the signs are right, it triggers the dowser's conscious mind by causing his arm muscles to "involuntarily" twist the witching stick earthward.

Map dowsing—mentioned in Chapter 12 on German psychological warfare—operates on the same principle. The dowser suspends a pendulum over a map of the area where the object—water, gold, enemy ships, Mussolini, or even UFOs—is expected to be found. When the pendulum begins to swing or circle above a particular spot on the map, the dowser marks the spot as the location of the object, unless for some reason he declares the "vibrations" wrong. The pendulum is sometimes also used much in the same manner as the Ouija board to spell out messages. The movements of the Ouija marker across the board are produced by the same involuntary muscular movements that guide the dowser's stick or pendulum.

As in the case of the much more dissociated "automatic writers," the messages spelled out by pendulums and Ouija boards come not from "the other side," but from the unconscious.

ASTROLOGICAL "READINGS" AND COUNSELING

The astrologer similarly uses the horoscope as a sort of Ouija-board foil to his unconscious. As I show in Book 0, the distribution of planets and houses in the chart is sufficiently random and general as to "fit" almost anybody. The system of astrology is so vague that it is easy to attain a score of 50 percent. All the astrologer has to do is fill in the details from what he consciously or unconsciously picks up from the client. It is this additional detail that makes the astrologer's interpretations and predictions seem so remarkably tailored to each client. The astrologer who fails to provide the "personal touch"—unless he's running a daily horoscope column—will soon find his clients losing interest.

In addition to the imprecision of astrological systems, astrological language is so general and vague that a horoscope reading often seems to fit nearly everybody. This permits the astrologer to concentrate— whether consciously or unconsciously—on the personal details that will astound the client and convince him that the "stars" can actually provide information and advice suited to his particular case. In *Outrageous Fortune,* Myra Kingsley unwittingly gives us an example of how she tailors her readings.[5] A mother had brought her young teenage son to discover what the "stars" had to say about his future career. While Mrs. Kingsley was drawing up his chart, she noticed him examining her collection of seashells with considerable interest, so she promptly focused on those aspects of his horoscope that indicated he should go into zoological research ("Pluto in conjunction with the sun"). The horoscope always provides ample opportunity for ingenious observation and intuitive guesswork.

While Mrs. Kingsley's advice in this case was colored by conscious observation, unconscious observation undoubtedly plays a large role in astrological counseling. However, to be able to identify the unconscious aspects of astrological readings would be very difficult if not impossible. Perhaps by evaluating a large number of readings and picking out those personal and important elements that do not exactly correspond to strict astrological tradition (which is unfortunately muddled), researchers could pick out specific unconscious urgings and advice. Yet, such unconscious triggering is far more common in everyday life than is generally recognized. When two people discover that they simultaneously are having similar thought patterns, we can be reasonably certain that some unconsciously perceived stimulus started them thinking along the same lines. Far from providing evidence of ESP or psychic phenomena, such spontaneous events merely indicate how much our unconscious minds actually participate in everyday, conscious living.

The astrologer can hardly avoid giving an unconscious slant to his interpretations. Even rank amateurs can often give startlingly accurate horoscope readings without realizing how they accomplish the feat. I have witnessed an amateur astrologer, casting only his third or fourth chart, attain an accuracy of 98 percent in a reading for someone he had only talked to on the phone a few times. Since some of his predictions contained specifics of health and marriage, he had to unconsciously pick up clues and indications through his conversations with the "client." Of course, luck and ingenious guessing were also involved, but it's highly unlikely he would have achieved nearly so high a score without the benefit of talking to his "client" beforehand.

This suggests another interesting test for unconscious triggering and slanting by astrologers: compare the scores attained when astrologers are permitted to interview their clients with similar "blind" interpretations based solely on the birth date, without client-astrologer contact. The difference in the scores should give an indication of how much information the astrologer picks up consciously and unconsciously by meeting and talking to the client. Perhaps by listening to recordings of the meetings, the researcher could identify the conscious clues given away by the client, thus separating the conscious from the unconscious elements.

Whether the astrologer picks up his clues consciously or unconsciously, his astrological "dowsing" can have a far more dangerous impact than his water-dowsing cousin. When the water dowser fails to find water, the client is merely out the money for dowsing and drilling. He still doesn't have a well, but at least he still has his land and his freedom. When the astrologer gives bad advice, the client may lose his career, his marriage, or his life.

The astrological "dowser" makes far greater claims than the water dowser. The latter merely claims to be able to find water or other objects, an unextravagant and reasonably harmless claim. The astrologer, on the other hand, claims to be able to psychoanalyze and counsel his clients in far less time and with far greater confidence than a professional psychiatrist. Astrologers dare—even delight in—giving career, love, and marriage advice that no professionally trained counselor would think of giving. Some astrologers even claim to be able to replace financial and political analysts, to outguess sports commentators, and even outpredict the psychics.

Since astrology claims no less than to be able to explain the workings of all life and events here on earth by magical planetary and stellar "influences," the astrologer feels justified in butting in and giving advice in whatever area of the client's life he wishes. We have already seen how Karl Ernst Krafft, Wilhelm Wulff, and Myra Kingsley felt no compunction whatsoever in advising clients in their love lives, careers, health, marriages, finances—even going so far as to influence political and life-and-death decisions. To be able to so blithely advise clients on such important matters must require an immense ego—verging on egomania—on the part of the astrologer.

While Myra Kingsley claims she is "acutely aware" of the effect she may have upon her clients' lives, one searches her book in vain for evidence of any display of conscience. For years, she advised one unhappy woman not to marry the "man of her dreams," that the signs were not yet right. I'm sure Mrs. Kingsley felt her advice was right, yet how could she be sure the woman might not be happier married, if only for a short time? The responsibility of giving such advice would weigh upon most people; Mrs. Kingsley apparently felt no such burden.

This, then, suggests that there is a certain type of personality that is attracted to astrological counseling. A psychological study of professional astrologers would be most interesting. Are they more egotistical, lacking in conscience and responsibility? Why would anybody *want* to give advice to others? Are they altruistically motivated to help, or are they satisfying some internal frustration, some dissatisfaction with the way they have "charted" their own lives?

Perhaps it's time for the astrologers themselves to be analyzed and advised. Modern science should be more interested in the psychological motivations of astrologers than in the alleged validity of their claims. Perhaps then we can understand why astrology is becoming so popular, why so many more people are now willing to give and receive advice based on the magical "dictates of the stars."

If anything, the claims of astrologers today are more extravagant than Roman and medieval astrologers who claimed to be able to find lost objects and answer questions, given only the time at which the question arose or the object lost. Modern astrologers claim to be able to tell the sex of an unborn child and to determine whether or not people are sexually compatible. Some, like Dr. Jonas, have even gone so far as to claim to be able to astrologically determine what days are "safe" to have sex!

But today it is in the realm of psychoanalysis that astrology makes its most extravagant claims. Popular astrology magazines are full of character analyses of politicians, film stars, and other public figures. Similar analyses are offered to the reader—for a price—by professional astrologers and astrological computing firms. Astrological advertisements claim to be able to improve one's outlook on life, to improve one's chances for a raise or career advancement, and even to improve the client's luck at gambling and horseracing! Such claims are much more than just extravagant. They are out-and-out lies, cruel deceptions designed to cheat a gullible public. How much physical and psychological damage such absurdly false astrological practices and advice cause cannot even be estimated. I can only point out that such claims for astrology are totally false and can be dangerous for the client who relies on such advice.

Before the legislators consider a bill licensing astrologers, they should take a good, hard look at what astrology is and how it affects believers and clients. Psychiatrists and psychologists are required to go through many years of training and testing before they are permitted to give psychological analyses and advice. Astrologers today are allowed to do the same with absolutely no psychological training, and the proposed California licensing would only test for competency in astrology and drawing up charts—simplistic knowledge which can be learned by nearly anybody. Licensing would do nothing to control the dangers of astrological counseling and would in fact lend an air of legitimacy to the ancient magical "art."

Astrological counseling has been with us for thousands of years, and the world seems to have survived its false and spurious advice up until now, but one cannot help but feel the world and its inhabitants would be far better off without it. The modern world is a very complex place, precariously balanced between ecological poisoning and atomic disaster. Good, solid rational thinking and advice are needed far more than the random, unconscious absurdities of astrology.

Astrology charted at least part of the courses of the Babylonian and Roman empires. If astrology is allowed to do so again today, we can be sure the consequences would be far greater. Today's instant communication and means of mass destruction could turn the magic of astrology into a nightmare. The example of Argentina's Colonel Rega should serve as warning: the type of person who turns to astrology and the occult is likely to be devoid of conscience and responsibility. When the "stars" say, "torture, bribe, and conspire," astrologers themselves are likely to be the first to follow their own advice.

Astrology has a psychological effect upon the astrologer as well as the client. As he becomes more and more adept at unconsciously picking up clues about clients, the astrologer becomes more and more a tool of his unconscious. Soon he begins to believe that his advice and interpretations actually come from the "stars." Then delusion sets in. As the astrologer becomes more and more involved in his "art," he begins to forget how simple the whole system is, how it's set up to insure at least reasonably accurate character analyses. In short, he forgets the statistical "secret" of astrology that he invariably learned when he first began drawing up charts and interpreting them. Book O will reveal this "secret" and try to remind astrologers why their "art" appears to give at least 50 percent accurate character analyses.

Perhaps, once this mathematical "secret" of astrology becomes recognized, clients and astrologers will stand less in awe of the ancient "art" that has done so much to deprive people of their freedom of choice, and which for millennia helped magician-priests control and manipulate their subjects. Astrology—for all its mystic appeal—actually serves quite mundane purposes. So the reader shouldn't be too disappointed to find the statistical "secret" of astrology also fairly mundane.

NOTES

1. I am indebted for details of Clever Hans's story to: Robert M. Goldenson, *Mysteries of the Mind: The Drama of Human Behavior* (Garden City, N.Y.: Doubleday & Co., 1973), pp. 262-79.

2. Niegel Calder, *The Mind of Man* (New York: Viking Press, 1970), pp. 188-90.

3. C. E. M. Hansel, *ESP, A Scientific Evaluation* (New York: Charles Scribner's Sons, 1966), p. 204, and Christopher Milbourne, *Mediums, Mystics and the Occult* (New York: Thomas Y. Crowell Co., 1975), pp. 2-3, 6-9.

4. D. H. Rawcliffe, *Illusions and Delusions of the Supernatural and the Occult* (New York: Dover, 1959), p. 345.

5. Myra Kingsley, *Outrageous Fortune* (New York: Duell, Sloan & Pearce, 1951), p. 97.

Book 0   The Statistical "Secret" of Astrology

In Chapter 14, we saw that there is a psychological "secret" to successful astrological character analysis and prediction: astrological "dowsers" pick up conscious and unconscious clues from their clients. These clues then turn up in the astrologer's interpretation of the client's chart as inexplicably accurate personal references and advice that convinces the client that the "stars"—seemingly so distant and impersonal—actually *do* have something to say to him personally. It is through astrological "dowsing" that followers of the ancient "art" have been fooled into thinking that the "stars" can somehow separate, and individually direct, the lives of each of the billions of people on earth.

A number of writers, most notably Louis MacNeice,[1] have already made this same suggestion: astrologers use the stars merely as props for their unconscious assessments of clients, much in the manner of crystal ball readers and palmists. Yet, to my knowledge, no writer has thus far suggested that the structural setup of astrology itself insures that almost any chart, any set of interpretations, will "fit" almost all clients to at least a 50 percent accuracy.

This, I would suggest, is the statistical "secret" of astrology. For millennia, astrologers have been telling both believers and skeptics that the odds against any particular chart and intepretation matching any random client are very high. This is out-and-out statistical deception; analysis of the horoscope and the way in which it's interpreted reveals that 50 percent accuracy is not an unreasonable success rate to expect of a cleverly written horoscope "reading."

While it's true that each and every person is a unique individual, different from all the other four billion people on the face of the earth, it is *not* true that each person differs from all others to the significant degree that astrologers would have us believe. The astrologer would like us to evaluate his performance as if the odds against a given chart matching a given random person were on the order of a hundred, or a thousand to one. But the true odds are much more like two to one. Statistical evaluations of astrologers' performances often give the astrologers inexplicably high scores, especially if they are tested on the entire horoscope rather than on just one particular aspect of the chart.

Why is this? How can a horoscope—with its dozen sun signs, houses, and ten separate planetary positions—possibly match almost any of four billion people? What strange "law" of statistics causes one of thousands of possible charts to "fit" any particular person out of billions?

The answer, of course, lies not in statistics, but rather in the physical layout of the horoscope chart itself.

As I demonstrated in Chapter 7, "Horoscopy," the horoscope consists of a number of separate elements: the twelve zodiac signs, the twelve houses attached to the earth, as many as ten planets including the sun and moon, the ascendant, decendant, midheaven, etc., not to mention angular planetary aspects, cusps, and a host of other even more esoteric features. Each of these separate elements provides a different, seemingly unrelated, attribute or characteristic to be assigned to the client.

Thus the sun sign is said to give the client's overall character and inner personality traits. Capricorns (those born under the "goat" sign) are told they are stubborn, tenacious, persevering, natural-born leaders with good minds and executive ability. However, if the sun happens to be located in the sign of Scorpio, the client is told he is suspicious, critical, and at best erratically creative. Now, the client may either "fit" his sun sign description to a varying degree of success, or he may *not* "fit" it to a varying degree of failure. Thus the client actually decides that he either "fits" his sun sign description, or he doesn't. This sort of decision is called a "binomial" decision because it results in one of two possible outcomes.

Since there are twelve different sun signs, it would seem that the probability of any one of the twelve matching a particular person should be 1/12th (8.3 percent). This is incorrect for two reasons. First several of the sun signs have overlapping attributes; for instance, Capricorn (the goat), Aries (the ram), and Taurus (the bull) all impart rather similar stubborn "influences" to those born under their sway. Second, each person has a number of sides to his nature, so that several different sun signs may equally well describe his character or behavior under differing conditions. For instance, a person may be stubborn one day, rather easy going and flexible the next, and heavily attracted to alcohol the third, so that his feelings and emotions may be alternately described as Tauran, Libran and Piscean (See Table 6-2).

In other words, it doesn't really matter what sun sign a person happens to be born under. The odds are still good that some aspect of his nature will correspond to the sign's magical "influences." I would suggest that at least half the signs will correspond fairly closely to most people or, to be more precise, to some aspect of their personality. In other words, 50 percent is a reasonable percentage to assign as the probability that a particular sun sign description will seem to fit a randomly chosen person. This is a far cry from the 8.3 percent probability that would apply if all the sun signs were totally distinct and if people were molded into a single, set personality type.

Fortunately, humans are far more interesting and complex than the simplistic classification of sun sign astrology. The world would be a very boring place indeed were people to remain so set in their behavior patterns and emotional responses. If Capricorns were only persevering and tenacious and Taurans singularly stubborn and plodding, both they and their associates would soon tire of their monotonous behavior.

Of course, the astute astrologer would immediately point out that there are many other elements of the chart that "take up the slack" and serve to describe other aspects of the personality than the limited sun sign attributes. For instance, the ascendant sign is said to describe one's outward personality, as opposed to the sun sign's inner qualities. The moon sign relates to the more fleeting nature of one's personality, as compared to the sun sign's control over character or individuality. Then, of course, there are the other eight planetary "influences" that are added onto the characteristics of the sun, moon, and ascendancy signs, not to mention all the earthy and mundane "influences" of the twelve houses. When the entire chart is constructed and interpreted, the astrologer has no less than nineteen or twenty separate horoscope elements to deal with, and often many more, depending on the number of planetary aspects (conjunctions, oppositions, squares, etc.), plus overlapping "influences" of planets found on the cusps or in particular decans, degrees, or transits.

A complete, "well-aspected" chart may provide the studious astrologer with as many as fifty to a hundred separate horoscopic elements from which to choose and juggle in matching his interpretation to the client at hand. Thus a really ambitious astrologer such as Krafft can find sufficient material in a client's horoscope to write pages upon pages of interpretation, cleverly slanting each elemental description to some particular aspect of the client's character and personality so that the sum total of the "reading" may seem to fit the person amazingly well.

This is to be expected. We have already seen that 50 percent is a reasonable figure to assign as the expected probability of any randomly chosen sun sign fitting any randomly chosen person. Similarly, since each of the other elements of the chart also describes some attribute of the client, 50 percent seems to be a reasonable probability figure for *all* elements of the horoscope.

Returning to my previous discussion of the "binomial decision," we can say that each element of the horoscope will either apply, or *not* apply to the client, depending on the astrologer's cleverness in wording the description, and whether or not the client has a wide-ranging character and personality. Furthermore, each "binomial decision" will have a probable success rate of about 50 percent (i.e. half of the elements of the chart are likely to give a reasonably accurate description of the client).

In short, astrology has the mathematical structure of a binomial multiple-choice test, in short, a true-false test!

Table O-1 illustrates this binomial game structure of modern astrology. Each astrological element (column 1: sun sign, Mars in the third house, etc.) provides, by means of the magical "principle of correspondences," a description of some attribute of the client's character and personality (column 2) which the client then scores as a success or failure, yes or no (column 3). The astrological game may have few or many elements, but its binomial multiple-choice nature remains.

As all students today well know, it's quite easy to obtain high scores on tests with multiple-choice questions, even when there are four or five answers from which to choose. All that's required is to apply the process of elimination and a little clever guesswork! And, if it's so easy to score high on multiple-choice tests with several possible answers, how much easier must it be for astrologers to "score" high on their *bi*nomial multiple-choice test?

Small wonder, then, astrologers often seem to give accurate character and personality assessments; even the rankest amateur should be expected to achieve a 50 percent score, just on the basis of chance alone. Throw in a little astrological "dowsing," and it's not hard at all to see how experienced astrologers achieve 80 percent, 90 percent, and even higher rates of success in horoscope readings of clients they have met or know.

Astrology has been set up over the ages to disguise its binomial parlor-game nature. Each separate element of the horoscope is cleverly said to relate to different aspects of people's personalities, so that the client looks at each feature of his chart as if it were independent, as if his overall character and inner personality type (sun sign) were unrelated to his outward personality (ascendant) or his outlook toward home life (fourth house).

This lack of independence among astrological elements in the horoscope is very crucial to the mathematical evaluation of the overall probability to be assigned to the horoscope interpretation. If the elements were independent, then we would simply multiply the individual probabilities for each element times each other. If we had mistakenly thought that the probability of success for each sun sign were 1/12 (instead of ½), and similarly 1/12 for the moon sign, etc., such multiplication of "independent" probabilities would yield $1/12 \cdot 1/12 \cdot 1/12 \ldots \cdot 1/12$, or some astronomically low probability on the order of 10^{-20} or so (.00000000000000000001). Not even the most hopeful astrologer would expect us to accept this figure as a reasonable assessment of the chances that his horoscope interpretation would match any randomly chosen client.

Of course, if we use the much more reasonable figure of 50 percent as the expected probability that any particular element of the chart will match the client, then the multiplication of "independent" probabilities would give $½ \cdot ½ \cdot ½ \ldots \cdot ½ = 2^{-20}$ (.000000954). This number is much larger number than 10^{-20}, but it's still far too small to give any realistic value to the expected probability that any random chart will match any random client.

Statisticians and mathematicians will immediately recognize the error in our above calculations: it is mathematically incorrect to multiply nonindependent probabilities. Only events that are totally independent and unrelated, such as separate tosses of a die or ESP guesses toward a randomly shuffled pack of cards, can have their probabilities multiplied together to give an overall assessment of the expected probability for the entire experiment.

In the case of our astrological binomial multiple-choice parlor game, the various elemental descriptions are *not* independent. They are applied to a single person, the client. And what could be *more* dependent, more related, than the various attributes of one person's personality? If the client is stubborn one day and easy going the next, this will greatly improve the astrologer's chances for success and consequently lower the expected odds against chance.

How, then, *do* we evaluate the expected probability of success for a horoscope interpretation? Unfortunately, there's no mathematical way to calculate a priori the overall probability for an experiment with dependent events or elements. Only careful, repeated experimentation could provide us with a physically real assessment of the astrologer's expected chances to match his interpretation to the client. There are just too many variables: how well-rounded the client is, how clever and experienced the astrologer, how success or failure is evaluated, and so on. Then, too, we have no way of evaluating the psychological factors, the astrological "dowsing" we discussed in Chapter 14, all of which will combine to greatly increase the astrologer's expected score.

However, as suggested throughout the book, and as indicated by the success rate shown in Table O-1, 50 percent seems a reasonable figure. Just as 50 percent is the likely probability that any one particular element of the horoscope will provide a "successful" interpretation, so it's equally likely that any other element of the chart will also successfully relate to other aspects of the client's personality. And if 50 percent of the astrological elements of the horoscope give successful interpretations, then the overall expected score should also be 50 percent. In other words, half of the horoscope, and thus half of the astrologer's interpretations, should apply to any client who happens to come along.

The "secret" is that not all the same elements of the chart will match different clients. The sun sign description may match this one, the ascendant that one, and the moon sign yet a third client. But the overall score will be about the same—50 percent.

This, then, is the statistical "secret" of astrology.

Thus have astrologers over the ages managed to fool clients that their "art" provides valuable information for the client and his future. The astrologers' motives may have varied from simple greed to grand political schemes, but the mathematical and psychological methods of astrology have remained essentially the same. However cleverly astrology may be set up, it relies mainly on deception, conscious and unconscious psychological factors, and the client's ignorance of the "art."

Astrology is a false "art" not only because it is a system of magic and its alleged "influences" totally nonexistent, but because it is cleverly set up to deceive and confuse. Astrology's true nature has long eluded believers and opponents alike. Yet, for all its deception and falseness,

Table O.1 Astrology's Binomial Multiple-Choice Game Structure

Astrological Attribute	Description and Interpretation	Score
Sun Sign.................	Overall character and personality type	yes
Ascendant	Outward Personality and physical body..........	no
Moon Sign	Personality changes and favorable transits	yes
Mars in Gemini	Intellectual energy and restlessness...........	yes
Jupiter square Neptune	Troubles in the occult................	no
. . .	. . .	. . .
	Overall score: approx. 50% yes	

astrology has had immense impact upon man, upon his societies, institutions, and even upon his thinking. Some writers and critics have even suggested that astrology was essential for the development of man's logical and scientific rationality, and, certainly it did play a part. It is impossible, of course, to judge the sum total of astrology's merits. We cannot balance its possible benefits to man against its many obvious deceptions, false forecasts, and disastrous results. Astrology has been with us for thousands of years, for better or for worse, and will no doubt remain with us for a while longer.

Yet, ultimately, one cannot help but feel that advancing scientific knowledge and modern man's dawning rationality will lead to astrology's final and total demise. The benefits of dealing with reality rather than fantasy should eventually cause man to abandon all such false and deceptive occult systems by which ancient leaders and priests controlled their people.

One day, astrology will be looked upon only as an historical curiosity, and as a societal mechanism of adaptive and selective value. No doubt, the astrological debate will continue for some time, perhaps even for more millennia, but as man learns more and more about the realities of the universe in which he finds himself, the vast gulf between the simplicities of astrological magic and the complex fascinations of reality will become more and more apparent.

The very fact that astrology still exists today and is believed in by millions of people indicates that modern man is not nearly so civilized and rational as he thinks. Civilization began only a few thousand years ago, an almost infinitesimal period of time in the life span of the earth. Present scientific knowledge predicts that man has another fifty thousand years before the next Ice Age destroys and obliterates most of today's civilized areas.

Fifty thousand years is a long time. If man can manage to avoid self-destruction through pollution and/or nuclear disaster, civilization may yet advance sufficiently to deserve its name.

In the long-term view, then, our present occult upsurge is but a minor irrational ripple in the wave of advancing knowledge and rationality. Only if the ripple happens to join forces with some other more powerful whirlpool of irrationality, such as Hitler's fanatical racism or today's radical terrorism, could it grow strong enough to once again endanger and engulf mankind.

This is not to minimize the potential dangers of occultism, but rather to assess the realities of the situation. Occultism is on the rise, certainly. But so is rationality. Occultists may be reacting to, and rejecting, the unrestrained growth of technology and the attendant loss of simple human values, but once such iniquities and stupidities are purged from our modern technological societies, man will no longer have any need for occult fantasies as a means of escape from harsh realities.

Reality need not be harsh, or cruel; technology does not have to lead to destruction or loss of human values. True, the greed, hypocrisy, discrimination, and oppression inherent in our present political systems are driving, and will to continue to drive, the unhappy have-nots and the oppressed to seek alternative solutions up to and including violent revolution. But revolutions have long been a part of man's history.

True revolutions deal with reality, with oppression, discrimination, and greedy leaders. The present occult upsurge is not a true revolution, since it encourages a return to fantasy, not reality. If anything, interest in the occult distracts the revolutionary, destroys true revolutionary fervor. For example, America's counterculture revolution became totally ineffective in the late 1960s as Eastern and occult ideas distracted the attention of leaders and followers alike away from political action.

Those who bury themselves in the occult soon lose sight of reality.

This, then, is my prognostication for the future of astrology: Its present upsurge in popularity will continue for a few years, perhaps for as long as a decade, and will level off at a level of popularity not much greater than what exists today. If one person in seven or eight today believes in astrology in America, we should expect no more than one in five believers at the height of its popularity. No longer can astrology attract as many followers as it has in the past.

Then, I predict, astrology will begin its final fall from grace, its final decline.

Already, there are distinct signs of a backlash, perhaps best illustrated by the statement prefacing this book, "Objections to Astrology," signed by 192 leading scientists, nearly half of all those invited to sign. This is the first time any public statement has been issued by the scientific community attacking the false premises and practices of astrology. For usually conservative scientists to take such a strong stand indicates that there is a powerful undercurrent among thoughtful, rational people to reject occult nonsense and fantasies.

Fewer and fewer people today are willing to "suspend disbelief" and accept ancient myths on "faith." More and more, people are demanding facts, proof. Even astrologers today are not accepting their magical "art" entirely on faith. Many are searching more and more for objective, scientific proof. This is a healthy sign; one only asks that they maintain an open mind and judge the facts dispassionately.

As I have repeatedly stressed, there have as yet been no properly conducted statistical tests of astrology which have at all suggested that it contains any "hidden grains of truth." Nor is it very likely that any such statistical confirmation of astrological theory will be forthcoming; astrology began as a system of magic, and magic it will remain.

The modern scientific fields of astronomy, cosmology, and relativistic physics have shown that the universe is a far larger, far more complex place than the small and tidy "All-is-One" world of our ancestors. On the surface of the earth, the fascinating fields of biological clocks, ecology, genetics and molecular chemistry are demonstrating that life is so interrelated, so dependent upon extremely complex earthly factors and processes, that any possible physical effects of the stars and planets are almost entirely lost in the press of reality.

Astrology would limit man to the arbitrary "dictates of the stars." Man cannot afford to do this if he is seriously interested in confronting and solving the problems before him. Evolution does not wait for stragglers; astrology may have served as an effective adaptive and selective societal mechanism for our Neolithic and civilized ancestors, but we can be sure it is ill-adapted to solving the complexities and problems of our modern world.

Life here on earth, in all its myriad forms, is the result of billions of years of physical, chemical, and biological evolution. Man is but one step, albeit a big one, in the evolutionary process. To think that man's character, personality, and destiny can be controlled by the simpleminded magical "influences" of astrology is to vastly misunderstand reality and underestimate man's potentiality.

Ultimately, of course, the choice belongs to the individual. Each person must decide if he is willing to be controlled and buffeted by arbitrary and oppressive societal mechanisms. Occultists must decide if they are willing to submit to the darker psychological sides of their natures. And astrologers must decide if they are willing to accept the magical "dictates of the stars" while psychologically influencing and controlling their clients who, in turn, must decide if they are willing to be so manipulated.

Belief in astrology, as in any occult "art," requires some loss of rationality, some loss of conscious, individual expression and control, and—ultimately—loss of freedom, the very thing man claims to value most. It is for this reason that I suspect astrology will eventually lose the battle and abandon its age-old hold on believers and followers. Rational, thinking man—for all his fears, for all his insecurities—loves his freedom far too much to delegate control of his life to others, be they astrologers, politicians, or priests.

As the facts about astrology become known, and as science continues to prove astrological hypotheses and assumptions false, present believers and practitioners will begin to lose "faith," begin to see their "art" for what it really is: nothing more than a magical system for controlling others.

NOTES

1. Louis MacNeice, *Astrology* (Garden City, N.Y.: Doubleday & Co., 1964), p. 13.

Appendix

Objections to Astrology

A STATEMENT BY 192 LEADING SCIENTISTS

Scientists in a variety of fields have become concerned about the increased acceptance of astrology in many parts of the world. We, the undersigned—astronomers, astrophysicists, and scientists in other fields—wish to caution the public against the unquestioning acceptance of the predictions and advice given privately and publicly by astrologers. Those who wish to believe in astrology should realize that there is no scientific foundation for its tenets.

In ancient times people believed in the predictions and advice of astrologers because astrology was part and parcel of their magical world view. They looked upon celestial objects as abodes or omens of the Gods and thus intimately connected with events here on earth; they had no concept of the vast distances from the earth to the planets and stars. Now that these distances can and have been calculated, we can see how infinitesimally small are the gravitational and other effects produced by the distant planets and the far more distant stars. It is simply a mistake to imagine that the forces exerted by stars and planets at the moment of birth can in any way shape our futures. Neither is it true that the position of distant heavenly bodies makes certain days or periods more favorable to particular of kinds of action, or that the sign under which one was born determines one's compatibility or incompatibility with other people.

Why do people believe in astrology? In these uncertain times many long for the comfort of having guidance in making decisions. They would like to believe in a destiny predetermined by astral forces beyond their control. However, we must all face the world, and we must realize that our futures lie in ourselves, and not in the stars.

One would imagine, in this day of widespread enlightenment and education, that it would be unnecessary to debunk beliefs based on magic and superstition. Yet, acceptance of astrology pervades modern society. We are especially disturbed by the continued uncritical dissemination of astrological charts, forecasts, and horoscopes by the media and by otherwise reputable newspapers, magazines, and book publishers. This can only contribute to the growth of irrationalism and obscurantism. We believe that the time has come to challenge directly and forcefully the pretentious claims of astrological charlatans.

It should be apparent that those individuals who continue to have faith in astrology do so in spite of the fact that there is no verified scientific basis for their beliefs, and indeed that there is strong evidence to the contrary.

Bart J. Bok, *emeritus*
professor of astronomy
University of Arizona

Lawrence E. Jerome
science writer
Santa Clara, California

Paul Kurtz
professor of philosophy
SUNY at Buffalo

SIGNERS

Nobel Prize Winners

Hans A. Bethe, *professor emeritus of physics, Cornell*
Sir Francis Crick, *Medical Research Council, Cambridge, Eng.*
Sir John Eccles, *distinguished professor of physiology and biophysics, SUNY at Buffalo*
Gerhard Herzberg, *distinguished research scientist, National Research Council of Canada*
Wassily Leontief, *professor of economics, Harvard University*
Konrad Lorenz, univ. prof., Austrian Academy of Sciences
André M. Lwoff, *honorary professor, Institut Pasteur, Paris*
Sir Peter Medawar, *Medical Research Council, Middlesex, Eng.*
Jacques Monod, *Institut Pasteur, Paris*
Robert S. Mulliken, *dist. prof. of chemistry, Univ. of Chicago*
Linus C. Pauling, *professor of chemistry, Stanford University*
Edward M. Purcell, *Gerhard Gade univ. prof., Harvard Univ.*
Paul A. Samuelson, *professor of economics, MIT*
Julian Schwinger, *professor of physics, U. of Calif., Los Angeles*
Glenn T. Seaborg, *univ. professor, Univ. of Calif., Berkeley*
J. Tinbergen, *professor emeritus, Rotterdam, The Netherlands*

N. Tinbergen, *emer. professor of animal behavior, Oxford Univ.*
Harold C. Urey, *professor emeritus, Univ. of Calif., San Diego*
George Wald, *professor of biology, Harvard University*

George O. Abell, *chmn., Dept. of Astron., U. of Cal., Los Angeles*
Lawrence H. Aller, *professor, Univ. of Calif., Los Angeles*
Edoardo Amaldi, *prof. of physics, University of Rome*
Richard Berendzen, *dean, Coll. of Arts and Sci., American Univ.*
William P. Bidelman, *professor, Case Western Reserve Univ.*
Jacob Bigeleisen, *professor, University of Rochester*
D. Scott Birney, *prof. of astronomy, Wellesley College*
Karl-Heinz Böhm, *professor, University of Washington*
Lyle B. Borst, *prof. of physics and astronomy, SUNY at Buffalo*
Peter B. Boyce, *staff astronomer, Lowell Observatory*
Harvey Brooks, *prof. of technology and public policy, Harvard*
William Buscombe, *prof. of astronomy, Northwestern Univ.*
Eugene R. Capriotti, *prof. of astronomy, Ohio State Univ.*
H. E. Carter, *coord. of interdisciplinary programs, U. of Arizona*
J. W. Chamberlain, *prof. of astronomy, Rice University*
Von Del Chamberlain, *Smithsonian Institution*
S. Chandrasekhar, *prof. of astronomy, Univ. of Chicago*
Mark R. Chartrand III, *chmn., Hayden Planetarium*
Hong-Yee Chiu, *NASA*
Preston Cloud, *prof. of geology, U. of Cal., Santa Barbara*
Peter S. Conti, *prof. of astrophysics, Univ of Colorado*
Allan F. Cook II, *astrophysicist, Smithsonian Observatory*
Alan Cottrell, *master, Jesus College, Cambridge, England*
Bryce Crawford, Jr., *prof. of chemistry, Univ. of Minnesota*
David D. Cudaback, *research astronomer, Univ. of Calif., Berkeley*
A. Dalgarno, *prof. of astronomy, Harvard*
Hallowell David, *Central Inst. for the Deaf, Univ. City, Mo.*
Morris S. Davis, *prof. of astronomy, Univ. of No. Carolina*
Peter van de Kamp, *director emeritus, Sproul Observatory*
A. H. Delsemme, *prof. of astrophysics, Univ. of Toledo*
Robert H. Dicke, *Albert Einstein prof. of science, Princeton*
Bertram Donn, *head, Astrochemical Branch, Goddard Space Center,*

NASA

Paul Doty, *prof. of biochemistry, Harvard*

Frank D. Drake, *dir., Natl. Astron. and Ionosphere Ctr., Cornell*

Lee A. DuBridge, *pres. emeritus, Calif. Inst. of Technology*

Harold Edgerton, *professor, MIT*

H. K. Eichhorn-von Wrumb, *chmn., Dept. of Astron., Univ. of South Florida*

R. M. Emberson, *dir., Tech. Services Inst. of Electrical and Electronics Engineers*

Howard W. Emmons, *professor of mechanical engineering, Harvard*

Eugene E. Epstein, *staff scientist, The Aerospace Corp.*

Henry Eyring, *distinguished prof. of chemistry, Univ. of Utah*

Charles A. Federer, Jr., *president, Sky Pub. Corp.*

Robert Fleischer, *Astronomy Section, National Science Foundation.*

Henry F. Fliegel, *technical staff, Jet Propulsion Laboratory*

William A. Fowler, *institute prof. of physics, Calif. Inst. of Tech.*

Fred A. Franklin, *astronomer, Smithsonian Astrophysical Observatory*

Laurence W. Fredrick, *prof. of astronomy, U. of Virginia*

Tom Gehrels, *Lunar and Planetary Lab., Univ. of Arizona*

Riccardo Giacconi, *Center for Astrophysics, Cambridge, Mass.*

Owen Gingerich, *prof. of astronomy, Harvard*

Thomas Gold, *professor, Cornell*

Leo Goldberg, *director, Kitt Peak National Observatory*

Maurice Goldhaber, *Brookhaven National Laboratory*

Mark A. Gordon, *Natl. Radio Astronomy Observatory*

Jesse L. Greenstein, *prof. of astrophysics, Cal. Inst. of Tech.*

Kenneth Greisen, *prof. of physics, Cornel*

Howard D. Greyber, *consultant, Potomac, Md.*

Herbert Gursky, *astrophysicist, Smithsonian Institution*

John P. Hagen, *chmn., Dept. of Astronomy, Penn. State Univ.*

Philip Handler, *president, National Academy of Sciences*

William K. Hartmann, *Planetary Science Inst., Tucson, Arizona*

Leland J. Haworth, *spec. assist. to the pres., Associated Univs.*

Carl Heiles, *prof. of astronomy, U. of Cal., Berkeley*

A. Heiser, *director, Dyer Observatory, Vanderbilt University*

H. L. Helfer, *prof. of astronomy, Univ. of Rochester*

George H. Herbig, *astronomer Lick Observatory, U. of Cal.*

Arthur A. Hoag, *astronomer, Kitt Peak Natl. Observatory*

Paul W. Hodge, *prof. of astronomy, Univ. of Washington*

Dorrit Hoffleit, *director, Maria Mitchell Observatory*
William E. Howard III, *Natl. Radio Astronomy Observatory*
Nancy Houk, *Dept. of Astronomy, Univ. of Michigan*
Fred Hoyle, *fellow, St. Johns College, Cambridge Univ.*
Icko Iben, Jr., *chmn., Dept. of Astronomy, U. of Illinois*
John T. Jefferies, *director, Inst. for Astronomy, U. of Hawaii*
Frank C. Jettner, *Dept. of Astronomy, SUNY at Albany*
J. R. Jokipii, *prof. of planetary sciences, Univ. of Arizona*
Joost H. Kiewiet de Jonge, *assoc. prof. of astron., U. of Pittsburgh*
Kenneth Kellermann, *Nat. Radio Astronomy Observatory*
Ivan R. King, *prof. of astron., U. of Cal., Berkeley*
Rudolf Kompfner, *professor emeritus, Stanford University*
William S. Kovach, *staff scientist, General Dynamics/Convair*
M. R. Kundu, *prof. of astronomy, Univ. of Maryland*
Lewis Larmore, *dir. of tech., Office of Naval Research*
Kam-Ching Leung, *dir., Behlen Observatory, Univ. of Nebraska*
I. M. Levitt, *dir. emer., Fels Planetarium of Franklin Institute*
C. C. Lin, *professor, MIT*
Albert P. Linnell, *professor, Michigan State Univ.*
M. Stanley Livingston, *Dept. of Physics, MIT*
Frank J. Low, *research prof., University of Arizona*
Willem J. Luyten, *University of Minnesota*
Richard E. McCrosky, *Smithsonian Astrophysical Observatory*
W. D. McElroy, *Univ. of Calif., San Diego*
Carl S. Marvel, *prof. of chemistry, Univ. of Arizona*
Margaret W. Mayall, *consul., Am. Assoc. of Variable Star Obser.*
Nicholas U. Mayall, *former dir., Kitt Peak Natl. Observatory*
Donald H. Menzel, *former director, Harvard College Observatory*
Alfred H. Mikesell, *Kitt Peak Natl. Observatory*
Freeman D. Miller, *prof. of astronomy, Univ. of Michigan*
Alan T. Moffet, *prof. of radio astron., Calif. Inst. of Technology*
Delo E. Mook, *assist. prof. of physics and astronomy, Dartmouth*
Marston Morse, *prof. emer., Inst. for Adv. Study, Princeton*
G. F. W. Mulders, *former head, Astron. Section, NSF*
Guido Münch, *prof. of astronomy, Cal. Inst. of Technology*
Edward P. Ney, *regents prof. of astronomy, Univ. of Minn.*
J. Neyman, *director, statistical lab, Univ. of Cal., Berkeley*
C. R. O'Dell, *project scientist, Large Space Telescope, NASA*
John A. O'Keefe, *Goddard Space Flight Center, NASA*

J. H. Oort, *dir., University Observatory, Leiden, Netherlands*
Tobias C. Owen, *prof. of astronomy, SUNY at Stony Brook*
Eugene N. Parker, *professor of physics and astron., U. of Chicago*
Arno A. Penzias, *Bell Laboratories*
A. Keith Pierce, *solar astronomer, Kitt Peak National Observatory*
Daniel M. Popper, *professor of astronomy, UCLA*
Frank Press, *prof. of geophysics, MIT*
R. M. Price, *radio spectrum manager, Natl. Science Foundation*
William M. Protheroe, *prof. of astronomy, Ohio State University*
John D. G. Rather, *Dept. of Astronomy, Univ. of Calif., Irvine*
Robert S. Richardson, *former assoc. dir., Griffith Observatory*
A. Marguerite Risley, *prof. emer., Randolph-Macon College*
Franklin E. Roach, *astronomer, Honolulu, Hawaii*
Walter Orr Roberts, *Aspen Inst. for Humanistic Studies*
William W. Roberts, Jr., *associate prof., University of Virginia*
R. N. Robertson, *Australian National University*
James P. Rodman, *prof. of astronomy, Mt. Union College*
Bruno Rossi, *prof. emeritus, MIT*
E. E. Salpeter, *professor, Cornell University*
Gertrude Scharff-Goldhaber, *physicist, Brookhaven Natl. Lab.*
John D. Schopp, *prof. of astronomy, San Diego State University*
Julian J. Schreur, *prof. of astronomy, Valdosta State College*
E. L. Scott, *professor, University of California, Berkeley*
Frederick Seitz, *president, The Rockefeller University*
C. D. Shane, *Lick Observatory*
Alan H. Shapley, *U.S. Dept. of Commerce, NOAA*
Frank H. Shu, *assoc. prof. of astronomy, Univ. of Cal., Berkeley*
Bancroft W. Sitterly, *prof. of physics emer., American Univ.*
Charlotte M. Sitterly, *Washington, D.C.*
B. F. Skinner, *prof. emeritus, Harvard*
Harlan J. Smith, *dir., McDonald Observ., Univ. of Texas, Austin*
Sabatino Sofia, *staff scientist, NASA*
František Šorm, *professor, Institute of Organic Chemistry, Prague, Czech.*
G. Ledyard Stebbins, *prof. emeritus, Univ. of California*
C. Bruce Stephenson, *prof. of astronomy, Case Western Reserve*
Walter H. Stockmayer, *prof. of chemistry, Dartmouth*
Marshall H. Stone, *professor, University of Massachusetts*
N. Wyman Storer, *prof. emeritus of astronomy, Univ. of Kansas*

Hans E. Suess, *prof. of geochemistry, Univ. of Cal., San Diego*
T. L. Swihart, *prof. of astronomy, Univ. of Arizona*
Pol Swings, *Institute d'Astrophysique, Esneux, Belgium*
J. Szentágothai, *Semmelweis Univ. Med. School, Budapest*
Joseph H. Taylor, Jr., *assoc. prof. of astronomy, Univ. of Mass.*
Frederick E. Terman, *vice-pres. and provost emeritus, Stanford*
Yervant Terzian, *assoc. prof. of space science, Cornell*
Patrick Thaddeus, *Inst. for Space Studies, New York, N.Y.*
Kip S. Thorne, *prof. of theor. physics, Cal. Inst. of Technology*
Charles R. Tolbert, *McCormick Observ., Charlottesville, Va.*
Alar Toomre, *prof. of applied mathematics, MIT*
Merle A. Tuve, *Carnegie Institution of Washington*
S. Vasilevskis, *emer. prof. of astronomy, Univ. of Cal., Santa Cruz*
Maurice B. Visscher, *emer. prof. of physiology, Univ. of Minn.*
Joan Vorpahl, *Aerospace Corp., Los Angeles*
Campbell M. Wade, *Natl. Radio Astronomy Observatory*
N. E. Wagman, *emer. dir., Allegheny Observatory, U. of Pittsb.*
George Wallerstein, *prof. of astronomy, Univ. of Washington*
Fred L. Whipple, *Phillips astronomer, Harvard*
Hassler Whitney, *professor, Inst. for Advanced Study, Princeton*
Adolf N. Witt, *prof. of astronomy, Univ. of Toledo*
Frank Bradshaw Wood, *prof. of astronomy, University of Florida*
Charles E. Worley, *astronomer, U.S. Naval Observatory*
Jeffries Wyman, *Instituto Regina Elena, Rome*
Chi Yuan, *assoc. prof. of physics, CCNY*